MEMORIALS

AND

CORRESPONDENCE

OF

CHARLES JAMES FOX.

MEMORIALS

AND

CORRESPONDENCE

OF

CHARLES JAMES FOX.

EDITED

BY LORD JOHN RUSSELL.

VOLUME II.

AMS PRESS
NEW YORK

Reprinted from the edition of 1853, London
First AMS EDITION published 1970
Manufactured in the United States of America

International Standard Book Number:
    complete set: 0-404-05470-6
    volume 2: 0-404-05472-2

Library of Congress Catalog Card Number: 75-115362

AMS PRESS, INC.
New York, N. Y. 10003

PREFACE

—◆

The present volume contains further materials for
Mr. Fox's Life, and in elucidation of the history of
his times, till the end of the year 1792. I have with
some difficulty altered the order adopted by Lord
Holland and Mr. Allen, making it more chronological;
and I have added some remarks from time to time
upon the great questions which, sixty years ago,
divided the opinions of the country.

In these papers, as in those contained in the former
volume, the frank, sincere, simple, and affectionate
nature of Mr. Fox pierces through all the super-
incumbent clay of a period of low morals, and factious
politics. The historical records of the time are very
imperfect, and I had no longer the help of Lord
Mahon's calm and steady light to aid, if not to direct
me. Differing from him, as I often do, it is impossible not to recognise in Lord Mahon an author
anxious to ascertain and avow the truth.

Lately, however, a publication of the Duke of Buckingham has given to the world singular and authentic information regarding the influence by which Mr. Fox was defeated, and the men by whom he was deserted. Too easily was the victory gained over a statesman who never would condescend to an intrigue, and never would betray a principle.

The end of this volume brings us to the brink of the war of the French Revolution. Attention has been lately called to this period in a pamphlet of singular clearness and force; * and the calumniated wisdom of Mr. Fox has been contrasted with the popular folly of his rival.

It will be my business, if I should be able to continue this work, to point out the utter want of foresight by which the conduct of Mr. Pitt was marked when he led the people of England into a crusade against the people of France.

* " 1793 and 1853."

CHESHAM PLACE, *April* 13, 1853.

CORRESPONDENCE OF

CHARLES JAMES FOX.

BOOK THE FOURTH.

PART THE SECOND.

* WE are about to enter on a most important part of Mr. Fox's political life. In fact, the course he took in 1782, 1783, and 1784, gave a direction to his whole career, and deprived him of that power to sway the destiny of the State, which would have been happy for his own fame, and conducive to the welfare of his country.

The death of Lord Rockingham enabled Lord Shelburne to succeed to the post of First Lord of the Treasury; but it also left a vacancy in the leadership of the Whig party, which Mr. Fox and Mr. Burke were alone competent to supply.

It has been said that the birth and connexions of Mr. Fox determined in his favour the question of the leadership; but the fact is, that while Mr. Burke was the greater philosopher, and the more profound reasoner on general principles of government, Mr. Fox

had far more readiness in debate, a more popular style
of eloquence, and more judgment in the practical
conduct of affairs. I have been told by Mr. Dudley
North, that when the managers, during the impeachment of Mr. Hastings, retired to consult together, it
was usual for Mr. Burke to close all debate by saying,
" Let us defer to the superior judgment of Mr. Fox."

But while the pre-eminent qualities of Mr. Fox
pointed him out as the successor of Lord Rockingham,
it seems strange to us that Mr. Burke, with his genius
and his standing in the Whig party, should not have
been a member of the Cabinet, either of Lord
Rockingham or of the Duke of Portland. The
exclusion of such a man seems to us unwise and
unjust : at the time it does not appear that it was
resented by Mr. Burke, or by any of his friends.

While Mr. Fox derived from the death of Lord
Rockingham increased importance, there arose at the
same time a new luminary whose bright rays spread
over the hemisphere.

William Pitt, the second son of Lord Chatham, was
born in 1759, ten years after Mr. Fox. His education
was very different from that of his great rival. He
was not sent to a public school like Mr. Fox, nor
was he taken by his parents to a foreign gambling-
table, and initiated early in the vices of a profligate
age. He was educated at home, and with such
regard to economy, that when he was sent to Cambridge, we find that one of his earliest calculations
referred to the comparative cost of keeping his horse
at grass, or in the stable. His private tutor had

taught him Greek and Latin. Lord Chatham himself
recommended to his Cambridge teachers to give much
time to the study of Thucydides. As an instance how
well this precept was obeyed, the late Lord Harrowby,
as he himself told me, being with Mr. Pitt at his
country-house, when he and Lord Grenville, waiting
for Mr. Pitt in his library, had taken down a Thucydides, and had arrived at a passage they could not
make out, Mr. Pitt coming in, took the volume and
construed the passage with the greatest facility. No
less successful was his study of mathematics ; so that,
having entered Cambridge at the age of fourteen, he
remained there till he became well qualified in the
science and learning of that celebrated university.
Elected to a seat in Parliament at the age of twenty-
one, his first efforts caused wonder and admiration.
Logical in his argument, clear in his arrangement, he
possessed from the very beginning the command of a
diction flowing, majestic, regular,

" Strong without rage, without o'erflowing full."

Not less remarkable was the confidence and presence
of mind which he displayed from the beginning.   Mr.
Adam told me of an instance of these qualities which
struck him and others with surprise not unmixed
with anger at the presumption of the boy-statesman.
Mr. Pitt was accusing the Minister of grave neglects,
when he perceived a conversation going on between
Lord North and (I think) Lord George Germaine, in
which Mr. Welbore Ellis interposed.   Mr. Pitt paused :
" I wait," he said, " till the Nestor of the Treasury

Bench has composed the differences of Agamemnon
and Achilles." Not less cool and confident was the
reply which Lord Holland has reported when an
injudicious friend expressed his wish to see the two
orators battle as their fathers had done before them.

Mr. Pitt, then, entered into public life with the
advantages of his great father's reputation; with
his own unblemished character; with a facility,
innate or acquired in early youth, of expressing his
thoughts in a manner to arrest attention; with great
readiness in reply; a mind disciplined to the use of
arguments, precise, connected, and sustained; and
with a fund of knowledge always available to the aid
of a powerful understanding. He differed in many
respects from his father; he had neither the feeling
nor the fancy of that mighty orator. But there was
the same commanding gesture; the same unsuspected
integrity, and in early youth he had the *stirpis
Achilleæ fastus*, which enabled him to confront Fox,
to withstand the raillery of Sheridan, and put aside as
fanciful and impracticable the large views of Burke.

We shall now give from Horace Walpole, from
General Fitzpatrick, from Lord John Townshend, and
from Mr. Adam, evidence from which Lord Holland
has drawn reflections favourable to the statesman with
whom he was so nearly connected in sympathy as
well as related in blood. Some remarks of my own
will be added on the events of a time so important in
its influence upon all subsequent periods.*—J. R.

Horace Walpole gives the following account of the
Shelburne Administration :—

"Fox and their junto having resigned, Lord Shelburne took possession of the Treasury, and adorned his new board with the most useful acquisition, and by the most artful address, of his whole Administration. This was by offering the seals of the Exchequer to young William Pitt, who, with youthful and thence pardonable vanity, readily accepted them, and the more difficult task of enlisting himself as the rival of *Charles Fox, who had fondly espoused him, and kindly, not jealously nor fearfully, wished to have him his friend.* Young as Fox was, Pitt was ten years younger; and what a fund of knowledge were ten years in possession of such a master-genius as Fox, besides the prodigious superiority of solid parts! Yet Fox left by neglect some advantages to Pitt. The one trusted to his natural abilities, and whenever he wanted them, never found them fail. Pitt, on the contrary, attended to nothing but the means of gratifying his ambition. His application * was not a moment relaxed, and he was not less abstemious and temperate; even attention to his health was unremitted, as if he feared that hereditary gout would traverse his career as it had often broken in upon his father's. No juvenile avocations diverted him from his studies, nor left reproaches from the grave on his character. Fox seemed to leave pleasure with regret, and to bestow only spare moments on the government

* In the latter part of his life Pitt was very indolent, and certainly during the greater part of it drank much wine, but Walpole loves contrast and antithesis.—V. H.   Walpole speaks here only of the early part of Mr. Pitt's career.—J. R.

of a nation ;—Pitt, to make industry and virtue the ladders of his ambition. Fox's greatness was innate, and if he had ambition, it was the only passion which he took no means to gratify. He disguised no vice ; he used no art ; he despised application ; he sought no popularity. A warm friend, and almost incapable of being provoked by one ; void of all inveteracy, and only an enemy when spirit called on him to resent, or the foe was so great that he was too bold not to punish, as he showed the next year by insisting on the dismission of the Lord Chancellor and the Lord Advocate. Pitt cultivated friends to form a party, and had already attached many considerable young men to himself."

" It is singular and perhaps totally a novel combination of circumstances that Charles Fox and William Pitt, the second sons of Henry Lord Holland and William Lord Chatham, who themselves were second sons, should become rivals and the first men in the House of Commons, as their fathers had been little more than twenty years before."

" Pitt had not the commanding* brilliancy of his father, nor his imposing air and person ; but his language was more pure and correct, and his method and reasoning better. Fox had not the ungraceful hesitation of his father, yet scarce equalled him in subtlety and acuteness. Yet no man ever exceeded him in the closeness of argument, which flowed from him in

* I suppose Walpole is right in this, but Pitt's language became more brilliant by constant practice ; and his delivery, at all times imposing, was yet more so, when the orator was known to be the most powerful minister in Europe.—V. H.

a torrent of vehemence, as declamation sometimes does from those who most want argument. He alone was a match for the nervous sense of Thurlow, and could dismount the wit and pleasantry of Lord North. Without that conciliatory jocoseness, and without the exuberant imagery of Burke, Fox's allusions were beautiful and happy ; and he often possessed that superior kind of wit, which, without being sought, results from the clearness of ideas and knowledge of the world, and which combines by intuition, not by fancy. It was one of Fox's merits, that though he idolised the imagination of Burke, the quickness and fire of Hare, the genteel irony and *badinage* of Fitzpatrick, and the gaiety of Sheridan, he never aimed at wit himself, which was not his peculiar talent. Good sense and reasoning were his native language, and he neither sought what he had not, nor studied to make the most of what he had. Nature had given him genius, and to her he left it to furnish him with occasions of displaying it. If he affected anything it was vice : all his abilities and good qualities were born with him. Intrepid, he did not fear even reproach. Art he was either incapable of or despised. I do not believe that he had one bad black or base object. It was a pity that he was as inattentive in having a good one. He acted as the moment impelled him ; but as his conception was just, and his soul void of malice or treachery, he meditated no ill, yet might have advantaged himself and his country more, had he acted with any foresight or any plan."

The passage above, though like all Walpole's writings too antithetical and forced to be literally correct, and at variance as usual with him, with much he has written before and afterwards on the same subject, contains many just observations on Mr. Fox, and exhibits a lively and true picture of his easy, spirited, and wise conversation—of his affectionate, generous, and honest temper—and of that which Grattan denominated the "negligent grandeur" of his character in debate and in action.

The latter part of Walpole's account of 1782 does not seem to be kept in the form of a Journal. There is *no day* entered after July of that year, but the last pages of the book, as well as the remarks, relate to Lord Shelburne's Administration, and transactions which took place after his appointment to the Treasury in July.—v. h.

In the autumn the following letter was written by

MR. FITZPATRICK TO LORD OSSORY.

"*Saturday night, November* 23rd, 1782.

"Dear Brother,

"Parliament is to be prorogued till Thursday sennight. It is said that Lord Shelburne has notified to the City the reason of it to be that Peace is in forwardness. Various conclusions are drawn from this by various politicians. You may form your conjectures as well in the country as in town, for every man seems to have his own. Some think he has the Peace in his pocket, and that he has

only to negotiate with the *powers* at home. Lord
North has had a meeting of his friends, to whom he
has announced his being free from all engagements
whatever. What the Duke of Richmond told me
proves true. I had this morning a note from General
Conway to inform me that the King had appointed
me aide-de-camp. I dare say when I see our *beau-
frère* he will tell me that he did it. Charles is
arrived, but I have not seen him since the news of
the day. Adieu.

" Yours affectionately,

"R. F."

MR. FITZPATRICK TO LORD OSSORY.

" *Monday night, December 2nd,* 1782.

" DEAR BROTHER,
            " M. de Rennervalle* (or whatever his name
is) arrived this morning at nine o'clock, which occasioned the stocks to rise immediately five or six per
cent. Since that, I understand they are fallen again.
Many people aver positively that there never has been
any reason to think Peace in such forwardness as
T. Townshend's letter seemed to imply. I saw
Lord Shelburne yesterday ; he told me we were all
to know the event as soon as they could hear from
Paris. Nothing, however, transpiring, I think he
will hardly venture upon a second prorogation.
Neither Lord Grantham nor T. Townshend knew of
Rennervalle's† arrival at twelve o'clock this morning,
till Sir Charles Bunbury informed them of it, and

---

* Rayneval.   † Rayneval.

it is said that none of the Cabinet knew anything of Peace being in forwardness or probable till they saw T. Townshend's letter to the City. Lord Shelburne says he understands nothing of the House of Commons, but that they show him a *very good list.* I told him I believed he would find himself mistaken, and so I do if it is put to the trial. I write just to tell you what is known, that is, that *nothing is known*, because Chewton told me you were undecided whether you should come or not."

1783.

January 2nd. In the loose notes of H. Walpole it appears that both the Duke of Richmond and Conway were at this time disposed to break with Lord Shelburne. Conway, in reporting the Duke of Richmond's inclinations, said he "thought he had a mind to reunite with Charles Fox." Walpole said that breaking for the reason assigned (viz., the offer to France of something in the East Indies, without the knowledge of the Cabinet), would be breaking for less than Charles Fox did ; and Walpole seems, through Conway, to have dissuaded the Duke of Richmond from resigning.

January 23rd. "Duke of Richmond declared to the King, that, disapproving of Lord Shelburne's assumption of too much power, he would go no more to Council, but as he had begun and could carry on great savings in the Ordnance, he would keep it, if the King desired it, which he did."—H. W.

January 24th. " Keppel resigned the Admiralty."
—H. W.

January 31st. " Lord Loughborough and Eden trying to unite Lord North and Fox, Lord Advocate Sir Grey Cooper and Robinson to unite him (Lord North) with Lord Shelburne."

February 5th. " Lord Carlisle resigned the place of Lord Steward, on pretence that American loyalists were sacrificed. Some say, because Lord Carmarthen was preferred to him for the embassy to Paris. Some, because Eden wrought on him, and he wished to get back to Charles Fox, as the extreme unpopularity of Shelburne made it probable that he would not keep his power long. Lord C. had quitted Ireland abruptly on the change, had been made Lord Steward by Charles Fox, leaving Eden in the lurch. On Fox's resignation, Lord Carlisle had deserted him, and now, perhaps, was persuaded by Charles Fox and Eden to resign, as a signal that Lord Shelburne was falling. Shelburne's insolence and folly advanced his fall daily. He consulted nobody but William Pitt, flattered the Duke of Richmond, neglected Lord Camden, Duke of Grafton, Conway, and everybody else, trusting to maintain himself entirely by the King. He had neither treated directly with Lord North nor with Charles Fox, and they, either hoping he would, or waiting to see the Peace concluded, had lain quiet, and given no marks of displeasure."

February 5th. " Lord Loughborough and Eden warmly endeavoured to unite Lord North and Fox (on Peace), Robinson and Sir Grey Cooper to join

Lord North and Shelburne ; Duke of Richmond wished Shelburne and Fox to unite."—H. W.

February 12th. " The Peace growing very unpopular, Lord Shelburne became alarmed, and began to treat with the two opposing parties, first with Charles Fox, through Lord Keppel, who owned to Conway he did not wish it to succeed, nor did it. For Fox insisting on the Treasury for the Duke of Portland, Lord Shelburne (who certainly did not mean to sacrifice himself in order to serve himself) said the King insisted on his keeping it. He then treated with Lord North, and acquainted Duke of Grafton, who objected strongly, and said he should not like to sit in councils with Lord North and that party. 'Shelburne said, ' Oh, it was not meant that Lord North should have influence in the Council, but would the Duke object to that party having a few places ? ' The Duke said, ' He would consider of it, and could not give a positive answer.' Lord Shelburne had begun to sound Charles Fox and that party by Duke of Richmond and Lord Keppel; but, finding that they insisted on the Treasury for Duke of Portland, he sent Mr. W. Pitt in form to Charles Fox, in order to have it to say that they had refused on account of places. The treaty (with Lord North) was negotiated by the Lord Advocate, but Lord North was irresolute, and it did not succeed ; yet even on the 13th, while it was pending, Lord Shelburne foolishly made the Duke of Rutland not only Lord Steward in the room of Lord Carlisle, but made him of the Cabinet Council, a most unusual honour for a Lord Steward, and filling up one of the best posts with which he might have trafficked with Opposition. All his measures were rash, indigested, and unconnected."—H. W.

February 17th. "Charles Fox, on rejecting Lord Shelburne's offers through Pitt, acquainted Lord North, who had also refused them, and Lord North and Charles Fox immediately leagued; though, as Fox declared in House of Commons on the 17th, no further than to censure preliminaries." In giving an account of the debates and votes on the Peace :—" In fact, many Scots were for Lord Shelburne, and most connexions were so broken and divided by the late changes, that scarce one, or even family connexions, remained united. The Lord Advocate and Andrew Stuart, a subtle, able man, who had obtained Shelburne's protection for his brother-in-law in India, kept many Scots to him. In the Commons, some of the staunchest friends of Fox and the Cavendishes left them because they had joined Lord North, and some of North's friends deserted him because he had united with Fox."

On the debate in Commons, "Lord North spoke with great temper. Charles Fox admirably, beginning with saying, that the Ministers seemed to have neglected everything to study, recollect, and reproach him with all his actions, sayings, and most careless words. The Lord Advocate abused his late friend, Lord North, most grossly, and said, 'the new amour of Lord North and Charles Fox had produced nothing but abortive puerility—the motion.' He boasted that on their next motion he should retort Fox's sarcasms, but, probably from reflecting on the latter's success, he did not speak on the following Friday. He was justly reproved by Fox and Sheridan, and having said he would act with any man who agreed with him in principles, they asked him if he agreed with Shelburne's on representation? No. On reformation? No. On East India? No—or only by Shelburne coming over to his opinion. Charles Fox reflected on his uncle, the Duke of Richmond, and said Lord Shelburne had outrun all the demands of the Associations in so hard a manner, that it looked as if he meant to make men sick of reformations."

" Pitt and the Lord Advocate both reckoned the game desperate ; and it soon grew more so. It was evident that Fox and Lord North agreed, and that the Cabinet were much divided. The Duke of Richmond fluctuated. Conway was not pleased."

February 20th. " The Duke of Grafton resigned the Privy Seal ; he had long been dissatisfied ; the refusal of Salisbury for Bishop Hinchliffe ; the promotion and admission, without consulting him, of the Duke of Rutland to Cabinet, had disobliged him. He stated the last to King and Lord Shelburne, who, when he said he should resign, replied, ' I cannot deprecate that,' and Duke of Grafton, who meant only to quit the Cabinet on that treatment, told the King he would resign his place. Lord Shelburne slightly mentioned to Conway—but not as asking advice—that he had thoughts of standing in spite of the House of Commons. Conway treated the thought as most imprudent."—H. W.

February 21st. Lord John Cavendish's motion to censure the Peace, of which Walpole disapproves as scandalous and unpopular. " Such gross indecorum," adds he, "was perhaps occasioned by the desire of saving Lord North, their new ally, as both he and they owned he was become, from any retrospect, the neglect of which they could not justify if they went into articles against Lord Shelburne. Thus, by this junction, Lord North got himself whitewashed by his bitterest enemies. Mr. Powys, Mr. Cecil Wray, and others, were very severe on this new junction, which Mr. Fox had declared in Parliament he never would make. They both quitted Fox and that party with whom they had acted. The motions of Lord John were carried by 207 to 190."—H. W.

" It was now evident Lord Shelburne could not stand his ground. None of the supplies for the year were voted. At last, on the 23rd, he called a Cabinet, and in the evening a large assembly of his adherents, to both which meetings he declared his resolution of resigning his post."

February 24th. " Lord Shelburne resigned. That very day, before any invitation from the King, the Duke of Portland, designed by the united factions as the ostensible Minister, went to Duke of Richmond and entreated him to stay in his place and reunite with his old friends, who would have all the power, as Lord North had but two places in the Cabinet. The Duke of Richmond thanked him, but said he could not see his own name standing to so many protests against Lord North, and consent to act with

him.   He had blamed his friends for retiring in the
summer, and hoped they would not blame him for
retiring, as he intended to acquaint the King he
should do so."—H.W.

We may now return to the correspondence of one
of the actors more immediately concerned :—

MR. FITZPATRICK TO LORD OSSORY.

"*Tuesday, February* 18*th*, 1783.

" DEAR BROTHER,

          " I am not very sorry that your indolence
prevailed upon you to stay in the country, as I should
have feared that your *pacific* disposition and that
general partiality to Peace, that strengthened the
Administration in yesterday's question, might have
inclined you to follow the example of some of your
brother country gentlemen (I mean of those who
know black from white), and to have voted in favour
of a Ministry you wished to destroy.   But what hurt
us infinitely more than the general propensity to
peace was the apparent junction with Lord North.
Powys took an early part in the debate in support of
Administration, and many of the independent supporters of the Whigs followed his example.   Lord
North's phalanx, as you may suppose, were less
capricious, and by the division we carried our
amendment by 16.   The amendment, as you will
perceive, was very *soft*, suited to the *modesty* of their
Address, and calculated for the squeamish stomachs of
scrupulous friends, which were not, however, strong
enough to digest it.   Lord North, according to his

character, was, in concerting the question, amazingly indecisive; he would agree to no censure, though the amendment we carried must necessarily be followed by one, which, however, must of course be gentle, as from his official situation, Shelburne cannot be the object of it, and nobody wishes to bear hard upon either Lord Grantham or Poor Tommy.* What will be the change of Administration it is difficult to foresee; the *coup de pied* is given to Lord Shelburne. Who will succeed him is a matter for speculation. I think North will hardly undertake it alone, and I think those who undertake it with him will risk their credit with the public upon very unsafe ground. Lord Gower made a miserable shuffling figure, and voted against the Ministerial address, with all his friends divided in the House of Commons, Vernon and Wrottesley against, and Lord Trentham with us. Lord Shelburne received a hearty dressing from Lord Loughborough; and the Advocate the most severe one I ever remember to have heard from Charles in the House of Commons. We had the mortification of carrying our question by Lord North's alliance; but Ministers had the disgrace of being supported by Jenkinson and Rigby. The call is Wednesday, but I suppose it will be put off. I cannot be insolent enough to go to Shelburne House, though I think he must allow that both you and I told him fairly what he had to expect. He has upon the whole certainly made a most ridiculous figure. Adieu.

" Yours ever,

" R. F."

* Mr. Thomas Townshend.

SAME TO SAME.

"*Wednesday,* [19*th February,* 1783.]

" Dear Brother,

" The House was called to-day, but I cannot learn what time was fixed for calling over our defaulters. On Friday a committee is to be moved for, and resolutions, &c. No news yet, but various reports. The Duke of Grafton resigned before the debate upon the Peace, on account of Lord Shelburne's style of treating the Cabinet, having added the Duke of Rutland without informing them. I have not been near Shelburne House, as you may suppose, under the present circumstances. People say he is mad enough to be inclined to fight on ; the truth is, that forcing a change in the present moment is a very ticklish business, and I make no doubt that if he could involve the country in war, he would be glad to reproach the *factious* junction with Lord North with having done it. I will write to-morrow if there is anything worth saying.

" Yours,

"R. F."

SAME TO SAME.

[22*nd February,* 1783.]

" Last night we had a second victory in the House of Commons upon a stronger question, and with the additional majority of 1 ; to the Administration it is *cita mors,* but not *victoria læta* to us; the apparent juncture * with Lord North is universally cried out

* Union, amity.—Johnson.

against, though, at the same time, all moderate and reasonable men approve of it as the only means of establishing any government in the country. Charles made a most admirable speech; but as the chief merit was the *policy* of it, probably it would not be so well understood out of doors as Pitt's, which was upon the highest stilts that ever his father was mounted. Pitt was understood to announce the resignation of Ministers, if the question went against them; yet the report of the day is that Shelburne holds a contrary language. The King is gone to Windsor, and I believe feels this is a more decisive defeat than the former. I dare not venture to Shelburne House to tell our *beau-frère* that if he is mad enough (which, however, I do not believe) to allow the House of Commons to meet in the present state of things, he must be removed by an address of the House. I find that most of the country gentlemen, who have voted against us in these questions, are ready for such a measure. The formation of the new Ministry is the great point at present, and the difficulty (independent of public appearances) is to secure Lord North, whose weakness of character and indecision has been even more conspicuous than ever since this *unnatural alliance.*

" Unless a *real good Government* is the consequence of this juncture, nothing can justify it to the public. I am anxious about Louisa as well as you, but am afraid that calling or inquiring might be misinterpreted. The good to be expected from all this is, that no one will venture to undertake the Government after Lord Shelburne's example. Lord Gower makes almost as ridiculous a figure as the Minister, having thought fit to oppose the last question after having shabbily supported the first. The Duke of Marlborough equally so, by having deserted Lord Shelburne after the first defeat. I am glad to hear you are coming, for in the present hurry it is impossible to write any accurate accounts of anything.

" Yours affectionately,

"R. F.

" I wish you had been present to have talked over these matters, for there never was a case more full of difficulties and dangers to the real friends of Whiggism and good principles."

The events which brought about the ill-fated and much calumniated Coalition are well known ; but the agency through which the agreement was conducted has never been explained to the public. Rumour attributed much of it to Eden (afterwards Lord Auckland), and to Wedderburne ; but I believe with little or no foundation. Lord North was sincerely disposed to retire, and Pitt, and yet more probably the King, would willingly have sought assistance among the late Minister's followers ; but before any such agreement was ripe, Mr. Pitt, instead of trusting to the reported probability of Lord North's acquiescence and retirement, was said to have insisted on a renunciation, on the part of all Lord North's followers who should join him, of all connection with a man so stigmatised by failure and disgrace.　At least, Mr. Dundas (Lord Melville), who had it must be presumed submitted to that ignominy himself, told his old friend and associate, Mr. Adam, that " Pitt was ready to negotiate with Lord North's party on the basis of excluding Lord North personally."* At this Adam, ever warmhearted and friendly, was naturally " incensed and provoked,"† and he communicated his indignation to George North, who was intimate with Mr. Fox's intimate friend, Lord John Townshend; the three were mainly instrumental in prevailing on Lord North and Mr. Fox to form a coalition, which Burke, with his usual vehemence, passion, and inconsistency, and others, with an impatient desire of office, were earnestly recommending.　In 1830, I wrote to Lord John Townshend to inquire the particulars of this negotiation and transaction.　I transcribe the letters I received from him, as characteristic of one of Mr. Fox's most intimate friends in those days, and as exhibiting a lively picture of what was going on at the time :—

"BRIGHTON, *June* 15*th,* 1830.

" DEAR LORD HOLLAND,

　　　" In answer to your questions, I should certainly say that George North, myself, and Adam,

---

* This I had from Mr. Adam's own lips in February, 1835. [A more detailed and correct account than memory and conversation could furnish of what passed between Mr. Adam and Mr. Dundas on this occasion, will be given afterwards from memorandums made at the time by Mr. Adam, which were obligingly communicated by Sir Charles Adam to Mr. Allen while he was preparing these collections for publication.]

† His words.

were the most active and instrumental negotiators in the business of the coalition. In truth, I should say, that without the immediate and direct communication that was happily established after many difficulties between Lord North and your uncle, through the intervention of George North and myself, through whom the *most* private and confidential correspondence was easily carried on, the coalition never could have taken place. Lord North had the firmest confidence in his son, and I need not tell you that your uncle reposed the same in me. It has always been the pride of my life to think so. George North and I had laid our heads together long before the *first overtures* were begun, in order to plan the best means of effecting this object, and of counteracting the opposition to it, which it was evident would be made by many of the violent and unreasonable on both sides, of which there were plenty, and most especially of Lord North's party, *who were far more hostile* to the junction than the subordinate Whigs. The latter were more obedient to their leaders, but the ascendancy which some of Lord North's rogues and fools had occasionally over him was something astonishing when one considers the strength of his mind and very superior understanding. But it was not long before we got rid of these pests, and having Lady North and the whole family, sons and daughters, strongly with us, we succeeded in driving the whole pack of rogues from his presence. When you ask if Burke, on your uncle's side, and Eden on Lord North's, had much to do in it, I should say

undoubtedly, yes, very much, especially Eden, no one
knowing better how *to work* upon the rotten part of
Lord North's party. He was therefore highly useful,
though I don't think he had any great weight with
Lord North, who seemed to think that his (Eden's)
bias led him more to your uncle, to whom he professed the most ardent attachment, chiefly owing, I
believe, to his own connection with Lord Carlisle, an
earnest advocate for coalition.

"If Burke had been adverse we must have dropt all
idea of the thing, as he had the greatest sway, I might
almost say command, over Lord Rockingham's friends,
with the exception of the Duke of Devonshire, who,
besides his personal attachment to your uncle, thought
him in every respect a far superior man to Burke,
whose total want of judgment and discretion he was
fully aware of. Burke, however, had no great hand
beyond this in the work, and it was lucky, as we
thought, that he had not, as he might any one day
have marred everything, according to custom, in some
wrong-headed fit of intemperance. Fitzpatrick's aid
was invaluable, his excellent judgment mainly contri-
buting to the success of the measure and removing
unexpected difficulties that occasionally arose. No
one's opinions, you know, *had half so much weight*
with Mr. Fox as your uncle Richard's. Sheridan was
then beginning to acquire some of that influence he
afterwards more fully possessed over your uncle, and
which, not many years after that, he entirely lost—
you know how. Well, Sheridan, do you know,
instead of being adverse to the coalition, as I dare

say you have often heard the vapouring rogue declare, was, on the contrary, I assure you, one of the most eager and clamorous for it.   His hatred of Pitt, and his anxiety to get into office, were motives sufficient. It is true he had no hand in carrying the measure into effect, for nobody had any sort of trust or confidence in him.   Think of his impudence afterwards, in boasting that he had always deprecated the coalition, and foretold its disastrous consequences.   I have now given you a long and tedious, but a faithful history.   I fear you will regret your indiscretion in asking me any questions on the subject, not expecting such a detail.

" Ever yours, dear Lord Holland,

" Most truly,

" J. TOWNSHEND."

Upon my acknowledging that Sheridan had cajoled me into a belief that he had strenuously deprecated the coalition, Lord John sent me the following letter, which I also transcribe here, though it relates more to transactions of the ensuing year than to 1783.

"BALLS, June 23rd, 1830.

" DEAR LORD HOLLAND,

"I have laughed heartily at your account of Sheridan's having duped you into a belief of his noble sacrifice of judgment and opinions to the wishes of others, by his acquiescence in the coalition and handsome support of a measure he originally disapproved. In his great wisdom, it seems he foresaw (foretell he

certainly did not) all the ill consequences of the imprudent step.   These secret thoughts, however, he kept
carefully locked up in his own breast, never uttering
a syllable of disapprobation of the measure, in the
course of it, to Mr. Fox, to Fitzpatrick, or myself, or to
any one of his intimate friends, till more than a twelvemonth afterwards; when, I allow, he was one of the
loudest in his lamentations and condemnations, though
I don't think he had the impudence, *even then*, to
say that he had been prepared for the events that
followed.   When the India Bill had passed the Commons by so large a majority, Sheridan, I remember,
as well as most of us, scouted the idea of its being
thrown out possibly in the House of Lords, which,
indeed, could not have happened, but for the King's
personal and immediate canvass, and the sly but able
manner in which he conducted himself.   Eden, too,
was one of the most sanguine, and ridiculed the fears
of George North, who had much better intelligence
than he had.   The very day before the vote in the
Lords, Eden assured us we might rely on the Duke of
Marlborough and various others, and that he found
Moore, the Archbishop of Canterbury, *more than
friendly*.   ' I own,' said Lord North afterwards, ' I
never quite liked this awkward phrase, *more than
friendly*.'

   " I never saw a man more downcast and chapfallen
than Sheridan, after the decision in the House of
Peers, where Boreas's troops deserted him by
dozens; very few, excepting his brother, the Bishop
of Winchester, Loughborough, Sandwich, my father

(who, by the way, was personally canvassed by the King), and Lord Stormont, remained firm and stout. The latter (Stormont) most especially active and serviceable. Your uncle too, I must own, was strangely deceived into a belief that after our great majority in the Commons, there was no danger whatever from the Lords.

"Having all these matters as fresh in my recollection as if they happened yesterday (for nothing in politics ever interested me so much), I scribble away *currente calamo*, without connection, and in a manner that must confuse you. But if, as I am inclined to suspect, you have any notion of giving a history of the coalition, and the important consequences of it, I should like to talk with you, as I can certainly give you an accurate detail of many, very many, curious circumstances, and of some which are totally unknown, or have been strangely misconceived and misrepresented. In this one respect, therefore, my communications to you may be, as you say, a valuable *chronicle of facts*. But what I should most wish, if ever you should take up your pen on this subject, is not only that you would vindicate the motives which induced those two great men to coalesce, and to give a picture of the fair, disinterested, and honourable feelings of them both during the whole of the negotiation, and that you would rescue them (and it is no more than strict justice to do so) from the false imputation of great rashness and folly, in having too eagerly dashed into this junction, without any regard to principle, or even the common prudence and foresight that was to be expected from two such statesmen as these.

"The first point, I mean the motives and the honourable conduct, were even at the time, I think, generally acknowledged by the candid and impartial part of the public, and very soon afterwards the cry was entirely dropped in the House of Commons, excepting a few fools like Martin, who said the House ought to have a starling kept in the lobby to vociferate from day to day, ' No coalition !' upon which Lord North, with his usual good humour observed, there was perhaps a great deal of good sense in this patriotic recommendation, but that it was surely unnecessary, as the House had already the advantage of possessing a ' *Martin* ' fully competent to execute the important duty, and quite as fit for the office as any ' starling ' that could be found. The House laughed heartily, and there was very little further cry against the coalition. But the second point requires more examination, and is more difficult to prove. The fact, however, is certain, and cannot be contradicted, that soon afterwards, and until the King showed his teeth on the occasion of the India Bill, which was *really* unpopular, and made so by Burke's ungovernable temper, and Jack Lee's extreme indiscretion ; till then, I don't hesitate to say, that the coalition had lost all its unpopularity, the country had become more than reconciled (don't remind me of the Archbishop's disposition towards us, more than friendly), but in truth the country had quite come round to us, and your uncle was, I think, more popular than ever, at least with the sober and thinking part of the public, and the junction of Pitt with Jenkinson, Dundas, Jack Robinson, &c., was more astounding and more condemned than the other. But then came the India Bill! &c., and all Burke's folly.

"I must have wearied your patience, but if you have been annoyed, recollect you have brought it on yourself by your own indiscretion.

"Ever truly yours,

"J. TOWNSHEND."

As Lord John Townshend, in the first of these letters, mentions his father with reference to the Coalition Ministry and India Bill, I cannot help relating a saying of that lively and humorous old man on the occasion. He said, "he had always foreseen the Coalition Ministry could not last, for he was at Court when Mr. Fox kissed hands, and he observed George III. turn back his ears and eyes just like the horse at Astley's, when the tailor he had determined to throw was getting on him."

[Very copious details have been left by Mr. Adam, of the occurrences that led directly and immediately to the coalition of Lord North with Mr. Fox, some of which were imperfectly known to Lord John Townshend, who, with George North, eldest son of Lord North, had the principal share in reconciling them and bringing them to act together.]

[Mr. Fox having resigned on Lord Rockingham's death, with about twelve of the Rockingham party who were in office, and with a great following of those

who were not in office, Lord Shelburne, though he
obtained the aid of Mr. Pitt, who had declined to
accept of any place in the former Administration,
found himself compelled to strengthen his government with such of the adherents of Lord North as
could be prevailed upon to join him. The most
valuable of these acquisitions was Mr. Dundas, to
whom he wrote a most flattering letter, offering him
the Signet for life, the place of Treasurer of the Navy,
and the recommendation to all offices that should
fall vacant in Scotland. On receiving this letter,
Mr. Dundas came up to London; but, to his credit
be it said, he declined to accept those brilliant offers
till he had Lord North's approbation.]

[When Parliament met in December, 1782, it was
composed of three parties; first, of that of the
Ministry, consisting of the friends of Lord Shelburne,
of such of the Rockingham Whigs as had remained
in office after the resignation of Mr. Fox, and of such
of the old adherents of Lord North as either held
offices themselves, or supported the present Ministers
from dislike or fear of Mr. Fox; secondly, of Lord
North's party, consisting of persons devoted to him
from affection, from attachment to the principles of
government he had always maintained, or from
expectation that the disunion of his enemies and the
supposed favour of the Court would bring him back
again to power; and, thirdly, of Mr. Fox and his
personal friends, and of the great body of the
Rockingham Whigs, who had no confidence in
Lord Shelburne.]

[It was evident that if none of these parties fell to pieces, two of them must, sooner or later, coalesce, and overpower the third. The question was, which were to lay aside their former differences and form a junction? Those of the Rockingham party, who had remained in office with Lord Shelburne, were desirous of a re-union with Mr. Fox. The Duke of Richmond, Lord Keppel, and Mr. Pitt himself were inclined to this coalition. Lord Shelburne, on the contrary, with Mr. Dundas, Mr. Rigby, Mr. Jenkinson, and other old supporters of the American war, preferred a junction with Lord North. The following extract from a letter of Mr. Jenkinson to Mr. Adam, dated the 4th January, 1783, shows the views of the two different sections of the Ministerial party after the short session in December, 1782 :—

"You may be sure that there is not the least truth in what St. John told Lord N., of a proposition being made to Charles Fox. The Duke of Richmond and Keppel may be always working at this, but Lord S. assures me that he will never have any connection with C. F.; and I confess I believe him. Mr. Pitt is very much displeased with Lord N.'s last speech, and this disturbs Shelburne. I have done all I can to pacify him, and have made him disposed to send a message through me to Lord N.; but we agreed not to come to any resolution on that head till we have another conversation. I wish that somebody of weight would talk to Mr. Pitt, and for that reason I should rejoice if the Advocate (Mr. Dundas) was come to town."]

[The preliminaries of peace had been signed, and

were laid before Parliament on the 27th of January, 1783. The terms were not in general approved of; and the Ministers thought a vote of approbation by Parliament absolutely necessary for their continuance in office. Lord North declared that he would oppose any vote of censure, but that he could not concur in a vote of approbation. " If they come for an address," said he, " they make us judges, and they must make out their case." In this posture of affairs, Mr. Dundas made a communication to Mr. Adam, which led to consequences of importance, and of a very different nature from what he intended.]

[Mr. Adam, be it remembered, was a personal friend of Lord North, and in habits of intimacy with Mr. Dundas. In the preceding October he had been sent for by Lord Shelburne and had an interview with him at Shelburne House. Many civil speeches were made, and hints of official situations dropped, but nothing was concluded, Mr. Adam being resolved to follow his profession, and attach himself to the fortunes of Lord North. But, though unconnected with Lord Shelburne, he was equally unconnected with Mr. Fox; and of his personal friends many were placemen, or supporters of Ministry, and very few partisans of Mr. Fox. When the possibility of a coalition between Mr. Fox and Lord North was first hinted to him by Lord John Townshend, he was far from encouraging it, and seemed to Lord John to be rather averse to it.]

[On Wednesday, the 12th February, Mr. Adam had an interview with Mr. Dundas, in which the latter told him that every prospect of an overture for coalition from the Ministry to Lord North " was at an end for the present ; that the conduct of Lord North had made it impossible ; that Lord Shelburne and he had pushed it, but that they could not get the other Ministers to agree to it ; that he himself did not like to talk to Lord North, as he had no proposition to make, and had never talked to him in that line,— Lord North having always said ' that he wished to hear of no bargain.' "]

[Adam said he had reason to think that Lord North would oppose every censure on the Peace, but that he would not agree to an Address of Approbation.]

[Dundas thought an Address absolutely necessary, and the impression left on Adam's mind was, " that no arrangement could be made with Lord North, unless he supported the Address explicitly, without deviating into any censure of the Peace in any one of its parts ; that such complete support was necessary to enable Lord Shelburne and Mr. Dundas to overcome the prejudices of the other Ministers, and in that way Lord North and his friends might be brought into office at the end of the session in a respectable manner, some of his friends having offices, and himself a great, but not a Cabinet place."]

[Dundas then told him, that some time ago Ministers had thought the best thing that could happen to them would be a junction of Mr. Fox with Lord North ; that Mr. Pitt had wished for it, thinking the Ministry would thereby gain supporters

from the adherents of both. Such a coalition, added
Dundas, would have overcome Pitt's objections to
Jenkinson and others, against whom his prejudices
are strong ; for he believes in Court influence, and all
such things. But that matter is now at an end, for
Pitt has been at last permitted to treat with Fox.
They have met. Pitt's proposition was that the
Treasury should stand as it is, and that they should
share fully in the other parts of the Government.
The conversation was short. Pitt drew himself up,
on Fox declaring he would have nothing to do where
Shelburne was concerned.]

[Dundas then said to Adam with strong injunctions
of secrecy, " It appears to me that the Government
with Lord Shelburne at the head of it is at an end.
I had not seen him from the time the message had
gone by Pitt to Fox till this morning. He sent for
me early. He asked me when I came into the room,
whether I had ever heard the story of the Duke of
Perth. I answered, 'No.' He then said, 'The
Duke of Perth had a country neighbour and friend,
who came to him one morning with a white cockade
in his hat. ' What is the meaning of this ? ' said the
Duke : ' I wish to show your Grace,' replied his
country friend, 'that I am resolved to follow your
fortunes.' The Duke snatched the hat from his head,
took the cockade out of it, and threw it into the fire,
saying, ' My situation and duty compel me to take
this line, but *that* is no reason why you should ruin
yourself and your family.' "]

[" I find," continued Lord Shelburne, " that it will

now be necessary for me to quit the Government;
and as you are beloved by all parties, I wished you to
have early notice of it, that you might be prepared
for what must happen. Fox and the Duke of Portland
will make up a Government with Pitt, for I cannot
hear of Pitt's high notions of not taking part in any
Government where I am not one. He shall not think
of resigning with me. Lady Shelburne is so dis-
tressed, that I cannot think of remaining longer in
this situation; and having worked the great work of
peace, I am not desirous to remain."]

[" Lord Shelburne," said Mr. Dundas, " spoke with
so much calmness, that I believe him sincere, and that
it will end in the resignation of Lord Shelburne, and
in the union of Pitt and Fox, which will be followed
by a dissolution of Parliament, and extinction of the
party of Lord North." " Can nothing," says Adam,
" be done with Lord North to prevent that calamity? "
" I see nothing," replies Dundas, " but Lord North's
support of the Peace, in which case his friends will be
gradually preferred, and at the end of the session
Shelburne and I must prevail over the prejudices of
Pitt and of the other Ministers; but at present I see
no prospect of a coalition with him."]

[At parting, Dundas said to Adam, " You will not
mention Lord Shelburne's intended resignation; but
you may say in general terms to Lord North himself,
and to Charles Townshend and his other friends, that
it is my conjecture there will be a government of
Fox and Pitt, with the Rockinghams and all Lord
Shelburne's friends but himself—that they will

dissolve Parliament, and there will be an end of
Lord North—that I see no means of preventing this
but a support of the Address, in which case the
difficulties will be got over; but at present no
coalition can be made."]

["Next morning," says Adam, "I waited on Lord
North. When I went in to him he told me he had
had a message from Mr. Fox the evening before of a
very civil nature, stating what had passed between
him and Pitt. I told him I had heard of it, and
informed him that it was on the footing that the
Treasury should remain where it was, which he said
it was very important for him to know." Mr.
Adam then related to him what Mr. Dundas has
desired him to communicate, and repeated it to
Mr. Charles Townshend. He again met with Lord
North at the Speaker's room, and was told by him
that, after consulting with Charles Townshend, he
thought it essential to prevent the threatened junction
of Fox and Pitt, and for that purpose he should
avail himself of Fox's communication. Adam
requested him to wait till they had again seen
Dundas, whom they were to meet at dinner.]

[Dundas had no private conversation with Lord
North, but he told Adam that "Pitt was softened
down on the subject of resignation, and though he
still protested against Shelburne quitting the Treasury;" he added, "unless the measure *originated*
from himself." At parting, Dundas repeated again
to Adam, that nothing would answer but an absolute
unconditional support of the Address, which he

read to him. The Address was a measure they
thought necessary, and Lord North must support it.
Adam remonstrated in vain against the peremptory
demand of support without allowing Lord North the
exercise of his own judgment.]

[Adam then went to Lord North's, and repeated to
him, to his son George North, and to Charles
Townshend what he had been desired to communicate. After mature consideration it appeared to
them all, that the only means of preventing the ruin
of their party was to have a communication with
Mr. Fox, and *that* immediately, in order that Mr. Pitt
might not be beforehand with them. Mr. Charles
Townshend was particularly clear and decided for this
measure, and it ended in George North's going to
Mr. Fox that evening and appointing a meeting with
him next day at two o'clock.]

[In revealing to Adam his private conversation with
Lord Shelburne it was evidently the intention and
expectation of Dundas that it would stimulate Adam,
by the fear of a dissolution, to use every possible
endeavour with Lord North to make him accede to
the Ministerial proposition, and with the same view,
no doubt, he made the same secret and confidential
communication to Robinson, Lord North's principal
agent ; but he overshot his mark. Instead of
terrifying Lord North into compliance, he roused
him to resistance, and made him avail himself without
delay of his son's inclination for, and connection with,
Mr. Fox.]

[Next morning Adam met Dundas at Mr. Rigby's.

Rigby insisted that Lord North must support the
Address—would hear of no medium between unqua-
lified support and decided opposition—derided the
notion of any merit in opposing a vote of censure,
unless it was accompanied by a vote of approbation—
and finally he and Dundas went to Lord North with
the Address in their pocket, which " they were sure he
could not refuse." Lord North, though he thought
their proposal insulting to him, received them with
civility, but would not say he approved of their
Address, on which Dundas wrote a letter to Lord
Shelburne in his presence, saying that he had read
the Address to Lord North, who would not say
whether he would support it or not; and having
shown this letter to Lord North, he despatched it to
Lord Shelburne. In relating these particulars to
Adam, Mr. Dundas lamented that Lord North's
obstinacy had ruined everything, and enumerated
the vast number of places, which Lord Shelburne
would have had to distribute among the friends of
Lord North, had he been more compliant.]

[On the same day, Friday, 14th of February, Mr.
Fox and Lord North had their first interview. They
met at the house of Mr. George North. They agreed
to lay aside all former animosity, Mr. Fox declaring
that he hoped their Administration would be founded
on mutual good will and confidence, which was the
only thing that could make it permanent and useful.
They agreed, also, that nothing more was required to
be done in reducing the influence of the Crown by
economical reform, and that on parliamentary reform

every man should follow his own opinion. Mr. Fox
having urged that the King should not be suffered to
be his own Minister, Lord North replied : " If you
mean there should not be a Government by departments, I agree with you ; I think it a very bad
system. There should be one man, or a Cabinet, to
govern the whole, and direct every measure. Government by departments was not brought in by me. I
found it so, and had not vigour and resolution to put
an end to it. The King ought to be treated with all
sort of respect and attention, but the appearance of
power is all that a king of this country can have.
Though the Government in my time was a Government by departments, the whole was done by the
Ministers, except in a few instances."]

[There was some little, and but little, conversation
about men or offices. They agreed to oppose the
Address, and Lord North drew up the amendment,
which was afterwards moved by Lord John Cavendish,
with the omission of a clause in favour of the American
loyalists, which was moved separately by Lord North.
Such was the substance of their first conversation, as
reported next day by Lord North to Mr. Adam.]

[This interview could not long remain secret. Next
day Sir James Lowther went to Mr. Rigby's, and told
him there had been a meeting the day before between
Lord North and Mr. Fox, at Mr. George North's;
and proposed that something should be done immediately to bring about an interview between Lord
Shelburne and Lord North. Rigby offered to convey
any message, if he had authority, from Lord Shelburne.

Sir James procured him the authority he desired, and he went accordingly. Lord North's reply was, " I cannot meet him *now*." " Then," said Rigby, " you are fixed in Opposition." Lord North said again, " I cannot meet Lord Shelburne *now*. It is too late."]

[The report of a coalition between Mr. Fox and Lord North spread rapidly, and filled with dismay those friends of the latter, who had connected themselves with the Shelburne Administration. Jenkinson, who had received private intelligence from Robinson that everything was settled between Fox and North, was in consternation. He spoke fairly and candidly of Lord North, and said he had been shamefully used, but lamented the step he had taken, which he imputed to the message sent to him by Dundas. Rigby said to Adam, " It was your communication that put an end to everything. Dundas, though he does not like to talk on the subject, owns that you said nothing you were not authorised to communicate." Rigby added that he should vote for the Peace, but wished Lord North might beat the Ministers ; and, with respect to himself, he was determined never to be in Opposition again. Dundas laid the whole blame of Lord North's recent conduct on Mr. Eden and Lord Loughborough. Adam replied, that the coalition had been brought about by the Ministers having treated with Fox as a friend, and offered to participate with him in everything except the Treasury, while they had insisted on Lord North's support in the first instance as the terms of his getting anything. Dundas owned that he had had a proposition to Lord North in his pocket, but withheld it till Lord North should first declare he would support the Peace. To Adam's suggestion that all parties might unite, with the exception of Lord Shelburne, who was so obnoxious to the Rockingham party that they would have nothing to do with him, Dundas replied, " It was strange the impression entertained of Lord Shelburne's character, but it was so."]

[On the resolutions of censure on the terms of the Peace moved by Lord John Cavendish, an effort was made by Robinson to terrify Lord North from supporting the motion by the reports of defalcations among his friends ; but these reports turned out on inquiry to be utterly without foundation. Through the whole of these proceedings, Robinson seems to have been as much disinclined to a coalition with Mr. Fox, as Eden and Loughborough were in favour of it.]

[Lord Shelburne having resigned, an attempt was made by Dundas to prevail on Mr. Pitt to undertake the Government. He had at one time succeeded, and much joy and triumph did he and Rigby express thereat, with many gibes and taunts against Adam and Lord North. On Thursday morning, the 27th of February, Mr. Pitt had agreed to accept ; but, in the course of the same day, he repented and declined. His consent had been obtained by Dundas assuring him that Lord North himself would not take an active part in Opposition ; but, reflecting on the uncertainty of this assurance, he would not proceed upon it.

Both Adam and Dundas expressed their wish that Pitt could be included in the new arrangement. Dundas said he had done all in his power to bring it about; but he found it impossible, and as to himself, he was attached to Pitt for the rest of his life. He afterwards said, "Pitt is impracticable on the subject of Union; he proscribes Lord North, and does not even express himself clearly disposed to unite with Fox. He has a high opinion of Fox's abilities, and had always wished to have him in the Government; because he thought it impossible to conduct great and difficult affairs with such abilities to criticise them. But now he seems much estranged from him."]

[Some days elapsed before any communication was made to Lord North on the part of the King. Meeting Lord Guilford as he came from the Queen, whose Chamberlain he was, his Majesty went up to him, wringing his hands, and saying, "Did I ever think, my Lord Guilford, that Lord North would have delivered me up in this manner to Mr. Fox?" Lord Guilford replied, that he was sure it was not Lord North's intention to do what was disagreeable to his Majesty; but he understood his Majesty had got over any difficulty on that head by the interview between Mr. Fox and Mr. Pitt.]

[Aversion to Mr. Fox, from whatever cause it originated, seems to have been at that time the predominant principle in the King's mind. Lord Shelburne showed Mr. Dundas a letter he had received from his Majesty, in which, with some exultation, he said that he had been always sure the interview

between Fox and Pitt would end as it did, owing to
the *rudeness* of the former. Those who knew Mr.
Fox will be able to appreciate the prejudice under
which that observation was made.]

[Was it not the discovery of this deep-rooted
aversion in the royal bosom which had of late, as
Mr. Dundas had observed, so " much estranged "
Mr. Pitt from Mr. Fox?]

I now resume the extracts from Walpole.

" The King was unwilling to part with Lord
Shelburne, or at least disliked the junction of North
and Fox, or was averse to receiving the latter and his
party ; at least he could not be insensible to the force
put upon him a second time in one year, and the little
or no option left him in naming his own Ministers.
This repugnance was no doubt fomented by Lord
Shelburne. The insolence of the victorious allies
soon added fuel to that secret flame. They had so
wantonly marked out the victims they intended to
make, particularly the two capital ones, the Lord
Chancellor Thurlow and the Lord Advocate, that they
and their friends soon concerted measures to baffle the
conquerors. Those two lawyers, with Lord Weymouth
and Lord Gower and Rigby, who had all united with
or were grown inclined to Shelburne, communicated
their discontents to the King, who received their overtures with alacrity from the Lord Advocate, and
actually wrote to Lord Weymouth, to desire his
support *against his new tyrants.* His Majesty wished
Lord Gower to accept the Treasury, but he had not
courage. In that distress the Lord Advocate, one of

the boldest of men, proposed to the King to send for the very young Chancellor of the Exchequer, William Pitt, not yet past 23. The offer was no doubt dazzling, and so far worth accepting, as to *obtain the chariot for a day*, was glorious at his age, and to one so ambitious. It was placing him at the head of a party, —a rank which he must always preserve, in or out of place. The young man had the discretion, however, to ask time to consider, and on the 27th he excused himself to the King from undertaking the charge of Prime Minister. He certainly, says Walpole in a note, consented for a few hours, but soon retracted. Lord Shelburne dissuaded him, from jealousy, but there might be another reason—the King made the offer very drily and ungraciously. In fact it was in every light wise; in a personal one it showed mode-ration. No supplies were voted, nor would be granted by a hostile majority. A victorious majority too of a popular assembly, if thwarted, grow violent, and the disappointment of those, who have expected to share the spoils of their enemies, impels their party on all excesses. Nor would Pitt himself appear but as the substitute of Lord Shelburne, against whom an impeachment might be voted. On the contrary, giving a career to the hopes of the triumphant, was the best way to hurt them. Most men, not con-nected with the new and strange junction, could but be scandalised at it, and *were*. Compassion for the insult to the King would weigh with others. All who should be dismissed would become more envenomed enemies, and all the partisans of Fox who should be provided for, or of Lord North who should not be restored, would not be less incensed. The probable rapacity of the victors would furnish matter for abuse. The character of Fox would be an inexhaustible fund of objections, and the yet unstained one of Pitt, with a large following of young men who worshipped him, would soon raise him to a formidable height. He might contemplate, too, as certain devotees, the Yorkshire associations, &c." (Here follows more speculation on his probable adherents among the reformers, not worth transcribing.)

March. " T. Townshend created a peer. He had detached himself entirely from Fox and the Cavendishes; had addicted himself to Lord Shelburne." (A speculation follows, on the state of the House of Lords, and a long diatribe on Lord Shelburne's pensions, to the Chancellor, Lord Grantham, and Sir Joseph Yorke, as well as to Barré and Dunning.)

" The King continued to closet Lord Advocate and Lord Gower, and the few he trusted, of whom Jenkinson was the chief, trying every method to avoid submitting to take the Duke of Portland and Fox. His counsellors were as inveterate as his Majesty, but had less boldness—finding which, he told the Lord Advocate that sooner than yield he would '*go to Hanover*,' and had even prevailed on the Queen to consent. He had meditated such abdication at the time of the riots for Wilkes. He had carried that intention farther the last year, having held the royal yacht in readiness a fortnight for that purpose. If the Queen consented, it was probably to humour

a person in a passion, rather than contradict, as it
gives credit, and time to soothe. This, perhaps, the
Queen did, for on the 4th March, in the evening,
the King sent for Lord North, and, after long and
most earnest endeavours to persuade him to break his
coalition with Fox, and retake the first post himself,
(both which Lord North positively refused, recommending the Duke of Portland ;) the King told him
in wrath, " he would not put the Treasury into the
hands of a head of a faction."

Here follow some minute remarks of Walpole on
the mistaken policy of the King, in sending for Lord
North instead of applying to Duke of Portland
directly, which he (Walpole) argues, and I think
proves, cemented rather than shook the coalition
between the Whigs and Lord North, " by giving the
latter an opportunity of showing and *vaunting* his
fidelity."

March 5th. In the morning " the King sent again
for Lord North, but repenting before his arrival, dismissed him immediately, saying, ' he had not yet
resolved what to do.' But the secret lay deeper than
even his general aversion to the Cavendish faction. His
son, the Prince of Wales, had of late thrown himself
into the arms of Charles Fox, and this in the most
undisguised manner. Fox lodged in St. James's
Street, and as soon as he rose, which was very late, had
a levee of his followers, and of the members of the
gaming-club at Brookes'—all his disciples. His
bristly, black person, and shagged breast, quite open
and rarely purified by any ablutions, was wrapped in a

foul linen night-gown, and his bushy hair dishevelled.* In these Cynic weeds, and with Epicurean good humour, did he dictate his politics, and in this school did the heir of the crown attend his lessons and imbibe them. Fox's followers, to whom he never enjoined Pythagorean silence, were strangely licentious in their conversations about the King. At Brookes', they proposed wagers on the duration of his reign, and if they moderated their irreverent jests in the presence of the Prince, it was not extraordinary that the orgies of Brookes' might be reported to have passed at Fox's levees, or that the King should suspect that the same disloyal topics should be handled in the morning that he knew had been the themes of each preceding evening. The Prince not only espoused the cause of the Coalition, but was not at all guarded in his expressions. He was even reported to have said aloud in the Drawing-room, " that his father had not yet agreed to the plan of the Coalition, but, by God, he should be made to agree to it."

"The anguish to a mind that had from the Prince's childhood anticipated jealousy, rendered the already-conceived antipathy to *Fox a rankling ulcer.* How far his suspicions went I do not know, but while he kept all Government at a stand, and was searching for a succedaneum, it transpired that he had consulted the Lord Chancellor and Lord Ashburton on the still

---

* This description, though of course a strong caricature, yet certainly has much humour, and I must needs acknowledge, from my boyish recollection of a morning in St. James's Street, some truth to recommend it. —V. H.

nearer question of his son. One or both whispered the consultation, if not the purport. At first it was supposed to have been on the Prince's debts; but as they did not appear considerable, it was believed that the royal parent had demanded of the two lawyers what redress he could have against a man who had alienated from him the affections of his son. Rumour added, that the blunt and surly Chancellor had replied, ' that he would have no peace till his son and Fox were secured in the Tower.' I do not pretend to give credit to the violence, nor am certain that even the interrogatory was proposed. Yet the extreme vehemence, with which Fox and his associates, with the concurrence of his allies,* proscribed the Chancellor at this crisis, seems to imply some foundation in the story. Fox had lived upon amicable terms with the Chancellor, who had certainly supported Shelburne in the faintest and loosest manner.† Lord

* "The Prince of Wales said aloud at supper, at the Duke of Cumberland's, that he hoped that damned fellow the Chancellor would be turned out. This, combined with the proscription by Fox, seems to confirm the report of the Chancellor having expressed himself roughly on their connexion."—H. W.

There was sufficient ground for this ' proscription ' in the inconvenience lately felt by the Whigs from Thurlow's retaining the Seals in Rockingham's administration, and in North's wish to open the way to them for Loughborough, who was courting the whole Coalition and the Prince very assiduously. That Thurlow expressed himself roughly is most probable, but that he seriously advised the arrest of Mr. Fox and the Prince is quite a preposterous story; he had too much sense, too much law, and too much cowardice to do so.—V. H.

Walpole's account hardly implies any such advice.—J. R.

† This is very possibly true; but it does not follow that he did not thwart Lord Rockingham and Mr. Fox in the most vexatious way, and assist the King in thwarting them first and Lord Shelburne afterwards. In support of any body or any thing Thurlow was throughout his life, if not

North's friends had, till this minute, affectedly asserted
that Lord North would insist on the Chancellor's
retaining the Seals.   As he now abandoned him
abruptly, they were puzzled to excuse North or themselves, and strengthened the report of the offence.   In
truth, the Chancellor had never loved, and rather
despised Lord North; and the latter, if he protected
him for a time, did it more I suspect to deprecate his
resentment, than from zeal to serve him."

" Though the King had failed,. both in attempting
to form an Administration, or to detach Lord North
from his new friends, and would not yield to the
latter; and though there was, in reality, no Government—for Lord Shelburne had actually resigned, and
the other Ministers only transacted the ordinary business, without opening new matter—and though the
Houses continued to sit; yet his Majesty went to
Windsor, leaving everything in suspense.   And
though he returned to town at the end of the week,
and appointed a Drawing-room, it was put off, and he
was, or it was given out he was, ill."   (Then follows
a statement of the inconvenience and danger, both
from mutinies and French, arising from this want of
government.)   " The suspense still continued, and it
was evident to thinking men that whichever side had
most temper would get the better.   Fox was aware of
that, and said not a word in Parliament, and restrained
his friends.   Had they made any violent motion—as,
perhaps, the King expected and hoped—it was very

faint and loose, indolent and unsocial; but in opposing and thwarting he
could be earnest and zealous enough.—V. H.

likely that the Tories would have returned to him, and resented the force laid upon his prerogative. Of the votes Lord North had governed, he was not likely to retain half. The House of Lords was still less disposed to obey the Coalition. If Lord North demanded many places for his friends, the Cavendish faction would have refused them, fearing his predominating. If he obtained but few, and those for his family and particular friends, the number who had fallen with him, and would not be indemnified, would become his enemies; and to satisfy them all was impossible. Burke's reform had struck off many places; no more pensions could be given; and to satisfy Fox's dependents, all indigent, North's connections, the friends of the Cavendishes, and the rapacity of Burke and his family, there would be wanting more places than existed before his retrenchment."

March 12th. " When the interministerium had lasted seventeen days, the King sent again for Lord North, and told him he should form an Administration according to the plan he had proposed; but as he should not like to change again, he desired it might be broad enough. Lord North proposed to the King to see the Duke of Portland himself; but that the King refused, and told Lord North to desire the Duke to send him his arrangement *in writing*. This was as positively refused by the Duke, who sent word that if his Majesty condescended to employ him, it would be necessary for him to see his Majesty.

" Some days more were spent on messages of this

kind, yet with partial discussions, either between the King and his future Ministers, or amongst themselves. The King was peremptory against dismissing the Chancellor; Lord North as positive for Lord Stormont being Secretary of State, who would take nothing else. The King's friends complained that his Majesty was not allowed to make one of his own cabinet council; and he himself once, and but once, spoke to General Conway on the subject, and complained, that when he summoned them to settle his Administration, they replied they were not agreed amongst themselves.

"Coke of Norfolk, attached to the Cavendishes, gave notice that if no Administration were appointed by the 22nd, he would move to know the reason. This was probably to terrify the King. Coke had the promise of a peerage from Lord Rockingham."[*]

March 17th. "A great meeting was held at Lord Fitzwilliam's, whom the Cavendishes were nursing up as a young Octavius, to succeed his uncle Rockingham. The Duke of Portland presided, declaring nothing was settled, but hoped things were in a good way."

March 19th. The remaining Ministers held a cabinet on the tumults at Portsmouth, and "before they parted, they recommended to the Chancellor to advise the King to settle the Administration with the Duke of Portland."

* Mr. Coke was offered a peerage in 1782-3, and again in 1806, but both times declined the honour. Later in life he was created Earl of Leicester. —J. R.

March 20th. " The Chancellor, not to hinder the arrangement, declared to the King that he would not keep the Seals ; yet was the settlement not advanced ; for now Lord North,—who had at last, for accommodation as he pretended, consented to take the Seals of one Secretary, instead of Lord Stormont, with whom Charles Fox had declared that he could not nor would not act, so much did their principles differ,—acquainted the Coalition, on the 20th, that he had persuaded Lord Stormont to be President. At this they exclaimed, ' He had done it of himself, and without consulting them ;' and, though the Duke of Portland had been admitted to the King in the morning (Lord North, to force the King to comply, declaring he was tired, and would carry no more messages), and had been asked for his list, which he still would not give in writing, the party were so angry with Lord North, that at eight in the evening they dispatched the Duke of Portland to the King, to say the negotiation was at an end. However, they still consulted, and Fox's necessitous friends being very clamorous, and Lord North declaring that ' though he would support them, he would take no part,' * they deter-

---

* One much connected with Lord North, telling me of this coolness between him and Fox, added, " Lord North at first thought Mr. Fox was to support him, now he finds he is to support Mr. Fox, and therefore he will have done with them." Lord North had even on the 20th, in the evening, wrote circular [1] letters to call a meeting of his friends to acquaint them with his reasons for breaking off with Fox.—H. W.

---

[1] I doubt this fact, and I suspect that Walpole exaggerates the necessary discussions between two chiefs of a coalition party on forming a Ministry, into

mined to say that Lord North had *not* violated the
agreement, though they *had* said he had; and, in two
hours after sending the Duke of Portland to the King,
to declare off, they, at ten that night, begged Lord
North to acquaint the King that they would recommence it. The Duke, two hours before, on acquainting
the King that Lord North would take no part with
them, had offered to make an arrangement himself for
his Majesty. The King replied, coldly, ' I thank your
Grace; I will not give you that trouble.' On the
contrary, he sent for W. Pitt the next day."

March 22nd. " Mr. Coke made his intended
motion, but waived it on the Coalition declaring that
they believed his Majesty would soon appoint an
Administration."

March 23rd. " The Duke of Portland was again with
the King, and carried a list of the intended Cabinet;
but the King would not look at it, demanding to see
the whole list, which the Duke would not produce, but
continued to press the Cabinet list upon him, saying,
' I implore your Majesty to look at it,' but the King
held his hands behind him, and would not take it.
I believe it was the next day that the Duke wrote
to the King, and to palliate the refusal of the whole
list, assured him *they did not intend to remove anybody
about his person, or in the household.* Whatever day
it was, on the 23rd the King wrote both to the Duke
and Lord North a few words, to declare that all

dissensions and ruptures that never occurred. At least, the friends of Mr. Fox,
most averse to the Coalition, have never given me any impression against Lord
North's conduct at this period.—V. H.

negotiation with them was at an end ; and he sent
again for Mr. Pitt : and on the 24th it was universally
believed he had undertaken the Administration, till
Mr. Coke, in the House of Commons, declaring that he
would repeat his motion, unless Mr. Pitt would say
that he had accepted the first place, Mr. Pitt rose and
declared that he was *not* Minister, nor knew of any
arrangement formed.   A most remarkable debate
followed, Mr. Fox accusing the King's secret friends
of breaking off the negotiation, which at first seemed
levelled at the Chancellor ; but afterwards, looking
full at Jenkinson, the latter rose with great emotion,
and did in effect own that he was the secret Minister,
though he protested he had never gone to the
King but when sent for; and he appealed to Lord
North whether he had ever found obstructions from
him.   Of that, Lord North fully acquitted him ; and
then took occasion to protest, that he and his friend
had had no difference for twenty-four hours.   The
Address was carried."

Walpole remarks three mistakes in the policy of
the King, of Jenkinson, and of Mr. Pitt.   The first,
in the King not closing in the first instance with the
Coalition ; the second, in Jenkinson avowing his secret
correspondence with the King; the third, in Pitt
declining the Administration.   In assigning the
reasons which should have induced the King to close
with the Coalition, he says, among other things, " The
bad character of Fox and his friends, and the great
emoluments he would have bestowed upon them,
would have given infinite offence ; and Lord North

and Lord Stormont,* the latter of whom had been excluded by Fox from the Secretary's seals, would not have agreed.

" On the Address being voted on the Monday, the King immediately went to Windsor that evening to hunt next day, in all likelihood to carry away the Prince of Wales from Fox. He returned on the 25th, received the Address, gave a gracious but no explicit answer to it."

March 26th. " General Conway being with the King on the business of the Army, the King spoke to him a little on the present strange situation, though not so much as he wished, to give him an opening to advise the King to take the Coalition;—the more honest and handsome in him, as he expected they intended to lay him aside, not one of them having talked to him of their politics, though the Duke of Portland and the Cavendishes kept up intimacy with him, but they had left him out of their proposed Cabinet. Burke, too, had of late paid great court to him, though cold and hostile towards him when he would not resign with them ; and Burke had lately declared in the House that the Army never had had so useful and indefatigable a Commander-in-Chief, and he believed never would have. The King said to him, ' It was a strange debate on Monday,' and then complained that the Duke of Portland had refused to show him

* It is just to remark that Lord Stormont, a stiff, formal man, of high Tory principles, to whom Mr. Fox seemed at first to have so much repugnance, always conducted himself during their political connexion with great honour and fairness, and that Mr. Fox has frequently told me that he behaved well.—V. H.

the list of their arrangements. Conway replied : ' Yes,
sir ; of the great posts I thought they had.' ' No,'
said the King, ' none but the Cabinet ; not the Lord-
Lieutenant of Ireland. But I can tell them Lord
Temple will not stay with them ; and *you*, what have
you done to them ? ' said the King, artfully. ' I
know nothing,' said Conway ; ' nobody talks to me,
nor I to any of them.' ' Why, they have left you out
of the Cabinet,' said the King ; ' I suppose they
design to have no Commander-in-Chief. And what
will the Duke of Richmond do ? ' continued the King.
Conway said, ' he did not know,' and the King changed
the discourse."

March 29th. " The King sent again for Lord
North, at night, and pressed him to be Minister, but
he refused ; and having said in reply, ' The Duke of
Portland is ready to be so.' ' Then,' said the King,
' I wish your lordship good night.' "

March 31st. " Mr. W. Pitt resigned. Lord
Surrey made his two motions—one, to inquire who
prevented the Administration—the other, to desire
one. The first was universally disapproved, and the
Tories discouraging the other, both were dropped.
Yet Charles Fox attacking Jenkinson warmly, his fear
probably fixed the King's resolution, for on the
1st of April he sent once more to Lord North, and
said, ' Well, so the Duke of Portland is firm.' ' Yes,
sir.' ' Well, then, if you will not do the business, I
will take him.' ' I have told your Majesty I cannot.'
' Well, then, tell him he may come and kiss my hand
to-morrow.' Accordingly, on the 2nd of April the

Duke of Portland was made First Lord of the Treasury; Lord John Cavendish again Chancellor of the Exchequer; Lord North and Charles Fox, Secretaries of State. The King received the Duke of Portland and Charles Fox graciously. To Lord Carlisle, who had now changed sides three times in one year, and whose resignation had been the signal for blowing up Lord Shelburne, he did not speak; and Lord North he received with the utmost coldness, and continued to treat with visible aversion. Thus, from February 24th to April 2nd the nation had been without any head of Administration.

" The Duke of Portland, on quitting the King, went directly to the Duke of Richmond, and begged him to remain Master of the Ordnance. The latter desired time to consider of it, but expressed dislike of acting with Lord North, yet• *rather inclined to stay in place*.

" Thence Duke of Portland went to General Conway, made excuses for his being left out of the Cabinet, and pressed him to remain at the head of the Army, which Conway, having ascertained from the King his approbation, consented to do."

April 3rd. " The new Ministers, pressed, as they said, by Lord North, who wished to restore Lord Townshend to the Ordnance (but I rather think hoping to fix the Duke of Richmond's irresolution, in which they acted unwisely, as, had they let him alone, I am persuaded he would have gone on with them,) sent for the Duke's answer. He was offended, threw up the Ordnance, and they were disappointed.

" Fox, in his first audience of the King, vindicated himself on the aspersions thrown on him, as insti- gating the Prince of Wales to disobedience; protested he had never said a word to the Prince, which he should not have been glad to have his Majesty hear; he had promised nothing to the Prince, but to get his family settled. 'Oh,' said the King, 'that will be all in due time.' Fox hinted plainly at the Chancellor as the author of these aspersions, which the King shuffled off—but this proved that *that* had been the true cause of the Chancellor's disgrace—and he not resigning, and it being reported that he would not, Fox, by the King's leave, sent to him for the Great Seal. Yet the impression remained, and the King was said to call this *his son's Ministry*. When the Duke of Richmond resigned, the King was so pleased with it, that he seemed quite reconciled to the Duke and laughed at Lord North to him."

April 7th. " Fox rechosen for Westminster,—there was some hissing, but no opposition, nor was there any to Lord J. Cavendish at York."—H. W.

The only authentic sources from which Walpole at this time derived his information were General Conway and the Duke of Richmond, but principally the former.

We may now refer to the letters of Fitzpatrick, an actor in these events. They show that, in some respects, the account of Walpole is inaccurate. There does not appear to have been in the course of those transactions any breach between Mr. Fox and Lord North :—

RICHARD FITZPATRICK TO LORD OSSORY.

"Brooks's, *Saturday night,*
" *8th March,* 1783.

" I dined to-day with Lord Fitzwilliam at a Coalition dinner, which went off with great success. In the course of it, Lord N. received a note from the King, and has been with him to-night. I have just heard here that nothing passed except a renewal of former conversations and former proposal to him to undertake it, which was of course declined. This is all I know at present, and it is now past eleven.

" Yours affectionately,

" R. F.

" P.S. Charles has just told me that the above is exactly the state of the case."

SAME TO SAME.

" *Wednesday evening,* 12*th March,* 1783.

" This morning (and not before) the King sent for Lord North, and desired him to acquaint the Duke of Portland that he was desirous of forming an Administration upon a broad bottom, and had no objection to his being at the head of it ; that he wished them to settle the arrangement of it, and send it to him. The Duke of P. and Charles are going to Lord North's this evening to talk the matter over ; but Lord N. seems to agree with them that the King ought to see

the Duke of Portland to conclude the business. I
will write again to-morrow.

" Yours,

"R. F."

SAME TO SAME.

" *Thursday night*, 13*th March*, 1783.

" Nothing is yet absolutely settled, but probably
the whole will be so to-morrow. It seems to look as
if the point of Secretary of State would be given up,
but the dismission of the Chancellor insisted upon. I
have not had any opportunity of speaking to the Duke
of Portland, but I suppose I shall to-night ; and
probably Charles has already talked to him.

" Yours,

" R. F."

SAME TO SAME.

" *Friday,* 14*th March*, 1783.

" The business is not yet finally settled ; but it is so
far advanced that Lord North has sent to the King to
let him know, that they have so far agreed as to wish
that he should see the Duke of Portland. I believe
Carlisle will be Secretary of State, which is the best
that could be, supposing that point to be given up
to Lord North.

" Charles tells me I must be Secretary at War, if
all difficulties are obviated. It is a great undertaking,
yet I feel ashamed of declining it. When you come

to town, I will explain further to you my notions upon
this. Adieu.

" Yours,

"R. F."

SAME TO SAME.

"*Saturday night*, 15*th March*, 1783.

" The whole negotiation has broken off this
morning, most unexpectedly. The Duke of P. and
Lord North had agreed on all arrangements last
night, but Lord Stormont declined accepting either
the President of Council or Privy Seal. The Secretary of State (which had been given up to Lord North)
was fixed for Lord Carlisle. This being the state of
the case, Lord North went this morning to the King,
who enquired if the Chancellor was intended to
remain ; Lord North informed him that the Duke of
Portland and Charles would not act with him in the
Cabinet, upon which the King declared that unless
they consented, no Administration could be formed on
a broad bottom, as he wished ; and insisted that
Lord Stormont should be Secretary of State. Lord
North told him that he knew the Duke of Portland
and his friends would not acquiesce in these arrangements ; accordingly, they did not. I believe Lord
North considers himself as ill used by the King, who
empowered him to fix his arrangements with the Duke
of Portland by a *carte blanche*, and probably the
arrangements may have been so far known as to
offend many persons who think themselves neglected.

This was probably the original view of the Court. But as the treaty breaks off upon the most popular ground, something is expected certainly in the House of Commons on Monday. Possibly the King may give way again to-morrow, and consent to everything; but, unless he does, some motion will infallibly be made on Monday. Lord Surrey intended it before, if measures had not been taken for forming a Ministry. If the King is stout, there seems a probability of warm proceedings on Monday, and I take it for granted you will wish to be here. I cannot think the Chancellor will be mad enough to encourage him in resisting. Perhaps they will try Pitt again. A great meeting of Whigs is fixed for to-morrow night, at Fitzwilliam's, upon a supposition of announcing an Administration; but it will now be for the purpose of stating what has passed. Our friends in general seem to think the King has behaved as might have been expected; Lord North perfectly well, though, perhaps, he may not be bold enough to persevere; but that this proceeding will secure even all those of the House of Commons who hesitated to approve before. I write no more, concluding you will come, at so critical a moment.

"R. F."

MR. FOX TO MR. FITZPATRICK.

[No date.]

"I have only time to tell you that in consequence of the interview this morning, we are to meet at Lord North's to-night, and settle an arrangement. The

King does it *de la plus mauvaise grace possible*, and
there are several unsatisfactory circumstances in the
manner in which he has left it with the Duke of
Portland. Lord North will be Secretary of State,
which I am very glad of.

" Yours ever,

"C. J. FOX.

" I think this had better not be said, I mean the
unsatisfactory part of it."

* I now return to the remarks of Lord Holland.
In speaking of Mr. Fox's resignation, on the death of
Lord Rockingham, he says :— *

Perhaps the subsequent conduct of Mr. Fox, and
more particularly the coalition with Lord North (the
other equally questionable and yet more unfortunate
step of his public life), was a necessary and unavoidable consequence of the resignation. Of the manner
in which that coalition was accomplished, I know little
or nothing that is not recounted in the preceding
pages. For the ground on which it was to be justified,
or could be extenuated, the reader must look to the
correspondence, anecdotes, and authorities I have
transcribed, and to the various speeches of Lord
North and Mr. Fox, however imperfectly preserved,
in the Parliamentary Reports. If judged by the
event, and Mr. Fox acknowledged to his friends that
it was a step only to be justified by success, it must
be pronounced indefensible. Mr. Fox never entirely
recovered the disgust which it unjustly, but naturally,

produced in many minds, and especially in the minds
of those who affix the highest standard to public
virtue. The intemperate language in which Burke,
and the vehement invectives in which Mr. Fox had so
recently indulged against Lord North, were remembered and cast in their teeth in proof of inconsistency
and apostacy. They were collected and printed under
the title of ' Beauties of Fox, North, and Burke ; ' and
it is not easy to escape from the dilemma of having
been guilty of much unfounded and exaggerated
personalities against a Minister of whom they had not
the bad opinion which they professed ; or of having
courted and coalesced with a man whom they thought
covered with delinquencies, and dangerous to the
Commonwealth, for the purpose of gratifying their
resentment against others, or for the still more sordid
object of obtaining place, power, or emolument. Yet
acknowledging with shame and regret such censures,
not only *dici potuisse,* but *dicta fuisse* and *non potuisse
refelli,* all the circumstances, nevertheless, well considered, and all the characters, parties, and individuals
well, impartially, and historically weighed, it will be
found that the Coalition was, though an outrage on
public feeling, in no sense on either side a dereliction
of public principle. Neither the Whigs nor the
friends of Lord North sacrificed any opinion or
principle. Even when they differed in the latter end
of the American War in their votes and measures,
they *in fact* more nearly agreed in their objects and
their principles, and even in their designs, than they
did with a numerous but less prominent class of

supporters of that war. All, or nearly all the latter joined against their old nominal but moderate leader, Lord North; and they enlisted themselves under those who, in profession at least, had been and were still more bitter and uncompromising enemies of their policy and principles than the Whigs or Mr. Fox. Lord North, with admirable good-humour, and Mr. Burke, with infinite wit and fancy, very frequently exposed this union of Tories and Jacobites with Republicans,—viz., Lord Gower, Mr. Dundas, Mr. Jenkinson, Mr. Robinson, and all the high prerogative faction, with Lord Camden, Lord Shelburne, Mr. Pitt, and the remains of Lord Chatham's party. There had been on Lord North's first retirement from office a great clamour, on the part of the more republican branch of the Opposition party, against the impunity with which the conductors and instruments of the American War were permitted by Lord Rockingham's friends to escape censure and punishment; but on the first separation between the Whigs and Lord Shelburne, and immediately on the appointment of the latter to the Treasury, the very same men who had thus inveighed against the impunity of Lord North and his adherents earnestly deprecated in conversation and in public all vindictive and retrospective measures. They courted pretty obviously the support and co-operation of the faction, denominated the King's friends.

Whatever odium ultimately attached to the Coalition it did not for a considerable time weaken the two parties of Mr. Fox and Lord North in the

House of Commons. It hardly seems to have affected their popularity out of doors very materially. Notwithstanding the disgust it is supposed to have created, and notwithstanding the growing popularity, splendid, and improving talents, as well as unblemished character of Pitt, it certainly did not reconcile the Parliament or the country to Lord Shelburne's Administration. The Parliament on the 21st of February, 1783, censured the preliminaries of Peace, and the country bore the defeat of the Ministry, even on such a question as Peace, with singular patience. The obstacles thrown in the way of the Coalition Ministry by the King did not seem combined with any predilection for the retiring Premier, and that Premier always suspected the Court of secretly conniving at his downfal. The King, however, was, on the 2nd of April, 1783, compelled to admit to his councils the men dictated by the Coalition, namely,—

DUKE OF PORTLAND . . .	First Lord of Treasury.
LORD NORTH . . . . }	Secretaries of State.
MR. FOX . . . . . }	
LORD STORMONT	President of the Council.
LORD CARLISLE	Privy Seal.
LORD JOHN CAVENDISH . .	Chancellor of Exchequer.
LORD KEPPEL	First Lord of Admiralty.

He was, notwithstanding his earnest endeavours to preserve Lord Thurlow, forced also by the inflexible determination of Mr. Fox, to put the Great Seal in commission, and the only appointment of the seven in which his wishes could be said in any way to have been consulted, was that of Lord Stormont, as

President of the Council, though even in that the King, and possibly Lord North himself, would have preferred giving him the seals of one of the Secretaries of State. The state of parties, and the reluctant acquiescence, or rather capitulation of the King, on the formation of the Coalition Ministry, may be gathered from the journals of Horace Walpole and Fitzpatrick.

The accession of the Coalition Ministry forms a new era, and though it did not last long, it was not barren of incidents and events illustrative of Mr. Fox's character, as well as public conduct.

It may here be remarked, that although immediately previous to the formation of the two Administrations of Lord Rockingham and Lord North, Mr. Fox was as much pressed by debt and pecuniary distresses through indulging in habits of dissipation (so often the theme of animadversions on his private life) as at any previous or subsequent period, yet, in the arrangements of neither of those Ministries did he ever suggest, claim, or accept of any office, pension, or reversion, which could repair his broken fortunes.

It may also be observed, in answer to the animadversions upon the great unpopularity of the Coalition, that Lord John Cavendish and Mr. Fox, on vacating their seats for office, were re-elected without opposition by the freeholders of Yorkshire and the electors of Westminster; the elections at that time most indicative of public opinion.

The second appointment of Mr. Fox to the office of Secretary of State, in 1783, was a yet more bitter pill to George III. than the first in 1782. The royal

enmity to that party of which Mr. Fox was now
virtually the leader, had, during the short interval,
been embittered by increased acrimony. The Coalition
had aggravated those feelings. There is also reason
to suspect, with Walpole, that the intimacy between
the Prince of Wales and Mr. Fox, which subsisted, and
was increasing during that period, greatly exasperated
the King. He never loved his son—he had always
treated him distantly and unkindly. He probably
ascribed, though most unjustly, his excesses and imprudence to the advice, influence, and manœuvres of one
whose own dissipation afforded plausible grounds for
such a suspicion ; whom he had long regarded as a
political antagonist, and towards whom, for that and
many other reasons, he felt implacable resentment. Accordingly, his Majesty, though perhaps yet more deeply
hurt at Lord North's conduct, both in correspondence
and conversation marked how disagreeable any intercourse with Mr. Fox was to his feelings. Mr. Fox, on
the other hand, was uniformly attentive, complaisant,
communicative, and respectful. George III. was not
even then entirely insensible to the propriety of his
behaviour. He had the grace, many years afterwards,
to bear some testimony to those qualities of Mr. Fox.
For when, in 1806, compelled by the force of
circumstances and public confidence, he consented to
appoint him for a third time Secretary of State, and
to restore him to that Council from whence, in a
moment of anger, he had thought fit to dismiss him,
he told him, with more grace than was usual with
him, that wide as their differences, and strongly as he

disapproved of many parts of Mr. Fox's career, he had always known that " he was a gentleman," and he added, that it was some comfort, under any circumstances, to transact business with those who deserved that appellation. This compliment, I apprehend, related to Mr. Fox's demeanour in 1782 and 1783. The King had observed, contrary to his expectations, an entire exemption from petulance, vanity, arrogance, pride, or presumption. Possibly he contrasted the absence of all such disagreeable qualities with what he had experienced in the earlier periods of his reign from public men placed in similar situations, Lord Chatham, Duke of Bedford, and more especially Mr. George Grenville. His correspondence and intercourse was, however, always constrained and repulsive. He soon indeed became, as Mr. Fox expresses it, " *Civil, but no more*," to his Ministers. He expressed satisfaction, and even surprise, at the conciliatory conduct of the Duke of Portland in particular, and he was as distant to Lord North as to his colleagues. It is barely possible that, even at that period, he met from the Duke of Portland not only with that courtesy and respect which are due from a Minister to the chief magistrate of the country, but a compliance better suited to a royal palate, such as his associates were not disposed to administer, and such as they were not aware that he himself displayed in the closet. Be that as it may, it is certain that both in and out of office the Duke of Portland experienced fewer marks of royal displeasure than any man of his rank connected with persons adverse to the system and policy of George III. He was, however, far from inactive or courtly on one business, which drew the attention of the Coalition Ministry soon after its formation ; viz., the household establishment of the Prince of Wales. The Duke of Portland supported, and I believe suggested, the large grant of 100,000*l.* per annum. The proposal roused all that jealousy and distrust which the Prince's marked partiality for the party in power had engendered in the King's mind. Accordingly, an opinion prevailed that it would break up the Ministry. In truth it was near doing so. The Prince was naturally enough delighted at the prospect of such an establishment, and much encouraged by the Duchess of Cumberland, as well as his personal dependents and flatterers, not to forego or relax his pretensions. Mr. Fox, with his characteristic generosity, did not shrink from incurring the odium both at court and in public. He had always regarded the King's treatment of his son as unjust; on some points relating to the Duchy of Cornwall, as illegal; and on all, unhandsome and unkind. He was, therefore, warm in his endeavours to procure for him as good terms as were equitable and right, and easily, perhaps too easily, persuaded that 100,000*l.* a year was not too much. At the same time he on that occasion, and on all others, earnestly exhorted the Prince to be temperate and respectful in his language ; to abstain from all indecent canvass, and to discountenance the tittle-tattle tale-bearing and slander to which the Prince's society, or to speak more openly, the Prince's nature, had so manifest a propensity. When Mr. Fox found his colleagues, and

particularly Lord John Cavendish, averse to so large
an income, he felt the necessity of yielding, and
would no doubt, if consulted by the Prince, have
recommended a reduction in the application ; but he
assures Lord Northington, in a letter of 17th July,
1783, that but for the good advice which Lord Lake
and others gave the Prince, and the handsome and
spontaneous cession of the Prince himself signified to
the Ministry, he (Mr. Fox) would reluctantly, but
unavoidably, have encountered the charge of wrong-
headedness and servility ; and the yet greater pain of
differing with Lord J. Cavendish, Lord North, and all
the Cabinet, except Duke of Portland and Lord
Keppel. Had he resigned, he observes, none but
himself would have fought for an establishment with
any heart which Lord J. Cavendish and Lord North
thought extravagant ; but he adds that Lord North
was, however, as perfectly disposed to make *cause
commune* as a man could be. The King thus obtained
the sorry triumph of thwarting the wishes, and
reducing the proposed revenue of his son, though he
supplied the loss by 50,000*l.* per annum from his
own Civil List. Whether the public derived any
advantage from the economy cannot be hastily pronounced. That problem is not satisfactorily solved,
unless a comparison be instituted between the frequent
and subsequent payments of debts, both of the
Civil List and Prince of Wales' revenue (they being
natural consequences of the small original allowance
allotted to the Prince), and the sum to which
100,000*l.* annually paid would have amounted, if

accumulating till the new arrangement was settled on
his marriage.

Mr. Fox, on his second accession to power, had the
same objects in view abroad which he had pursued
unsuccessfully the year before—namely, the completion
of the work of peace by a definitive treaty, and the
establishment of some European system which should
balance the House of Bourbon. He engaged in both
these projects without loss of time. In obtaining the
first object—the treaty—he had to act with a minister
(M. Vergennes) in France, who, having concluded
the preliminaries with his predecessor, viewed with
some distrust the person who had succeeded him as
having been elevated to the Seals by a vote of censure
on the treaty he had negotiated. He had, too, to
contend with occasional reproaches from the King,
and some difficulties in employing the persons he
deemed best disposed and best able to promote his
object. Ministerial convenience required the appointment of the Duke of Manchester, and the removal of
the Duke of Dorset from Paris, both on account of
the very slender capacity of the latter, and of the
ascendancy the fashion and splendour of the French
Court had obtained over him ; but it would appear
that such a step was hardly taken before it was
represented both to the Duke of Manchester and to
the Court of Versailles as particularly disagreeable to
George III. The dexterous and conciliatory manner
in which Mr. Fox reconciled the King to it, may be
collected from his correspondence, as well as the good
temper, assiduity, firmness, and judgment, with which,

contrary to the fears of many of his colleagues, and the apprehensions or hopes of the King, he contrived to bring the definitive treaty to a conclusion early in September, 1783. In his endeavours to render the treaties with America and Holland more separate and friendly than those with France and Spain (though, with respect to the latter, such a project was suggested by the Duke of Manchester), he appears to have been baffled by the force of circumstances, and by the distant and cold co-operation of the King. George III. never lost an opportunity of twitting him with the humiliation produced by the vote of the House of Commons refusing to continue the war in 1782. There are some traces of a suspicion, but I think unsubstantiated, of a clandestine communication between Comte Vergennes and the English Opposition ; and there are also symptoms of the Americans, though full of confidence in Mr. Fox, being more reserved in their intercourse, from an apprehension natural but utterly belied by the fact, lest the introduction of Lord North and his adherents into his councils might have infused some portion of that anti-American spirit which had protracted the war, and was incompatible with any heartfelt reconciliation.

For the accomplishment of Mr. Fox's second object, the re-establishment of a system in Europe which should act as some counterpoise to the family compact of the House of Bourbon ; strengthened as it had been by the separation of the American provinces from England, and by the *éclat* which their successful interference for that purpose seemed to have thrown round the Courts of Versailles and Madrid; he had more advantages both personal and political than appeared, and he lost no time in showing that he was able and ready to avail himself of them. He had engaged the affections of the diplomatic agents employed abroad so entirely during his first short Administration, by the perspicuity of his views, the frankness of his communications, and the unaffected interest which he took in the personal concerns of those employed under him, that his restoration to office was hailed as a jubilee by nearly all of them. Their zeal was quickened by private friendship and gratitude, and their efforts were directed by a plain, prompt, and unreserved explanation of the views entertained at home, uniformly and conjointly to the same public objects. The same frank and honourable course seems to have inspired the other Courts with mutual confidence. The great reputation which Mr. Fox enjoyed for transcendent abilities, was not only confirmed by his public speeches and official papers, but by the private report of all who approached him, and by his extensive correspondence in various Courts. His letters were often communicated and generally admired by the Ministers and Princes of the respective countries, and more especially by the great King of Prussia and the Empress Catherine, for the ease and grace of their language, for the simplicity and soundness of their views, and above all for their artless and conciliatory exposition of designs in them-selves honourable and sagacious, and favourable to the

preservation of peace, and the independence of all
countries which constituted the great society of
Europe. Even long before the definitive treaties with
France and Spain were signed, the attention of
Mr. Fox was directed, and some progress was made
in establishing a counterpoise to the House of Bourbon.
The Court of St. Petersburg hesitated between an
intimate connection either with Austria or Prussia.
It leant with some partiality to the former; but
Mr. Fox, partly perhaps from the natural predilection
which one man of genius has for another, and partly
from an apprehension that the family connection
between Vienna and Versailles might lead to irresolution and clandestine intercourse between the two
Courts, seemed to set his heart on an intimate union
and concert with the King of Prussia, and on healing
entirely that breach which had subsisted more or less
for near twenty years between Berlin and St. James's,
and which it had been his earliest endeavour in 1782
to repair. He was, no doubt, somewhat tickled by
the decided and unusual personal approbation of his
character and his views which Frederick II. avowed
on his second accession to the office of Secretary of
State; but that monarch with equal frankness
acknowledged that affairs were not, in his opinion,
yet ripe for an entire change of system, though he
acknowledged the advantage of having in England
what he said he had long regretted the want of, a
Ministry on whose honour, stability, and abilities he
could rely. In the meanwhile several little obstructions
occurred in the completion of the definitive treaty;

partly owing to one or two hasty and indistinct concessions made to Spain in negotiating the preliminaries
by Mr. Fox's predecessors, partly to the personal
character of M. de Vergennes and the intrigues
going on in his councils; and partly perhaps to the
malicious pleasure, which, on the occurrence of every
little obstacle, George III. took in twitting Mr. Fox
with the humiliation to which the Opposition and
termination of the American war had exposed the
country.   However, the courtesy and respect with
which all intercourse with the closet was carried on
by Mr. Fox, the perspicuity of his statements, his
candour, good-humour and simplicity, may even,
from the notes preserved, be inferred to have been
gaining ground on George III. himself.   They would
no doubt in a short time have acquired as much
esteem and confidence as it was in so unamiable a
nature, so haughty and sullen a mind, and so
retentive a memory, to bestow on any man who had
once incurred his royal resentment.   But suspicions
relating to the Prince of Wales, which have been
already alluded to, retarded this natural effect of
transacting business with Mr. Fox; and it was not
long ere the fatal business of the East India Bill,
forced on, no doubt, in some degree by the exigencies
of the case, and by the pledges which all public
bodies of men and parties seem to have contracted,
but yet more by the passionate and intemperate
activity of Mr. Burke, revived the King's hopes never
entirely extinct, of extricating himself from the tram-
mels of the Whigs, and enabled him by the practice of

a little duplicity, and the aid of some ambitious and discontented patriots, as well as the old servile party of the Court, to accomplish his designs effectually.*

The French Ministry complained loudly of Mr. Fox, as much less tractable than the preceding Minister. I have often heard him and General Fitzpatrick joke at the description (so wide of the mark) given of his temper by M. de Vergennes: "C'est un fagot d'épines que ce M. Fox." Some traces of hostility to the French Court, and displeasure at our method of treating, may be found in his correspondence with the Duke of Manchester. But neither this circumstance nor the delicacy and tact with which he avoided, as much as possible, obtruding all unpleasant, and particularly American business, on the King, prevented that ungracious and resentful prince from enjoying maliciously, and aggravating spitefully, every little difficulty that arose. Delay of signature, unreasonable pretensions suddenly started by the enemy, and, still more, anything which could be construed into a slight, was studiously and instantly seized upon by his royal correspondent and master as no matter of surprise, but as the natural consequence of that Opposition of which his Minister had formed so conspicuous a part, and of those measures in February, 1782, which he had persuaded Parliament to adopt. Notwithstanding these appearances, Mr. Fox continued to assure his correspondents, and to persuade

* It will be seen by the Grenville correspondence that the King was never, as Lord Holland supposes, reconciled in the smallest degree to Mr. Fox as his Minister.—J. R.

himself, of the probable stability of his Ministry. He was satisfied that neither Lord Shelburne, nor Mr. Pitt, nor even the party termed emphatically the King's friends, had any concerted plan for forming a government, and though he never doubted the inclination, and indeed determination, of the King, to seize any favourable opportunity of dismissing him, he questioned his courage or activity in creating such an opportunity; and perhaps he thought, though very erroneously, that his own intimacy with the Heir Apparent would deter, rather than stimulate him, to resorting to immediate and premature defiance. In all these various causes of anxiety, and in none more than in those arising from rooted jealousy of the House of Bourbon and those connected with the state of the Royal Family at home, it is curious to observe the entire concurrence of opinion, and at the same time delightful to reflect, on the artless, unaffected, open and affectionate intercourse established, in the course of two or three months, between him and Lord North. If there seldom were political opponents who, during an honourable opposition to one another, were oftener betrayed by Parliamentary warfare into more intemperate invective on one side, or more cutting and successful ridicule on the other, there never were two such men engaged in the service of a common cause of a common country more entirely exempt from all distrust, and jealousy, or resentment. They were sincerely united in opinion and in affection, and in congeniality of sentiment and sweetness of disposition. Lord North, though neither so warm in his affections, nor so generous or devoted to a cause, was equally indulgent to others, equally devoid of guile and of gall, equally candid, reasonable and charitable, to his opponents, and equally disposed, though not so forward and eager, to maintain and promote a liberal system of government, and an uninterrupted enjoyment of popular rights. Both had the same disdain of hypocrisy, and the same abhorrence of tyranny, though the easy temper of the one would be satisfied with practically eluding the consequences, and defeating the purposes of such crimes; and the noble and vehement spirit of the other would, in spite, and perhaps in consequence, of the tenderness of his nature, pant to arraign, expose, and resist all approaches to injustice. Long as they had been engaged in hostility to each other, they were made to act together, and no union of public men could have been more propitious to the two great causes of Peace and Liberty, than a continuance of these two statesmen in power together.—v. H.

* We may now consult Walpole's account of the proceedings of the Coalition Ministry.*

Walpole remarks on the appointment of Lord Northington to be Lord Lieutenant of Ireland, after Lords Devonshire, Fitzwilliam, and Althorpe had refused it, and adds: "Mr. Fox gave him for Secretary Mr. Windham, a Norfolk gentleman, of good fortune, of most fair character, in *his principles much disposed to Republicanism*, and reckoned to have good parts; but so ignorant of the world, that if it was evidence of his virtue, I do not think it was of his sense, nor do I think he had a considerable share."

May. After mentioning what he calls Burke's indecent and outrageous rants against Governor Hastings, he adds : " He was no less extravagant in his own defence.   Powell, the confidant and creature of the first Lord Holland, and one Bembridge, both officers of the Pay-office, had been largely deficient in their balances, and were under prosecution.   Colonel Barré, the late Paymaster, had dismissed them. Burke not only restored them, but had not even communicated their restoration to his associate Ministers, who first learnt it by complaints made in the House of Commons, where Martin and Sir Edward Astley termed it an insult to the public. Burke flamed at those words in so *frantic* a manner, that Fox and Sheridan were forced to hold him down ; and both laboured to palliate his conduct, though so difficult to be excused.   In fact, for the two last winters, so intemperate had been Burke's behaviour, that many thought his intellects disordered."

May 7th. Mentions Mr. W. Pitt making a motion on the representation of Parliament, in a " very long, guarded, and fluctuating speech ; " but though he ridicules the pretended conversion of Dundas and Thomas Pitt to reform, takes no notice of Mr. Fox's speech or conduct on that occasion.

Lord Sandwich made Ranger of the Parks and his son, Lord Hinchinbrook, got also a place, " not very creditable," adds Walpole, " to tumble from First Lord of Admiralty to be a Ranger, nor more so for

Mr. Fox to countenance him, yet as decent as for him to have joined Lord North." Hence Walpole takes occasion to lament the want of principle, so prevalent in times when the people, he says, were sold, and the Crown humbled; and he proceeds to descant on the characters of the men then out of place, of which he gives no flattering picture. In that of Pitt he adopts his favourite and usual method of illustrating character, —contrast—and says :

" His attention to character and future experience are more likely to set him at the head of this country than any man, though his abilities are infinitely inferior to Mr. Fox's, who, the longer he remains in power, will reconcile mankind to him, and acquire their admiration and attachment ; for besides his superiority of parts he has as much quickness of common sense as some men have of wit. He sees to the bottom of everything, and views it in its true light, as rapidly as they skim surfaces, and descry resemblances or allusions. His good-humour is as constitutional as his common sense, and both are clear of affectation. Mr Pitt, like his father, is more factitious. Application has given him as much as nature ; but his natural parts would not have carried him far without that aid.* Mr. Fox, when not in office, thinks of nothing but his pleasures, nor of business but at the moment he is doing it in the House of Commons. Void of art

---

* The impression produced in Walpole is very different from mine, who was never an adherent of Mr. Pitt's, nor one of the extravagant admirers of his eloquence—but extraordinary quickness of intellect, and natural sagacity in debate, seemed to me to be among his most shining qualities ; what he wanted was originality, philosophy, and genius.—V. H.

or design, if nature had not made him the most powerful reasoner of the age, he would never have distinguished himself; he never stooped to the manœuvres of a politician. Had not Pitt so early aspired to be his rival, Fox would have cherished Pitt as his friend and disciple. Fox was charmed with his outset, and loved him. Pitt, with a boy's arrogance, intoxicated with success, pronounced presumptuously, ' Mr. Fox had never been answered.' When he forced Fox to answer *him*, it was with such facility of superiority, that Pitt had better have remembered that neither Thurlow, nor Dundas, nor both together, could defeat Fox. Pitt still was a phenomenon, when at all able to enter the *mélée* with such men as Fox, Thurlow, Dundas, and Lord Loughborough, all men of first-rate abilities." *
—H. W.

Walpole, after a severe and almost scurrilous character of Lord Shelburne, proceeds : " He had stolen the succession from Lord Rockingham, and he had trampled on Fox ; yet he neglected his own friends, affronted those that adhered to him, when

---

* When Walpole's propensity to disparage public men is considered, and when it is recollected that he never had the blind predilection of friendship for Mr. Fox, and was at the time of writing the above passage far from satisfied with his political conduct, it must be acknowledged to contain a striking testimony to the superiority of his talents, and to the attractive qualities of his disposition. Whatever we may think of Walpole's judgment or prejudices, he was not likely to admit too readily of a person, not within his own immediate circle of friends, that *he would command the admiration and attachment of mankind when in office*, that *his good-humour and common sense were constitutional ; that he was void of all art or design, never stooped to the manœuvres of a politician, and was the most powerful reasoner of the age.*—V. H.

Fox and the Cavendishes broke with him, and though he had so very recently concurred in tearing a well-planted Minister from the Crown, he was so blind as to suppose that his subservience to the Crown would balance all other factions.*   If he flattered himself that Lord North and Mr. Fox were irreconcilable he knew little of mankind.   Nothing is more true, than that men are always most enraged at those who have offended them last; nor is it less true, that when three men hate each other reciprocally, the two who have lost power will be most angry with him who has deprived them of it; nor was it possible for Lord Shelburne to prevent such a junction but by gaining either the one or the other.   The moment Lord North and Fox united, Shelburne's fall was inevitable, nor was it delayed a moment."

May 26th. " Mr. Powell, of the Pay Office, cut his throat. . . . On the evidence of Burke, Rigby, and others, the Coroner's inquest pronounced him insane."

" Lord J. Cavendish opened the taxes, and they proved popular beyond example; Lord Mahon, a wild young man, opposed them, and fell on Lord North, who turned him into ridicule.   Pitt supported him in one of his best speeches, in which his language was thought equal to his father's, his reasoning superior, and his spirit greater than he had hitherto exerted;

---

* Virulent and, as I believe, unjust, Walpole's language about Lord Shelburne may be, I am afraid he is right in supposing that he, Lord Shelburne, fondly supposed that by subserviency he might gain the Court; and that he and the Court together would be omnipotent.—V. H.

but injudiciously treating Charles Fox as flimsy and flippant, the latter showed how much more justly those epithets belonged to himself."

June. Tax on receipts—though an attempt made to raise a clamour against it by the Opposition—generally approved. " Sheridan said to be its author, and proved its best support. He improved daily in speaking, turned all the Opposition said into excellent ridicule, and always brought the House into good-humour with the Ministers."

June 11th. Walpole's account of the settling the Prince of Wales's revenue—censures the policy of Ministry in telling the King that they would get 100,000*l.* a year for the Prince, supposes Shelburne had promised as much, and the Prince would not have been satisfied with less. The King heard all the Ministers said, allowed them to proceed and summon the House of Lords, but having " seen Lord Temple in private, and it was universally supposed, offered him the Administration, which he as readily accepted, and *having even sent a servant of his own in livery, to stop the Duke of Richmond from going to France ;* on the 15th, when the Duke of Portland brought him the message in writing, for his approbation, which was to be delivered in the House of Lords, he sent him word not to deliver it, for he had changed his mind."

" The Ministers were thunderstruck, and disgusted to the utmost. The Prince was enraged, pressed them to resign, and had a fever with vexation. The Ministers knew not what to say to the two Houses, to

whom the intention had been notified, and where they
were called upon for a solution."

June 16th. "Ministers held a meeting, whence
they were to go and resign their employments, but
before they separated, the Duke of Portland was
summoned to the King, *who, in agony of tears, kissed
the Duke, confessed he had gone too far, and begged the
Duke to rescue him.* This strange weakness saved the
Ministers. Charles Fox went to the Prince, and prevailed on him to submit himself entirely to his father,
which at last he did, and the Ministers, who had thus
the King in their power, and the Prince in their
hands, extricated themselves with great address, and
pleased everybody. No revenue was demanded from
Parliament. The King gave 50,000*l.* a-year to the
Prince, out of his own income, with the Duchy of
Cornwall (the Prince's right) of 12,000*l.* a-year more,
and all that was asked of Parliament was 30,000*l.* to
pay the Prince's debts, and as much to set him out.
But the Prince declared he would never forgive
Lord Temple."

Walpole gives his conjectures, upon the causes of
the " sudden turn" in the King's mind, and supposes,
on very insufficient grounds, that Lord Bute was consulted through Andrew Stuart and his family, and
from timidity and apprehension of Lord Temple's
want of pliability, advised against a change. He
adds, "Lord Thurlow, too, the late Chancellor,
declared to Charles Fox his disapprobation of such a
change, though that might be to disguise his share in
it. He, the Advocate, and Lord Weymouth, were

certainly endeavouring secretly, in concert with the King, to make another change." *

"Lord Weymouth, who, though he had warmly endeavoured the exclusion of the present Ministers, and had pitifully and meanly stooped to stay in place with them, *was daily in private with the King*, or the Duke of Montague, late Governor of the Prince, and who, though the most shallow of men, was the person in whom the King had most confidence, and to whom *alone* the King ever spoke of his son, and who betrayed the King's sentiments by officiously seeking occasions to abuse the Prince."

"All the above particulars I believe to be true, and I had them from very good authorities. I do not answer for the following, but it was asserted. The King reproaching the Duke of Portland with their setting his son against him, the Prince gave the King a letter he had from the Duke, in which the latter had conjured the Prince to submit to his father, and given the best advice; that the King was charmed, and said "he did not know the Duke was so honest a man."

July 4th. On Lord J. Cavendish's bill for reform of Exchequer places, "Rigby proposed a clause, to put the Chancellor Thurlow on the same foot with the other tellers, as if he had taken the reversion when it was offered. He had bragged much of not taking it, and had thrown out hints as if such grants were illegal; but the reason was said to be, that he did not care to insert his son's name in the patent, whose

* It will be seen, in a subsequent portion of this volume, that Lord Temple himself discouraged a change of Ministry on this question.—J. R.

legitimacy was doubtful.   Charles Fox, whom he had lately termed a bankrupt, violently opposed the clause, as did Sheridan, and it was rejected by a majority of 8, and with great disgrace to Thurlow."—H. W.

" The King greatly unhappy : he told Lord H. (Hertford, I presume,) that he disliked the Ministers, but would give them fair play, and would play them no tricks ; yet he had tried to play them one on Pitt's Reform Bill.   He also said, that every morning he wished himself eighty or ninety, or dead.   He had long conversations frequently with Lord Stormont, whom with Mansfield, it was supposed, he wished to detach from the Ministry, as he daily tried others.   He told Lord North, 'You have often seen me keep my temper, but now I often cannot command it.'   The Lord Advocate was turned out, though he had vaunted that no man in Scotland would venture to take his place, but Charles Fox was not a man to be intimidated.   He insisted on the dismission of both Thurlow and Dundas, by far the two ablest of his opponents."—H. W.

August. " Expostulations of Charles Fox with General Conway on not obliging him with promotions in the army, nor acquainting him and Ministers with his measures—Conway justifies himself well.   Charles Fox had talked to Prince of Wales of setting Prince Frederick at the head of Army, either to flatter the Prince, or not thinking his a good life ; perhaps both reasons." *—H. W.

* Horace Walpole is, like most men, an ingenious inventor of bad motives.—J. R.

August 29th. " Mr. Fox wrote to Lord Mayor, that the definitive treaties were to be signed on the following Wednesday, September 3rd, by England, France, Spain, and America."

September 6th. " Definitive treaties arrive, signed." —H. W.

Here end the manuscript books of Horace Walpole's journal. The remainder of it, if it can be called a journal, is irregularly kept on loose sheets, and both in style and (what is more material) in information, is more incorrect than the manuscript in books.

H. Walpole, from the time General Conway sided with Mr. Fox on India Bill, and questions against the dissolution of Parliament, becomes in his journal an eager and violent partisan of the Coalition party. So much so, that I find amongst his papers, squibs and epigrams against the Duke of Richmond, as well as Pitt and his supporters ; but there is more dissertation and report of debates than secret history in this part of his papers, and I shall be sparing, or at least abridging, in my extracts.—v. H.

* Lord Holland has placed in the most favourable light the coalition between Mr. Fox and Lord North. Yet its authors seem to have condemned their own conduct by anticipation. " Nothing but success can justify it," is reported to have been the declared opinion of Mr. Fox. " Unless a real good Government is the consequence, nothing can justify it to the public," is the sentence of General Fitzpatrick. The want of its success, therefore, is its condemnation. Yet this alliance had consequences so lasting, and so unfortu-

nate, that it is worth while to look somewhat further into the reasons which were alleged for the coalition, and the causes of its failure.

1. It was alleged in the first place that it was necessary to counteract, by a wide Parliamentary union, the personal influence of the King.

But this personal influence had been mischievous, chiefly because Lord North's good-nature made him yielding to the King and popular with the public. Lord Shelburne had no such popularity, and was not likely to retain his power long, unless Lord North or Mr. Fox should join him. Besides, Lord North in his conversation with Mr. Fox declined any engagement on this ground, and turned off the subject by an allusion to government by departments, so that the security was not wanted, and if it had been, would not have been obtained by this measure. 2. "It was desirable to secure a good Government for the country." But the Coalition afforded no guarantee for such good Government. The force put upon the King was sure to excite in him the strongest desire to shake off his masters, and opportunity could scarcely fail him. It is a poor evasion to say, that without the East India Bill the Government could have gone on without a check. The Prince of Wales' allowance had nearly driven out the Ministry, and nothing but the King's, or rather Lord Temple's, sagacious perception that such a ground for a rupture would not be popular, preserved the Coalition on that occasion.

While the reasons for the Coalition appear ,thus

unsubstantial, the reasons against it were many and weighty. First, Mr. Fox's invectives against Lord North were either well or ill-founded. If well-founded he was not justified in joining a man branded not only with incapacity, but with duplicity, treachery, and falsehood. If ill-founded, which is nearer the truth, Mr. Fox owed it to public decorum not to proclaim to the world that his invectives were the offspring of an unreasoning passion. He could have found some better means of retracting or mitigating his invectives than by a political junction with the object of them. Nor was his reflection *Inimicitiæ breves, amicitiæ sempiternæ*, a just defence. The enmities he had engaged in were not private but public quarrels, and as they were not incurred, so they ought not to have been dropped from placability and good-nature. Mr. Prior remarks truly that Lord North readily forgave the uttering of these invectives, but the public never forgave their being retracted.*

Secondly, the particular occasion chosen for the Coalition was very unfortunate. The peace of 1783 was a very bad one, but it was not more so than might have been expected from the misgovernment of Lord North. Any peace which saved the honour of the country should have appeared venial to Mr. Fox; at all events the blame, if blame was justly due, should have fallen rather on the head of Lord North, than on that of Lord Shelburne. In the previous Ministry of Lord Rockingham, Mr. Fox had strongly expressed

* Prior's Life of Burke.

both in Parliament, and in his letter to the King of
Prussia, his sense of the calamitous state to which
the country had been reduced.   The author of those
misfortunes, Mr. Fox thought at that time, ought to
be punished ; he now aided him to return to power.
Thirdly, although it might be alleged that the
American War was over, and that Economical Reform
had been carried, the great distinctions of the Whig
and Tory parties had not been effaced.   The Duke
of Richmond, Lord Camden, Mr. Fox, Lord John
Cavendish, and Mr. Pitt, were favourable to Reform
of Parliament; Lord North, and Mr. Dundas, were
against it ; and although Mr. Burke differed from his
friends on this subject, yet on the great constitutional
doctrines of a control of the Crown by popular insti-
tutions, Mr. Burke, as well as General Conway, is to
be added to the statesmen I have named.   It was an
unnatural combination which united Mr. Fox with
Lord North and Lord Stormont, and even dispensed
patronage to Lord Sandwich ; while the Duke of
Richmond, General Conway, and Lord Camden,
were left to defend prerogative against a constitutional
Ministry.

Thus it appears that the failure of the Coalition was
not an accident, but a result involved in the elements
of which it was composed.   The King, forced by a
violent wrench to take back Mr. Fox, was an enemy
constantly on the watch against his Ministers.   The
nation was not very partial either to Lord North or
to Mr. Fox.   The continued miscarriages of the one
had humbled the national pride ; the private life of

the other alarmed public morality.   Nor did men
readily give their confidence to a man so vehement in
his language as Mr. Fox.   Sir Samuel Romilly
remarks, that men rather blamed Lord North for
joining Mr. Fox than Mr. Fox for joining Lord North.
At a later period, the people readily responded to the
severe reflection of Mr. Wilberforce, "that the
Coalition partook of the vices of both its parents ; the
corruption of the one, and the violence of the other."

Thus was broken and dispersed by its own dissensions that great confederacy of freedom, which,
nurtured in the adversity of the American War, had
revived the ancient virtues of Whiggism and made
the Senate shine with the lights of patriotism and
eloquence.   Thus vanished the hope of seeing a more
brilliant Fox and a more consistent Pitt ; the one
adorning and advising his country in the conduct of
Foreign Affairs, which he above all men understood ;
and the other applying to the management of our
finances the economical principles of Smith, and the
wise frugality of Sully.   The Coalition prevented a
consummation so desirable.   It was clear that Lord
Shelburne could neither introduce Lord North into
his Cabinet, nor could he resist the Whig party in
the House of Commons.   He himself foresaw that
Mr. Fox and Mr. Pitt must upon his fall unite.
Mr. Dundas, meaning to unite Lord North to Lord
Shelburne, forced Lord North into the Coalition
with Mr. Fox.   The rout of the Whig party ; the
Pitt Administration ; and the War of the French
Revolution ; were the results of this fatal event.

There is one remark, however, which must not be omitted. Mr. Fox and Lord North had no personal antipathies to overcome in uniting with each other. Lord Holland has described them truly as being both men of generous temper, of kind feelings, of simple, straightforward, and candid nature. But these sympathies did not compensate for the loss of a great public cause in the hands of men joined together by agreement on public grounds. The Coalition displaced the natural alliances of statesmen, and brought on a fierce contention, which deprived Mr. Fox of the support of the people, and weakened for the rest of his life the influence of his genius, his eloquence, and his wisdom.*

BOOK THE FOURTH.

———◆———

PART THE THIRD.

* THE conduct of Mr. Fox during his second period
of office was not less admirable than during his first.
Prompt and diligent in the transaction of business,
sagacious in the views he took, and luminous in the
instructions he gave, he guided his course by the
largest principles of government, and the most con-
summate knowledge of the interest of his country.

In respect to foreign affairs, his first care was to
seek for some improvement in the details of the
definitive treaty, without departing from the preliminaries to which the faith of the country was pledged.
But beyond the explanations and directions which this
task imposed upon him, he gave his mind to the
development of the plan which he had conceived when
the two branches of the House of Bourbon were
arrayed in hostility against us. This was to revive
the policy of Lord Chatham, and to cultivate the friendship of Prussia, with a view of employing a northern
alliance to counterbalance the weight of France and
Spain. Time was wanting for the consolidation of this

system ; Frederic was too old to enter into a new course, and the Empress too volatile to be fixed to any scheme of policy, except by means of frequent and unreserved communications.   Had such a policy ever taken root, it is probable that the system of Europe might have been maintained in peace, even amidst the hurricane of the French Revolution.

With respect to Ireland, the views of Mr. Fox were conciliatory, but not timid.   He held that the concessions of the past year had been ample and final. Had he not found the measure already far advanced, he would not even have added the renunciation of the authority, legislative and judicial, of England over Ireland.   But having done so much, and ready as he was at any time to consider Irish grievances, he was not disposed to treat with the Volunteers with arms in their hands.   He considered that, as soldiers coming forward to defend their country from an enemy, their part properly ceased with the peace ; and that, as armed men dictating laws to the Parliament, they could not be acknowledged without danger.   He prescribed, therefore, a refusal of any demands thus made, not on the ground of merits, but because they were thus made. While no man more strenuously asserted the cause of liberty, no man was more resolved to maintain the just rights of authority.   He would no more allow the Constitution to be subverted from without, than he would permit it to be undermined from within.

This mode of conduct, being frank and without design, was speedily successful.   Lord Northington, while he corrected some errors into which Mr. Fox had fallen from ignorance of local questions, adopted heartily and boldly the large policy of his friend and colleague. Upon this, as upon all other questions, Mr. Fox was in reality the Minister. He alone comprehended the vast extent of the administration of which he was the soul and the life.

Before the session of Parliament an overture reached him from Lord Thurlow. Till this time the King, with bare civility, had kept him at arm's length; and in one of his letters, indeed, he had remarked somewhat ominously, " in states as well as men, where dislike has once arose, I never expect to see cordiality." *

A very strong symptom of want of confidence was the refusal to grant any peerages. Lord Ossory, an Irish peer, nearly connected with Mr. Fox, was known to be desirous of an English peerage, but the favour could not be obtained. Suddenly Lord Thurlow intimated that if the Great Seal were delivered into his hands, the cloud which obstructed the rays of royal favour would be removed.

Upon this unexpected suggestion Lord Loughborough was consulted, and the opinion he gave was marked by sense, and, on the whole, by fairness. Whether the admission of Thurlow would have saved Mr. Fox from the vengeance which soon overwhelmed him, may well be doubted; in the Ministry of Lord Rockingham he had assumed in the House of Lords the utmost liberty of opposition to measures of the Cabinet to which he belonged. It may more clearly be said that the uncertainty which hung over

---

* September 7th, 1783.

the fate of the Coalition Ministry was changed to a
certainty by the rejection of the overtures of Lord
Thurlow. Whether that rejection were owing to
Mr. Fox's dislike of Lord Thurlow ; to the instinctive
feeling that in admitting him to the Cabinet they
would admit a spy and an enemy ; or to the unwillingness to give up Lord Loughborough, a friend, for Lord
Thurlow, an enemy, it is impossible to ascertain.

The question of an allowance to the Prince of Wales
gave rise to a momentary difficulty. The facts may
be fully gathered from the correspondence in this
volume. The India Bill was the decisive question of
this period. It will be useful, therefore, before proceeding to the correspondence, to clear up the facts
which were enveloped by Mr. Pitt and his friends in
so much artful misrepresentation.

The misgovernment of India had alarmed and dis-
quieted English statesmen of all parties. The Governor-
General had set at defiance, with flagrant audacity,
the laws of justice and good faith ; unwarrantable
aggressions, oppressive imposts, cruel punishments, had
marked his conduct for successive years. When the
Directors at home had purposed to recall him, the
Court of Proprietors, who possessed the power of a
negative, had refused their assent, and when they had
passed a vote of approbation, the Secretary of State, in
his turn, had refused to transmit the resolution to
India. Thus, while tyranny produced the greatest
evils in India, anarchy at home prevented the application of any remedy.

The remedy devised by the Cabinet of Mr. Fox was

to form a Board of Directors, to consist of seven persons, entrusted with all the powers of the Directors of the Company, assisted by eight other persons, qualified and empowered to manage the trading concerns of the Proprietors. The whole fifteen were to be named by Parliament, and to retain their power for four years. After that time the Directors were to be named by the Crown; any vacancy was to be supplied by the Crown; Earl Fitzwilliam, a man of the highest virtue and reputation, was named in the Bill, as Chairman of the new Board.

The questions which arise to any one, fairly considering this measure, are, was the evil so great as to require so strong a remedy? Was the remedy likely to be efficacious? In considering these questions, we must endeavour to view them in the light in which they were seen by the Government of 1783.

With regard to the magnitude of the evil, there can be little doubt. It has been said by intimate friends of Mr. Fox that he was hurried by the warm temper and bright imagination of Mr. Burke into the adoption of a measure which his cool judgment ought to have rejected; that the Coalition would have been successful had not the India Bill been introduced; that the failure of the Government of Mr. Fox and Lord North, was owing to the rashness with which a measure so ill-constructed was brought into Parliament.

It appears to me that those who thus argue do little honour to Mr. Fox. If he was bent on proving by success the wisdom of forming the Coalition, it is little to the credit of his penetration that he introduced, as

the great measure of his Ministry, a plan which, by
its irregular and mis-shapen features, was formed to
shock and disgust his country.   If Mr. Fox formed his
union with Lord North in the deliberate exercise of a
sound judgment, surely we must give him credit for a
similar deliberation when, in the recess of the summer
and autumn, he constructed the measure upon which
alone he feared any danger to the continuance of his
power.   Nor do the facts at all bear out the supposition that Mr. Fox was betrayed by the rashness of
Mr. Burke into a scheme of which he did not approve.
There do not appear any traces in the papers of
Mr. Fox of any outline drawn up by Mr. Burke, upon
which the India Bill was framed ; nor has any such
plan been produced from the manuscripts of Mr. Burke.
On the other hand, we know that the Bill was submitted to Lord North and Lord Loughborough, and
probably to other members of the Administration.

The plan itself was attacked both on the ground of
increasing the influence of the Crown; and of sub-
verting the influence of the Crown; of violating the
chartered rights of the Company, and shaking all
titles.   But, above all, it was argued that it tended
to place in the party of Mr. Fox a power inconsistent with the supremacy of the King and the due
balance of the Constitution.

When these objections come to be sifted, however,
they will lose much of their weight.   The Commissioners could not add very greatly to the influence of
the Crown, for being removable only by address from
the two Houses of Parliament, they would have been

very independent in the exercise of their patronage.
They would not, however, have possessed any powers
incompatible with the due authority of the Crown, for
the Secretary of State was still to exercise the supreme
control.   Neither was the Bill obnoxious to the popular and prevailing objection, that the seven Commissioners would have ruled India as absolute sovereigns,
for the benefit of one party.   In the first place the
dictatorship, if such it might be called, was only to
endure for four years.   In the next place, the power
divided among seven was to be exercised, not only
under a general, but under a minute responsibility ;
with reasons assigned for every act, and a close superintendence on the part of Parliament.   In the third
place, the mis-government of India had been so great,
that the whole four years might well be occupied in
remedying the injustice, in correcting the abuses, and in
sweeping away the corruptions of our Indian Government.   Lastly, the country would have had the guarantee of the character of Lord Fitzwilliam, a man
eminently virtuous ; unambitious by nature, mild and
benevolent in disposition ; more resembling the Nerva
and Trajan of Rome than the Clive and the Hastings
of our Indian empire.

There remains the further objection that the
chartered rights of the East India Company were to
be interfered with.   As one of the main evils which
had been suffered arose from the power of the
proprietors to overrule the decision of the Directors,
it would seem that some interference with these rights
was indispensable.   Mr. Fox had mentioned a signal

instance of the abuse of this power. The Directors
had determined upon the recall of Mr. Hastings.
The proprietors had placed their veto on this decision.
Such a power, exercised probably in corrupt connivance with a governor-general who enriched the families
of the proprietors, was inconsistent with the due government of a distant empire. But Mr. Burke gave a
complete answer to this objection when he said :—

"I therefore conclude what you all conclude, that
this body being totally perverted from the purposes
of its institution is utterly incorrigible ; and because
they are incorrigible, both in conduct and constitution, power ought to be taken out of their hands,
just on the same principles on which have been
made all the great changes and revolutions of government that have taken place since the beginning of
the world."

We may conclude these remarks by some extracts
from the speeches of Mr. Fox, which will illustrate
the great purpose with which the India Bill was
introduced :

"At the same time he said this, he was aware the
measure he had proposed was a strong one. He
knew that the task he had that day set himself was
extremely arduous and difficult ; he knew that it had
considerable risk in it ; but when he took upon
himself an office of responsibility, he had made up
his mind to the situation and danger of it. He had
left all thoughts of ease, indolence, and safety behind
him. He remembered an honourable friend near him
(Mr. Burke) had once said, half in jest, half in earnest,

"that idleness was the best gift that God had
bestowed upon man." But this was not a time for
indolence and regard to safety in a minister. The
situation of the country called for vigorous exertion,
for new measures, and for some risk ; he knew that a
minister who had no consideration but his own safety
might be quiet and safe; the consequence must be,
the country would be ruined. How much better was
it to venture what the exigency of affairs required ;
the minister, it was true, might be ruined, but his
country would be saved."

" He said, that if he should fall in this, he
should fall in a great and glorious cause, struggling
not only for the Company, but for the people of
Great Britain and India; for many, many millions
of souls."

" What is the end of all government ? Certainly the
happiness of the governed. Others may hold other
opinions ; but this is mine, and I proclaim it. What
are we to think of a government whose good fortune
is supposed to spring from the calamities of its
subjects, whose aggrandisement grows out of the
miseries of mankind ? This is the kind of government exercised under the East India Company upon
the natives of Hindostan ; and the subversion of that
infamous government is the main object of the bill in
question. But in the progress of accomplishing this
end, it is objected that the charter of the Company
should not be violated; and upon this point, sir, I
shall deliver my opinion without disguise. A charter
is a trust to one or more persons for some given

benefit. If this trust be abused, if the benefit be not obtained, and its failure arises from palpable guilt, or (what in this case is full as bad) from palpable ignorance or mismanagement, will any man gravely say, that trust should not be resumed, and delivered to other hands ; more especially in the case of the East India Company, whose manner of executing this trust, whose laxity and languor produced, and tend to produce, consequences diametrically opposite to the ends of confiding that trust, and of the institution for which it was granted ? I beg of gentlemen to be aware of the lengths to which their arguments upon the intangibility of this charter may be carried. Every syllable virtually impeaches the establishment by which we sit in this house, in the enjoyment of this freedom, and of every other blessing of our government. These kind of arguments are batteries against the main pillar of the British Constitution. Some men are consistent with their own private opinions, and discover the inheritance of family maxims, when they question the principles of the Revolution ; but I have no scruple in subscribing to the articles of that creed which produced it. Sovereigns are sacred, and reverence is due to every king ; yet with all my attachments to the person of a first magistrate, had I lived in the reign of James II., I should most certainly have contributed my efforts, and borne part in those illustrious struggles which vindicated an empire from hereditary servitude, and recorded this valuable doctrine, ' That trust abused is revocable.'

Mr. Burke, after a splendid speech, wound up in the following eloquent eulogium :—

" And now, having done my duty to the bill, let me say a word to the author. I should leave him to his own noble sentiments, if the unworthy and illiberal language with which he has been treated, beyond all example of parliamentary liberty, did not make a few words necessary; not so much in justice to him as to my own feelings. I must say then, that it will be a distinction honourable to the age, that the rescue of the greatest number of the human race that ever were so grievously oppressed, from the greatest tyranny that was ever exercised, has fallen to the lot of abilities and dispositions equal to the task ; that it has fallen to one who has the enlargement to comprehend, the spirit to undertake, and the eloquence to support so great a measure of hazardous benevolence. His spirit is not owing to his ignorance of the state of men and things; he will know what snares are spread about his path, from personal animosity, from court intrigues, and possibly from popular delusion. But he has put to hazard his ease, his security, his interest, his power, even his darling popularity, for the benefit of a people whom he has never seen. This is the road that all heroes have trod before him. He is traduced and abused for his supposed motives. He will remember that obloquy is a necessary ingredient in the composition of all true glory ; he will remember that it was not only in the Roman customs, but it is in the nature and constitution of things, that calumny and abuse are essential parts of triumph. These thoughts will support a mind, which only exists for honour, under the burthen of temporary reproach. He is doing, indeed, a great good; such as rarely falls to the lot, and almost as rarely coincides with the desires, of any man. Let him use his time. Let him give the whole length of the reins to his benevolence. He is now on a great eminence, where the eyes of mankind are turned to him. He may live long, he may do much; but here is the summit. He never can exceed what he does this day.

" He has faults; but they are faults that, though they may in a small degree tarnish the lustre, and sometimes impede the march of his abilities, have nothing in them to extinguish the fire of great virtues. In those faults there is no mixture of deceit, of hypocrisy, of pride, of ferocity, of complexional despotism, or want of feeling for the distresses of mankind. His are faults which might exist in a descendant of Henry IV. of France—as they did exist in that father of his country. Henry IV. wished that he might live to see a fowl in the pot of every peasant in his kingdom. That sentiment of homely benevolence was worth all the splendid sayings that are recorded of kings. But he wished perhaps for more than could be obtained, and the goodness of the man exceeded the power of the king. But this gentleman, a subject, may this day say this at least, with truth, that he secures the rice in his pot to every man in India. A poet of antiquity thought it one of the first distinctions to a prince whom he meant to celebrate, that through a

long succession of generations he had been the
progenitor of an able and virtuous citizen, who, by
force of the arts of peace, had corrected governments
of oppression, and suppressed wars of rapine :

> " ' Indole proh quanta juvenis, quantumque daturus
> Ausoniæ populis ventura in sæcula civem.
> Ille super Gangem, super exauditus et Indos,
> Implebit terras voce ; et furialia bella
> Fulmine compescet linguæ.'

" This was what was said of the predecessor of the
only person to whose eloquence it does not wrong
that of the mover of this bill to be compared. But
the Ganges and the Indus are the patrimony of the
fame of my honourable friend, and not of Cicero.
I confess I anticipate with joy the reward of those
whose whole consequence, power, and authority exist
only for the benefit of mankind; and I carry my
mind to all the people, and all the names and
descriptions that, relieved by this bill, will bless the
labours of this Parliament ; and the confidence which
the best House of Commons has given to him who the
best deserves it. The little cavils of parties will not
be heard where freedom and happiness will be felt.
There is not a tongue, a nation, or religion in India,
which will not bless the presiding care and manly
beneficence of this house, and of him who proposes
to you this great work. Your names will never be
separated before the throne of the Divine Goodness,
in whatever language, or with whatever rites pardon
is asked for sin, and reward for those who imitate the
Godhead in His universal bounty to His creatures.

These honours you deserve, and they will surely be paid, when all the jargon of influence, and party, and patronage are swept into oblivion.

"I have spoken what I think and what I feel of the mover of this bill. An honourable friend of mine, speaking of his merits, was charged with having made a studied panegyric. I don't know what his was. Mine, I am sure, is a studied panegyric; the fruit of much meditation; the result of the observation of near twenty years. For my own part I am happy that I have lived to see this day. I feel myself overpaid for the labours of eighteen years, when at this late period I am able to take my share, by one humble vote, in destroying a tyranny that exists to the disgrace of this nation, and the destruction of so large a part of the human species."

I now proceed to give the correspondence relating to the Coalition Administration.*

PRINCE OF WALES TO MR. FOX.

" Wednesday evening, 10 o'clock."

"DEAR FOX,

"Nothing could give me more satisfaction than the message that you were so good as to send me this morning. You know how sincerely you have my good wishes, and therefore will be convinced that I shall rejoice not a little if I again see you in administration, as I look upon it as the most fortunate event that can happen to us all. I mean, not only to myself in particular, but to the nation in general.   With respect to your friendly kindness to me, I shall ever be happy to acknowledge it with the gratitude it so justly deserves. I will not take up any more of your time at present than merely to ask you whether it will be convenient to you or not, my calling upon you, between court (if it is over in proper time) and dinner to-morrow.   You may depend upon my coming the moment I am released.   I can assure you no one can be more anxious than I am to see you at the present moment, as no one has your interest more sincerely at heart, and I hope you will ever look upon me as

" Your most affectionate Friend,

" GEORGE P."

SAME TO SAME.

" Monday night, ½ past 12 o'clock.

"DEAR CHARLES,

" When I left the Queen's House this evening, Weymouth was with the King.   I wish you would tell me in a short note how you interpret his frequent visits, and let me know whether you have heard anything fresh this evening.

" I am most sincerely yours,

"G. P."

SAME TO SAME.

" Queen's House, 4 o'clock.

" Dear Charles,

" I am now returned home, and if you have anything particular you wish to say to me, I am ready either to come to you or to receive you at the Queen's House, whichever is most convenient to you.   But if you should have nothing to say to me, I intend going out of town early this evening.

" I am,

" Most sincerely yours,

"GEORGE P."

SAME TO SAME.

" ¾ past 2 o'clock.

" Dear Charles,

" I am waiting for you at your own house ; pray come directly if you can, as I wish very much to speak to you.   I will not detain you three minutes.

" Yours most truly,

"GEORGE P.

" If you have not got your own carriage you had better take anybody else's."

SAME TO SAME.

" QUEEN'S HOUSE, 12 *o'clock.*
"*April* 30*th,* 1783.

" DEAR CHARLES,

" I did not return home till it was too late to answer your kind letter last night. I cannot express to you how very happy you made me by the contents of it, as I had always entertained the highest opinion of Dr. Cyril Jackson, and have always had the greatest friendship for him. You may easily conceive how much pleased I shall be at seeing him in so eligible a situation, and in a situation he must so much wish for himself. Before I conclude, allow me to thank you, my dear Charles, for your kind attention to me on this and every other occasion, and believe me,

" Ever most sincerely yours,

" GEORGE P."

SAME TO SAME.

"QUEEN'S HOUSE, 1 *o'clock.*

" DEAR CHARLES,

" I have a thousand excuses to make to you for not having answered your letter immediately, but I am only this instant awake, and therefore have only just had time to read your letter. I saw the Duchess of Portland yesterday, and took the liberty of desiring her Grace to deliver a message from me to the Duke of Portland, desiring him, if it was not inconvenient to him, to allow me to come to him to-morrow at eleven, instead of to-day. I ought to have explained this to you at Carlisle's when I desired you to meet me in Downing Street, on Sunday, at 11 o'clock, but it really quite slipped out of my memory. I must therefore entreat you to clear up the matter to the Duke of Portland, and make all proper apologies for me. I cannot, however, conclude without seizing the opportunity of thanking you for the part you have taken in bringing this essential business to me so near a conclusion, which, I can assure you, I shall never forget as long as I live.

" I remain,

" My dear Charles,

" Ever most sincerely yours,

" GEORGE P.

" P.S.—You may depend upon seeing me to-morrow at eleven."

SAME TO SAME.

" QUEEN'S HOUSE, June 18th, 1783.

" DEAR CHARLES,

"After what has already passed, I did not require this additional proof of your friendship and attachment ; and you will see by a letter I have this instant written to the Duke of Portland, how ready I am to take your advice, and that I leave it entirely to the Cabinet.

" Yours most sincerely.

" GEORGE P."

SAME TO SAME.

"CUMBERLAND HOUSE, ¼ *past* 9 *o'clock.*

" DEAR CHARLES,

" I have this instant received your kind letter. I am most exceedingly sensible of the kind and friendly attention you have shown me throughout the whole of this business, which is of so much importance to my happiness. Should anything arrive that you wish me to be immediately apprised of, pray send it to the Queen's House. I shall leave a servant there to bring me any letter that may come from you, wherever I am. James Luttrell I sent an express for immediately, but have not as yet sent to Lord Herbert, and according to your advice, the step not being as yet taken, I shall not send for him at all.

" I remain,

" Dear Charles,

" Ever most sincerely yours,

"GEORGE P."

LORD LOUGHBOROUGH TO MR. FOX.

"BEDFORD SQUARE, *Tuesday,* 6 *p.m.*

" DEAR SIR,

" After seeing the correspondence, it seems to me that nothing remains but to express an acquiescence in his Majesty's pleasure ; for it is impossible to propose without a message, or in any other terms than his Majesty thinks fit, continuing in office ; and if you were to go out, to propose in Opposition would

be odious and unavailing. I really do not see that
there are two lines to take, whether successful or not.
Submission for the present is the only reasonable
course. But it would be much better, and much
handsomer, if it were possible to dispose his Royal
Highness to give way respectfully, and with a dutiful
remonstrance profess himself ready to show his obedience, and to wait till his Majesty entertains another
view of the matter. If my idea appears just to you,
would it not be of great consequence that you should,
as soon as possible, try to persuade the Prince of
Wales to make a virtue of necessity, and gain the
public favour, by declining cheerfully any appearance
of contest, which makes better ground for him here-
after and can do him no prejudice at present. Excuse
me throwing out thus hastily what has occurred to
me, and believe me

" Most sincerely yours, &c.

" L."

MR. FITZPATRICK TO LORD OSSORY.

" June 17th, 1783.

" THIS letter will inform you of the fate of the
present Administration, and the short account of it is
this :—The King originally agreed that the whole
business of the Prince of Wales's establishment should
be settled by the Duke of Portland ; and his first
plan was that Parliament should be applied to for the
whole 100,000l. This was consented to. But upon
further conversation it was thought that a part from
Parliament, and a part from the Civil List, would be

more palatable in the House of Commons. The Duke of Portland apprised the King of this in a letter the day before yesterday, in answer to which he wrote a very angry letter, complaining of the departure from the first proposal. In answer to this the Duke of Portland wrote, that he did not mean the latter should supersede the first plan, which he was ready to propose to Parliament. The King answered this by saying, that he had not changed his opinion of their (his minister's) conduct by this letter; that he totally *disapproved* of the whole of their proposal; that he could not think of burthening the public, but was ready to give 50,000*l*. a year from the Civil List, which he thought sufficient; and that he found, notwithstanding all the professions of the present ministers for economy, they were ready to sacrifice the public interests to the wishes of an *ill-advised young man;* that he would never forget or forgive the conduct of the present ministers towards him. This, we suppose, has been settled with the enemy, and no measures are yet determined upon; but as we have a good attendance of friends in town, the wish is to do something to-morrow, and at least to die handsomely. Everybody thinks they cannot form any government that can have the appearance of lasting. This is coming to you by express, to hope you will come at any rate for to-morrow, though it is quite uncertain what may be done.

" Yours,

"R. F."

MR. FOX TO LORD NORTHINGTON.

"ST. JAMES'S, *June 17th*, 1783.

" DEAR NORTHINGTON,

" Lest in the hurry of this day nobody should have had time to write to you, I just steal a minute to tell you that there is great reason to think that our Administration will not outlive to-morrow, or, at least, that it will be at an end in a very few days. Your predecessor, it is supposed, will be the Duke of Portland's successor. The whole is quite sudden and was never dreamt of by me, at least till yesterday. You will, of course, not mention this till it is confirmed. The immediate cause of quarrel is the Prince of Wales' establishment, which we thought perfectly agreed upon a week ago.

" Yours ever,

"C. J. FOX."

" P.S. You may tell it to Windham."

SAME TO SAME.

"ST. JAMES'S, *June 19th*, 1783.

" DEAR NORTHINGTON,

" There is reason to think that the storm is for the present dissipated, and therefore I hope you have not mentioned to any one, except Windham, my last letter. The Prince has behaved in the handsomest manner, and his reasonableness under the hardest usage, is likely to keep everything quiet ; for how long, is a question which cannot for some days at least

be decided.   I hope in a few days to be able to write
to you a detailed account of the whole business, but
really have not now time.

" Yours ever,

"C. J. FOX."

SAME TO SAME.

[MOST SECRET AND CONFIDENTIAL.]

" ST. JAMES'S PLACE, July 17th, 1783.

" DEAR NORTHINGTON,

"I am sure you have too much consideration
for the various plagues and troubles of my situation
to attribute my silence to any neglect of you, but the
truth is that busy as I have been, I should before
this time have fulfilled my promise of explaining to
you the business of the Prince of Wales' establishment, if I had not understood that the Duke of Portland had written to you fully on the subject.   As to
the opinion of our having gained strength by it, the
only rational foundation for such an opinion, is, that
this event has proved that there subsists no such
understanding between the King and Lord Temple
as to enable them to form an Administration, because
if there did, it is impossible but they must have seized
an occasion in many respects so fortunate for them.
They would have had on their side the various cries
of *paternal authority, economy, moderate establishment,
mischief-making between father and son,* and many
other plausible topics.   As therefore they did not
avail themselves of all these advantages, it seems
reasonable to suppose that there is as yet nothing

I 2

settled and understood amongst them, and in this
sense, and inasmuch as this is so felt and understood
in the world, I think we may flatter ourselves that
we are something stronger than we were. In every
other view I own I think quite otherwise. The King
has certainly carried one point against us, and the
notoriety that he has done so may lead people to
suppose that he might be successful in others, if he
were to attempt them. Everybody will not see the
distinction between this and political points so strong
as the Ministers have done. Perhaps I do not myself,
but yet no man was more convinced of the necessity
of yielding than I. The truth is that, excepting the
Duke of Portland and Lord Keppel, there was not one
Minister *who would have fought with any heart in this
cause.* I could see clearly from the beginning, long
before the difficulties appeared, that Lord North and
Lord John, though they did not say so, thought the
large establishment extravagant, and you will, I am
sure, agree with me that to fight a cause, where the
latter especially was not hearty, would have been a
most desperate measure. Indeed all the advantages
we have hitherto derived, and are every day deriving,
from the deserved and universal good opinion which
is entertained of Lord J. Cavendish, would not only
have been flung away, but his name would have been
used against us ; for it is quite certain (at least it
appeared so to me) that his sentiments would have
been known enough to have this effect. Under all
these circumstances there appeared to me no alternative in common-sense but to yield with the best grace

possible, if the Prince of Wales could be brought to
be of that mind. I believe he was naturally very
averse to it, but Colonel Lake and others whom
he most trusts, persuaded him to it, and the intention
of doing so came from him to us spontaneously. If
it had not, I own I should have felt myself bound to
follow his Royal Highness's line upon the subject,
though I know that by so doing I should destroy the
Ministry in the worst possible way, and subject
myself to the imputation of the most extreme wrong-
headedness. I shall always therefore consider the
Prince's having yielded, a most fortunate event, and
shall always feel myself proportionally obliged to him
and to those who advised him. With regard to the
conduct of the Cabinet Ministers you will easily
collect from what I have said, that there was nothing of
that kind of division to which you and others naturally
looked. Lord North was perfectly disposed to make
cause commune as much as man could do. Lord
Stormont kept himself, I think, rather more distinct,
but not more than I expected, nor was there the least
suspicion that he had any greater share of the King's
confidence upon this occasion than the rest of his
Ministers. I do not think I have omitted anything
that can serve to throw light on this affair. I need
not point out to you that I have written all this in
the utmost confidence. There are parts very unfit to
be known by anybody, and especially what relates to
Lord John; for though there have been surmises in
the world relative to his opinion, and though Pitt
even alluded to them in his speech, yet the true state

of the case is not generally known, nor is it fit it should, for many obvious reasons. The same observation holds in regard to the manner of the Prince's yielding. In short the only thing that ought to be said is, that it was not a point upon which Ministers ought to dispute his Majesty's pleasure, and that they were the better enabled to yield by the generosity of the Prince, who was most ready to give up his own interest rather than be the cause of any confusion, or appear to be wanting in duty to the King. Well, but this matter being over, what is now our situation? I will tell you fairly what *I believe*, I mean it literally, for I should not be at all surprised to find myself mistaken. I believe the King is neither pleased nor displeased with us, that he has no inclination to do anything to serve us, or to hurt us, and that he has no view to any other Administration which he means to substitute in lieu of us. If this is so, we shall last the summer, and when Parliament meets, I own I am sanguine. The Coalition gains in my opinion both strength and credit, and the only source of weakness is the idea of the King's dislike. This idea will, no doubt, be a good deal confirmed by his making no English peers for us; but, on the other hand, our lasting out the summer will prove that his dislike is not such as to proceed to overt acts. The fear of which overt acts is in my judgment the only thing that prevents us from being abundantly strong in Parliament. Parliament is certainly our strong place, and if we can last during a recess, I think people will have little doubt of our lasting during the Session. Perhaps I see all this a little sanguinely, but I own when I look over our strength in the House of Commons, and see that all hopes of dissension between the two parts of the Coalition are given up, even by the enemy, while on the other hand, Shelburne, Temple, Thurlow, Pitt, &c. are some of them quite unarrangeable, and have, to my certain knowledge, hardly any communication one with the other, I cannot help thinking the fear of our being overturned in Parliament quite chimerical. However, the first business we shall have to bring on is of a very delicate nature, I mean the East India business, and if ever Opposition is likely to be formidable, it may be so on a question where they will be joined by many upon grounds of personal attachment to this or that Director, or to this or that Governor. This question once over, as I hope it will be by Christmas, I own I hope things will go on as smoothly as possible in a House of Commons where there is so able, so indefatigable, and so little scrupulous an opposer as Pitt. If we last the summer, the public will think that the King has made up his mind to bear us, and this opinion alone will destroy the only real cause of weakness that belongs to us. I repeat again that I may very possibly be mistaken in my conjectures about the King's intentions for this summer, but if I am right in this, I am much more firm in my speculations about the winter, which I can hardly bring myself to think can fail me. So much for our politics. I must now trouble you about some Irish business. In the first place I have been applied to by the Prince of Wales to write to you in favour of Dean Stopford, who

has a very small preferment, as I am informed, and
who would be glad of any step whatever. Whether
the present vacancy of the deanery of Ossory furnishes
an opportunity of doing the thing for him must
depend upon your engagements and intentions for
your own chaplains, but I need not say (especially
after the contents of this letter) that it will give me
great satisfaction whenever I am enabled to tell his
Royal Highness that his commands are obeyed. The
next business I am to trouble you upon is, Sir James
Erskine's, which I do not myself rightly understand, but I am informed will be no inconvenience
to you to grant. I am sure I cannot better recommend it to you than by bearing the testimony which
I owe to the perfectly handsome manner in which
Lord Loughborough has conducted himself towards
us ever since we came in, as well during the time
of our peril, as upon every other occasion. It
would really give me great concern that anything for
his nephew, after having got Conway to consent to it,
here, should fail in Ireland. These two points, therefore, I am bound to recommend to you in the strongest
manner, from every motive of political gratitude. The
third, to which I am now coming, I am solicitous
about, I own, much more from motives of private
affection than from any others. I mean Ogilvie's
application for the office of Registrar of Deeds. I
cannot perhaps better explain to you how strongly
these motives press upon me than by sending you a
letter I received from Lady Louisa Conolly in consequence of my having told her that I thought the place

might probably be given to Ogilvie. I will also add that my connection with the Duchess of Leinster and Lady Louisa Conolly, is not only that of a near relation, but of the most constant and uninterrupted friendship, and that to the latter in particular I am under more obligations than to any other person living. With respect to the thing itself I will only make two observations,—first, That I know Mr. Burton would immediately resign for Ogilvie, who would give him the profits of the place during life, and that it is not certain that he would resign to anybody else; secondly, that though the Duke of Leinster was cold about it some time ago, I believe he is quite otherwise now. I know Lord Charles, who has great influence with his brother, is very warm upon it.

"When I look at the length of this letter and consider the applications it contains, I begin to think, that instead of regretting my silence, you will wish I had deferred writing for ever. All I can say is, that I never do trouble you when I can avoid it. In these instances I have fairly told you my motives, which you will allow to be good ones. I am with the greatest sincerity,

" My dear Northington,

" Yours ever,

"C. J. FOX.

" P.S. I have only seen Windham for a moment, and have not yet had any conversation with him."

[FOREIGN AFFAIRS.]

In the first Cabinet of 8th April, 1783, the King was recommended to negotiate with the American Commissioners on commercial intercourse upon a footing of reciprocity, and Mr. Fox accompanied the minute with a letter to the King, saying, upon the subject of American intercourse, " It is intended to put off the bill now depending in Parliament till some progress is made in the negotiation, and to bring in a bill immediately for the purpose of repealing the prohibitory acts made during the war, and for removing the formalities which attended the admission of ships from the colonies during their state of subjection. Your Majesty will immediately perceive that the line proposed is to give as much facility to the trade between the two countries as is consistent with preserving the principles of the Act of Navigation. When Mr. Fox has the honour of waiting on your Majesty to-morrow, he will endeavour to give any further explanation which your Majesty may wish on this subject, and at the same time will take your Majesty's commands on the manner of opening this negotiation, and upon the person to be employed in it."

THE KING'S ANSWER.

" QUEEN's HOUSE, *April* 10*th*, 1783.
" 5 min. past 11 p.m.

" MR. Fox seems to feel so forcibly the singularity of the opinion given by the Canada merchants to Lord

North, which, they say, arises from the information
they have received from Mr. Oswald, that it is not
necessary for me to suggest anything on this subject,
except that I coincide with his opinion in the propriety
of proposing these regulations to the American Commissioners, though without much expectation of
success."

MR. FOX TO THE KING.

"St. James's, *April* 16*th*, 1783,
" 20 min. past 11.

" Mr. Fox trusts to your Majesty's goodness and
justice that your Majesty will give no credit to the
idle report which Count Bruhl thinks fit to write to
his Court.

" Mr. Fox takes this opportunity of assuring your
Majesty that he never heard, nor had reason to think,
that the removal of the Duke of Dorset was disagreeable to your Majesty, and that he is perfectly sure that
the Duke of Portland did not recommend that measure
from any ill-will to the Duke of Dorset, but merely
from the convenience which resulted to the arrangement from the present disposal of that appointment.

" Mr. Fox hopes your Majesty will not think him
presumptuous, or improperly intruding upon your
Majesty with professions, if he begs leave most humbly
to implore your Majesty to believe, that both the Duke
of Portland and he have nothing so much at heart as
to conduct your Majesty's affairs, both with respect to
measures and to persons, in the manner that may give
your Majesty the most satisfaction, and that whenever
your Majesty will be graciously pleased to condescend

even to hint your inclinations upon any subject, that it will be the study of your Majesty's Ministers to show how truly sensible they are of your Majesty's goodness."

MINUTE OF CABINET.

"Lord President, Lord Privy Seal, Duke of Portland, Lord John Cavendish, Lord Keppel, Lord North, and Mr. Fox.   Projects for definitive treaties with France and Spain submitted to the King.

" ST. JAMES'S, *April* 18*th*, 1783."

MR. FOX TO THE KING.

" ST. JAMES'S, *April* 18*th*, 1783.
"40 min. past 11 p.m.

" MR. Fox has the honour of sending your Majesty the two projects for the definitive treaties, together with the minute of Cabinet.   Mr. Fox will employ himself to-morrow morning in writing a dispatch to Mr. Fitzherbert, which, when it is submitted to your Majesty, will serve to explain the alterations made from the French projects and Spanish preliminaries, and the reasons for those alterations.   A blank is left for the logwood article, but Mr. Fox is not without hopes of being able to fill it up in the course of to-morrow.

" If your Majesty should wish for any verbal explanation upon this very great business, Mr. Fox begs to receive your Majesty's orders at what time he can wait upon your Majesty, as Mr. Fox humbly submits to your Majesty that it will be advisable to send off the messenger to-morrow night if possible."

THE KING'S ANSWER.

"QUEEN's HOUSE, *April* 19*th*, 1783.
" 25 min. past 9 a.m.

" THE projects of definitive treaties with France and Spain, and the dispatch which is to accompany them to Mr. Fitzherbert, must so fully state the reasons of the alterations from the preliminary articles that I do not mean to call on Mr. Fox for further explanation on this subject. Unnecessary discussions are not my taste, and the Cabinet, having by a minute approved of these projects, I do not propose to give myself any additional trouble with regard to them.

"G. R."

THE KING TO MR. FOX.

"WINDSOR, *April* 28*th*, 1783.
" 39 min. past 4 p.m.

" UNDOUBTEDLY the Emperor is in a most difficult situation, and it seems impossible he should keep the friendship of Russia without a total breach with France. Therefore, we must wait with patience till this is unravelled, which may the easier be done as there does not appear the smallest reason for taking any immediate step.

"G. R."

Mr. Fox in his first Ministry had, I believe, removed Mr. Hugh Elliot from Berlin to Copenhagen at the request of the King of Prussia, who was much

affronted with him for some good but saucy jokes on
him and his Government, and yet more for an outrage
in seizing the despatches of an American agent, and
reproaching the King for receiving him.

SIR JOHN STEPNEY TO MR. FOX.

[PRIVATE.]

"BERLIN, *April* 15*th*, 1783.

"DEAR SIR,

"I cannot omit by this first opportunity to
express the sincere satisfaction I felt at finding you
were reinstated in the same public situation in which
I left you when I quitted England last summer, and
to assure you of the pleasure I shall have in serving
immediately under your orders. I scarce need add,
that I shall follow them with the most exact attention,
and with very particular confidence. I do not know
whether you are informed that I was removed to this
Court without any solicitation on my part, and that in
some respects the removal was far from being advan-
tageous. I wrote, however, to Lord Grantham at the
time, that I should not think of asking for additional
appointments, unless I found, after some months'
experience, that it was impossible to go on without
them. Still less shall I say anything on this head as
yet to you. I shall delay the moment of entreating
you to lay such a request before his Majesty as long
as I possibly can, and if at last I shall be forced to do
so, I shall at the same time submit to your judgment
the recommending to this post some person of superior rank, fortune, and abilities, and the disposing of

me in any way you may think proper. This was the
tenor of what I took the liberty of saying to you last
year, and your very obliging and friendly conduct on
that occasion persuades me that I cannot be in the
wrong in repeating the same sentiment now.

" You will probably have heard from Mr. Elliot that
he had left Copenhagen for a few days, in order to
fetch his daughter from this place. He never communicated to me anything relative to his intentions,
nor was I acquainted with his arrival till after he had
left Berlin on his return. Mr. Elliot thought it necessary to enter the town under another name than his
own, and as he went out, declared himself in his
proper character. This, together with his arrival,
being entirely unexpected, has given rise to much conversation here. I therefore judge it proper you should
be made acquainted with the circumstance. At the
same time, I do not find that the Court pays so much
attention to it as it was at first expected, or that any
steps were intended which might have given rise to
disagreeable discussions between the two Courts.
Permit me to repeat the high sense I have of your
former obliging behaviour with respect to me, and to
assure you of the unfeigned attachment with which I
shall always remain, &c.,

" J. STEPNEY."

This mysterious adventure of Hugh Elliot was
followed by a duel with Baron Knyphausen.
Frederick II.'s displeasure with him is easily accounted
for, if his repeated sayings are true. When he was

inveighing against Frederick and Prince Henry to some admirer, and was stopped by the observation, " Vous conviendrez, pourtant, que ce sont de grands princes ? " " Oui, j'en conviens (said he), et de mauvais sujets." And when Frederick himself, at supper, tried to disconcert him, by asking him significantly if Hyder Ali had not beat the English, and if he was not, after all, a great man, " ce Hyder Ali ? " " C'est un prince, sire (he replied), qui dans son tems a assez bien fait la guerre ; mais maintenant (added he, fixing the King) ce n'est qu'un vieux roi qui radote." These may be witty repartees, but they are very ill-placed in the mouth of a foreign minister. Mr. Fox had naturally an aversion to foreign envoys who sought celebrity by mortifying the princes to whom they were sent.

EXTRACT FROM A LETTER FROM SIR JAMES HARRIS (LORD MALMESBURY) TO MR. FOX.

" MY DEAR SIR,

" You will, I am sure, give me credit for being rejoiced at your being reinstated in an office you filled with such uncommon ability, and for my sincerely wishing for the permanency of an administration in which you and your friends have so large a share [here follow application for removal, and strong professions of a friendship of twenty years].

"JAMES HARRIS."

SAME TO SAME.

" My dear Sir,

"I am greatly flattered by your very kind and
friendly letter of the 11th. My conduct towards you by
no means deserves the praise you bestow on it. There
is very little merit in acting with propriety when the
path is marked out by a perfect conformity of political
principles, and by a long personal regard. I shall
not trouble you with professions. You perhaps,
however, would distinguish mine from those hackneyed
ones generally made to men in power, yet I had
rather act as your friend than *say* I am so ; and that
part of your letter, where you mention you will put
this in my power, by enabling me to leave Russia as
soon as possible, is on every account very agreeable to
me. I have fully explained myself on this subject by
the messenger I sent away on Sunday, and I wait with
the greatest impatience for news of his arrival. He
will likewise bring you every information it has been
in my power to obtain on those points you mention
towards the end of your letter. Whatever favourable
impressions I may make will be owing to the judicious
and wise system you, sir, seem disposed to adopt.
Your return to office will restore that confidence which
the fluctuating position in which we have stood for
some time past had gone near to destroy. I shall be
happy if the next commission I may be charged with
here should be the most pleasing one, and to see that
perfect good understanding and intimate connexion

established between the two Courts of London and Petersburgh, that for near six years I have been labouring to produce.

" &c. &c.,

" JAMES HARRIS."

1st May, 1783. A minute of Cabinet and a letter from Mr. Fox sent to the King, with the project of the intended treaty with the States General, and announcing drafts and despatches thereupon to the Duke of Manchester.

THE KING TO MR. FOX.

" WINDSOR CASTLE, *May 7th*, 1783.

" THE despatches from Mr. Fitzherbert I return. As I did not object to the preliminary articles, I have no reason to complain of such advantages as may be gained in the definitive treaty not being equal to the sanguine hopes of some persons.

" The Duke of Chartres not having given any notice of his being here, and he not being a Sovereign or Prince Apparent, I have no directions to give concerning him."

THE KING TO MR. FOX.

"*June 15th*, 1783.

" THE opinion Sir James Harris gives in his private letter to Mr. Fox, that the Empress of Russia inclines to a treaty of alliance in conjunction with us, with Austria, not Prussia, is so conformable to every idea that has come from Petersburgh for above two years, that I am convinced it is founded, and this confirms me in the propriety of being civil to both Courts, and lying by till we really see by the events which must occur in a few months, what line we ought to pursue; by being too anxious we may do wrong, and the critical situation of Russia must soon oblige her to court us.

"G. R."

MR. FOX TO THE KING.

"*June 22nd*, 1783.

" Mr. Fox congratulates your Majesty on the fair prospect which is opened in Sir James Harris's despatch, of forming such a system as may make a counterpoise to the power of the House of Bourbon, and may under your Majesty's auspices preserve the peace of Europe. Mr. F. is aware that the levity of the Court of Petersburgh makes everything uncertain that is to come from that quarter, but so many circumstances now concur to show her Imperial Majesty the necessity of some plan of this sort, that Mr. Fox cannot help being more sanguine than ever he was before."

THE KING TO MR. FOX.

"Windsor Castle, *June 22nd*, 1783.

" My opinion coincides entirely with that of Mr. Fox, that appearances favour the idea of Russia beginning to wish a closer intercourse with this country ; but surrounded as the political atmosphere is at present with clouds, it is quite right to wait for events, when we shall be better able to judge what may with propriety be done.

"G. R."

MINUTE OF CABINET.

"St. James's, *July* 18*th*, 1783.

"THE object of this minute is to recommend to your Majesty to direct Mr. Fox to instruct the Duke of Manchester to propose the deferring of the sixth article of the Spanish treaty for six months, according to the words of the preliminaries; and in case this proposal is not accepted, agreed, but not unanimously, humbly to recommend to your Majesty to direct Mr. Fox to instruct the Duke of Manchester to sign it as it now stands."

EXTRACT FROM A LETTER FROM MR. FOX TO THE KING OF THE SAME DATE.

"THERE has been a great deal of discussion upon this matter; but it appearing to be still in our power to put our own interpretation upon the words ' *Continent Espagnol*,' and to determine upon prudential considerations whether the Mosquito shore comes under that description or not; it was the opinion of your Majesty's confidential servants present (except Lord Stormont) that the desirableness of getting the definitive treaties signed as soon as possible, ought to prevail, and Mr. Fox will accordingly, with your Majesty's approbation, write immediately

to this effect to the Duke of Manchester. The Duke
of Portland delivered Lord Keppel's opinion, grounded
on the expressions in Lord Grantham's private letter,
that it would not be advisable to refuse signing the
definitive treaty upon the ground of the Mosquito
shore."

THE KING TO MR. FOX.

"WINDSOR, *July* 19*th*, 1783.
"40 min. past 7 a.m.

" It is a very untoward circumstance that a
definitive treaty cannot be concluded without leaving
clear ground for fresh disputes ; but I do not mean
by this reflection to object to the opinion of the
Cabinet that the Spanish treaty should not, on account
of the sixth article, be longer delayed. Every difficulty in conducting peace, this country has alone
itself to blame ; *after the extraordinary and never
to be forgot vote of February*, 1782, and the hurry
for negotiation that after ensued, it is no wonder that
our enemies, seeing our spirit so fallen, have taken
advantage of it."

Much correspondence between Mr. Fox and the
Duke of Manchester, and much negotiation between
the latter and Count Aranda and M. de Vergennes
took place in the beginning of July, in which the
Duke of Manchester very earnestly and very successfully vindicates himself for having consented to the
sixth article, relating to the Mosquito shore, in
consequence of the concessions implied and expressed

by Mr. Fox's predecessor, Lord Grantham, before the
signature of the preliminaries ; and the Duke justifies
himself also from some loose imputations of negligence
which he suspects to have been thrown out against
him by the King, especially in a conversation with
Lord Ludlow. These letters would, *in extenso*, be
tedious and uninteresting, but the temper and judgment with which Mr. Fox handles the subject, afford
a specimen of the manner of transacting business,
which endeared him to all who served under him, and
inspired even the opposite party with respect for his
talents and esteem for his character.

MR. FOX TO THE DUKE OF MANCHESTER.

"My dear Lord,   "*July* 21*st*, 1783.

" You will see by the despatches which accompany
this, that your advice is followed, and that you are
authorised to accede to the sixth article, with all its
objections, unless you can prevail upon them to defer
the consideration of it for the present, which would
be most eligible on many accounts. Our great
objection is, that we make a concession not warranted
by the preliminaries ; and though we can certainly
defend ourselves against our predecessors, the more
material question is, how to defend ourselves against
the public. These considerations appeared to be so
strong, that there were not wanting opinions for
refusing absolutely to acquiesce, and even for risking
everything upon this ground. These opinions were,
however, happily overruled, and I only mention

them to impress you with an idea of how very important a service you will do us, if you can get this matter postponed, and the definitive treaty signed without it. What his Majesty meant by his conversation with Lord Ludlow is more than I can guess. This I am sure of, that there never was an accusation more unjust. It does not appear to me that a moment has been lost on your side of the water. I am sure you have been able to do more than anybody could have expected in the treaty with France. The only thing that could be wished to have been otherwise in the whole course of the negotiation, is, that you had taken an earlier opportunity of apprising me of this cursed clause in the sixth Spanish article. The reason why you did not, I take to be this : it was so much taken for granted where you are, and had been so uniformly acquiesced in in conversation from first to last, that you imagined I could not be ignorant of it. The unfortunate circumstance, too, of my having left the article quite blank in my project, prevented the words coming into consideration in the same manner as those of the other articles. However, whatever may have been the causes, my ignorance in this matter has certainly been unfortunate, because I certainly negotiated the business of the district and the boundaries upon different principles from those which would have guided me if I had known the latter part of the article. I am sure your Grace will do me the justice to believe, that I mention this not with a view to blame, but only to tell you openly and fairly the only thing that I wish to have been otherwise in the whole course of the negotiation. I assure you, at the same time, that the reason which I have suggested why it happened as it did, appears to me to be perfectly satisfactory, and I promise you, you shall never want the testimony which I owe you, of having acted, during the whole of this difficult negotiation, with uncommon assiduity, ability, clearness, and dispatch.

"I am, &c.

"C. J. FOX."

MR. FOX TO SIR JOHN STEPNEY.

"St. James's, *May 20th*, 1783.

" Dear Sir John,

"You will not be surprised that I am not yet able to answer your private letter. You know my good wishes to you, and you may be very sure of their continuance. The business contained in the following cypher will be a sufficient proof how much I rely upon your friendship, and how perfect a confidence I have in your discretion. It is possible that, at the distance where you are, you may suppose the near division in the Commons last night to be of more importance than it really is. A great number of Lord North's friends and ours voted against us; and, considering the great unpopularity of the question, what passed seems to me rather a proof of strength than weakness. I may be sanguine; but this is my real opinion; and, indeed, if I did not think there was great prospect of stability, you will easily believe that I should not, at this moment, have written what follows. [Thus far in his own hand : what follows is in cypher and decyphered in another.] I have pretty certain intelligence that the great plan of war with Turkey is laid aside, but that still there will be war between Russia and the Porte, in which the Emperor will not take a part. I wish you to communicate this intelligence *from me to the King of Prussia*, as a *matter of fact* that may be interesting to him, and as an event which, by creating a coolness between the Imperial Courts, may tend to that system which I had flattered myself to give birth to last year, under the auspices, and with the advice of his Prussian Majesty. It is very probable that my intelligence will be stale at Berlin by the time this reaches you ; but, at all events, it will show my sincere desire of acting confidentially with the King of Prussia, and my attention to this critical business, upon the issue of which the system of Europe must depend. You will recommend to the King of Prussia the greatest secresy upon this communication, as I would not have it known to any one that I have made mention of it ; and you will, of course, answer this in cyphers, and in a private letter, and take no notice of it in your public despatches. My reason for conveying this through you rather than Count Lusi, is not from any mistrust of, or from any dissatisfaction at his conduct, but for other reasons which it is not necessary for me to explain, and it will be but fair to tell his master.

" I am, with great truth, &c.

"C. J. FOX."

Sir John Stepney, in answer of June 3rd, informs Mr. Fox that he has been compelled to convey his communication to the King of Prussia through Count Finkerstein. In his cyphered despatches, dated Berlin, June 10th, and Berlin, June 14th, 1783, Sir John sends the answer from the King of Prussia, thanking Mr. Fox for his intelligence, but betraying great mistrust of Austria.

MR. FOX TO SIR JOHN STEPNEY.

"*July 27th*, 1783.

" DEAR SIR JOHN,

" The King of Prussia has sent me word by Lusi in the fairest manner that this is not now a time for our project, but that if ever a proper opportunity should offer he will let me know it. I have, of course, desired Lusi to thank him for me for this message, but I wish you would take some opportunity of signifying to him, through his Minister or otherwise, how very sensible I am of his candid way of dealing, and how very happy I shall be on all occasions to have his advice ; that all my wishes go to the project of last year ; and that his Prussian Majesty knows better than I that a Minister must be governed by times and circumstances and not by his wishes. In short, let him know that I feel his direct way of acting as I ought to do. His superiority to all other princes is certainly as great as ever it was represented to be. Pray let me know what is the true state of his health, and what sort of opinion is entertained of his succes-

sor. You may write a private letter in cypher now
if you have any occasion, as there is no immediate
danger of a change here. Indeed I am sanguine
about remote ones.

" C. J. FOX."

The letters from Sir James Harris from Petersburgh
to Mr. Fox, throughout the spring, are full of admiration, friendship, and gratitude, and contain many
proofs of the unsuccessful endeavours for detaching
the Court of Berlin from that of Versailles, and of
the disposition of the Empress to court the English
and Austrian alliance, with a view to her intended
projects on Turkey.

EXTRACT FROM A LETTER FROM MR. FOX TO THE KING.

"*6th August*, 1783.

" THE French Ambassador pressed Mr. Fox again
yesterday upon the subject of Turkish affairs, and
acquainted him that the Court of France would go
so far as to prevail upon the Porte to allow the
Empress to annex the Cuban entirely to her dominions,
and to put Crim Tartary upon such a footing as
would give her there everything of sovereignty but
the name. Mr. Fox meant humbly to have submitted
to your Majesty this day, whether it might not be
proper to send off a messenger immediately to Sir
James Harris with an account of this conversation, and
for this purpose has drawn the draft which attends

your Majesty with this, and will send the messenger to-morrow with your Majesty's approbation. Mr. Lawrens was yesterday with Mr. Fox to desire him to take your Majesty's pleasure whether it would be agreeable to your Majesty to receive a Minister from the United States. Mr. Fox knowing your Majesty's opinion upon this subject from what your Majesty did him the honour to say to him some time since, and feeling that it cannot be an agreeable subject to dwell upon, would have taken upon himself to have answered in the affirmative, if it had not been rather pointedly put to him *to take your Majesty's royal pleasure.* Mr. Fox most humbly begs your Majesty's pardon for troubling your Majesty with so much business, especially at this time, and would certainly avoid it if everything in this letter did not require dispatch."

EXTRACT FROM THE KING'S ANSWER TO THE ABOVE.

"WINDSOR, *August 7th*, 1783.
"7 p.m.

[The first part relates to a message to the Emperor of Germany about Prince Frederick's (Duke of York) visit to Vienna, which he never accomplished.]

" Mr. Fox is very right in keeping Sir James Harris apprised of every circumstance that falls from the French Ambassador on the Turkish affair. As to the question whether I wish to receive a Minister from America, I certainly can never express its being

agreeable to me; and indeed I should think it wisest
for both parties to have only agents who can settle
any matters of commerce; but so far I cannot help
adding, that I shall ever have a bad opinion of any
Englishman who would accept of being an ac-
credited Minister for that revolted state, and which
certainly for years cannot establish a stable
government."

THE KING TO MR. FOX.

" WINDSOR, August, 1783.
" 48 min. past 9 a.m.

" I cannot say the supposed letter of Mr. Hastings
gives great lustre to his prudential as well as moral
character, though it does not destroy the idea of his
activity.

" I cannot say that I am so surprised at France
not putting the last strokes to the definitive treaty
as soon as we may wish, as our having totally disarmed,
in addition to the extreme anxiety shown for peace
during the whole period that has ensued, the end of
February, 1782, certainly makes her feel that she
can have no reason to apprehend any evil from so
slighting a proceeding ! "

MR. FOX TO THE DUKE OF MANCHESTER.

" ST. JAMES'S, August 21st, 1783.

" MY DEAR LORD,
" I do not now recollect that there is anything
you can wish to hear from me upon, except the Article
of Presents. The King thinks our rule ought to be to

give whatever the French do, and this will do very well with regard to the mediators, Vergennes, and D'Aranda; but what are we to do with the four Americans? Whatever is given to them must be in money, or at least not in pictures, and will not one thousand pounds to each be thought a great deal, and yet how to distinguish between them and the Russians, who have not the character of Ambassadors any more than they. You will readily conceive that I have not been willing to mention this difficulty in the closet, nor shall I till I know how to remove it. If your Grace, or Mr. Maddison, from whose letters to Frazer I learnt what I know of the French intentions upon this matter, can help me to any expedient, I shall be very much obliged to you. For I am sorry to say (this is in perfect confidence) that the King's awkwardness upon these little matters relative to the Americans appears to me rather to increase than diminish. I hope and trust the French will be sufficiently mortified by the reception of their remonstrance (for such it was) at Petersburgh, and I flatter myself they will have still more reason to be so before the end of the business. Mr. D'Adhemar told me some time since that they should make a manifesto, complaining of the Empress's injustice, and of his most Christian Majesty not being seconded by other powers in his endeavours to prevent it. I hope to God they will do this, for I think nothing can make them so truly ridiculous.

" I am, &c.

" C. J. FOX."

DUKE OF MANCHESTER TO MR. FOX.

"PARIS, *August* 21*st*, 1783.

" MY DEAR SIR,

" I have nothing particular to write to you, but just to state that the reports here are very strong that the French Ministry will be changed; since the introduction of M. de Breteuil to the Council there has been great difference of opinion in the Cabinet, and it is generally thought that either M. de Vergennes, or M. de Castries, must soon go out. De Vergennes is very well with the King, but the Queen has expressed herself dissatisfied about the measures it is supposed he wishes to support in regard to the Russian disputes, as she interests herself strongly for her brother. M. de Castries is in great favour with her, but her society do not seem to like him, particularly the Chevalier de Vaudreuil, who is afraid that if he should become Minister he would bring in again M. de Necker, with whom he is strictly con-nected. These are the interior politics. In regard to peace, De Vergennes still makes excuses for not sign-ing, pretending great regard for the Dutch, and desiring to wait the return of the courier they have sent to Holland. This may make a long delay, as Berkenrode told me last Saturday he hardly expected the return these three weeks. I mean as soon as this week is out to make a peremptory requisition of Comte de Vergennes to name a positive day for signing, and hope I shall have by the next letters from you

directions for this purpose. It is the only mode that
will at present do here.

"I am, &c.

"MANCHESTER.

"P.S. You have given me no directions about the
presents that are expected by the negotiating Ministers.
They are pretty considerable. Mr. Frazer had a note
of them from Maddison."

DUKE OF PORTLAND TO MR. FOX.

"CHISWICK, *August* 25*th*, 1783.

[SECRET.]

"MY DEAR FOX,

"I by no means like the signature of the treaty
being deferred. It will certainly affect public credit.
Taylor's correspondent sends him word that Lord
Shelburne's last letter to Vergennes is of the 8th of
June, and was answered by the French Minister on
the 10th; that from the time of our coming in, there
are only *two* letters from Lord Shelburne, viz., on the
26th of May and 8th of June, that in the last he
congratulates V. on his good intentions to conclude
the definitive treaty, laments his not having had the
honour of completing the glorious work of giving
peace to Europe, which he had so much at heart,
assures Vergennes that the King's present servants
cannot hold their employments beyond the duration of
the Parliamentary recess, after which he hopes to have
the honour of corresponding with Vergennes again
upon public affairs. From the same quarter I learn

that Vergennes has letters from the Coast of Coromandel, informing him that Suffrein has lost 2000 men, and has as many down with fevers and flux, and that Bussy has joined him with four ships from Trincomalee, but no dates or force of Bussy's squadron are mentioned.

" Most sincerely yours,

" P."

THE KING TO MR. FOX.

" WINDSOR, August 24th, 1783.

" THE private letter of the Duke of Manchester gives an unexpected reason for Comte de Vergennes's delay of signing the definitive treaty, though I ever looked upon the introduction of so intriguing a man as M. de Breteuil in the Council as a dangerous measure for Comte de Vergennes, unless they understood one another. Yet I did not think a change in Ministry so near. Perhaps Breteuil, being unfriendly to the Court of Vienna, may be rather with Vergennes than Castries.

"G. R."

EXTRACT FROM A LETTER FROM THE DUKE OF MANCHESTER
TO MR. FOX.

" PARIS, August 26th, 1783.

" I HAVE talked with Mr. Hartley in regard to the presents to be given to the American Ministers, and proposed that a couple of 1000*l*. should be given amongst them, which he thought, with me, would be very handsome and satisfactory, and has undertaken to mention it in a friendly way to Dr. Franklin.

"There have been great cabals at Versailles, and M. de Vergennes is thought to be very tottering. The Queen, anxious to support her brother, has spoken very plainly to De Vergennes, who is said to have made a very firm reply. The King has a high opinion of him, and the Queen's Société are afraid that if M. de Castries should get the ascendancy, he will bring in again M. Necker, which would be particularly disagreeable to the Chevalier de Vaudreuil. At the same time M. de Breteuil, whom the Queen has introduced, differs much with the other Ministers.

"I have at present lost the assistance of Mr. Maddison. He is dangerously ill. It is a great doubt whether he can recover. His illness is so extraordinary and so rapid that it is the general opinion he has swallowed something which has poisoned him. Every endeavour will be made to save him ; should they not succeed, I must send my secretary Mr. Warner over with the treaty, which I shall dispatch the same day it is signed.

"I am, &c.,
"MANCHESTER."

LORD NORTH TO MR. FOX.

"WROXTON, *August* 27th, 1783.

"DEAR SIR,

"I am much obliged to you for your letter, which my son has delivered to me this morning. The delays of the French Minister in signing the definitive treaty are defended by him upon such frivolous and unsatisfactory reasons, that he certainly must mean something more than he says. What that is, it may be perhaps difficult to guess. The ratifications with America having been exchanged, one should think it is not the interest of France immediately to recommence a war, and yet there are some awkward appearances, especially on the part of Spain. I directed Mr. Nepean to send to you and the Duke of Portland a letter I lately received from Mr. G. Elliot, giving an account of a considerable armament preparing at Cadiz, an account of which he had received from Sir Richard Worsley, who had been lately there. Add this intelligence to the care taken by the Spanish Court that no information should pass into the garrison through the lines of St. Roche, and their unwillingness to destroy the works upon the Isthmus, I own I do not like the general face of the conduct of France and Spain, and think we ought to be upon our guard. I would, upon some pretence, and with as little parade as possible, delay for a time the further disarming of the fleet. The regiments destined for Gibraltar should sail immediately, and permission should be given to Sir G. Elliot to retain the regiments that are to be relieved, till he thinks he can part with them without danger. I do not know how the recruiting the old regiments goes on, but I think it should be recommended to the Commander-in-Chief to avail himself of the opportunities which the conclusion of the harvest will afford, and he should be permitted to give more than the usual encouragement, &c. It may perhaps not be amiss to endeavour to learn what conduct the mediators (especially Russia) will hold in case of any treachery on the part of France and Spain. Perhaps I may be too suspicious, but the total want of all honesty and decency which has usually (and particularly of late) prevailed in the Councils of the two branches of the House of Bourbon, added to the shuffling conduct of M. de Vergennes, gives me, I own, some uneasiness, which will not be removed till the definitive treaty is actually signed and ratified. The next letter from the Duke of Manchester will probably clear up the real intentions of M. de Vergennes, but from this moment we should take every precaution, and act with him as with a man in whom we can place no confidence whatever.

" I am,

" Dear Sir, &c.,

" NORTH."

SAME TO SAME.

" Wroxton, August 30th, 1783.

" DEAR SIR,

" Thank you for your good news. You have in a great measure relieved my anxiety. It did not arise solely from the want of that additional security which the peace acquires by the conclusion of the definitive treaty. France and Spain were already in point of honour and justice under the strongest obligations not to disturb again the public tranquillity. What alarmed me a little were the shuffling delays and unaccountable behaviour of M. de Vergennes, with the unfriendly conduct of the Court of Spain, and the reports of the preparations in the Spanish ports. Their present conduct appears, however, more fair and direct, and it is not to be supposed that they would publicly sign the definitive treaty at a moment that they harbour any immediate design of renewing their quarrel with Great Britain. You have done very right in giving immediate notice to the Lord Mayor, and I am much obliged to you for signing the Circular Letters, which were sent from my office upon the occasion. I am sorry to have been absent at this time, but I flatter myself that no inconvenience has arisen from my absence. I propose to be in London next week, and to remain there, or at Bushy, till after the royal christening. Ten days or a fortnight more for an excursion to the west of England upon business, is all that I shall desire during the rest of the year. Lord Derby has taken the Chancellorship of the Duchy, upon a footing very honourable for himself, and very convenient for the Administration.

" Adieu, dear Sir,

" Most sincerely and faithfully yours,

" NORTH."

LORD STORMONT TO MR. FOX.

" [PRIVATE.]

" September 2nd, 1783.

" DEAR SIR,

" I had this morning the honour of your letter, and heartily congratulate you on the conclusion of the definitive treaty. I find it very easy to reconcile myself to M. de Vergennes's ill-humour ; it will not hurt us; but, on the contrary, it shows the difference he finds between this Ministry and the last. It is, I think, scarce possible that the French could be weak enough to expect to engage us in any actual concert with them, but they probably did hope to draw from us general expressions, which they would have endeavoured to improve to their advantage, and would have represented at Petersburgh in such a manner as to support their own views, and divert to us a part at least of the Empress's resentment, which must now fall wholly upon themselves.

" The general turn of the Emperor's policy, and the opinion he has conceived of his own address, will naturally make him endeavour to the utmost to preserve both the French and the Russian alliance; but the scene that is now opened must, I think, render those alliances absolutely incompatible. The general influence of France upon the Continent will, of course, decline; and if we continue our attention to repair our losses, and to recover our strength, and watch opportunities as they may arise, I am in great hopes of our forming a proper Continental connection, without which I have ever thought this country cannot stand secure.

" I have the honour to be, with great truth

and regard,

" Dear Sir, your most obedient humble servant,

"STORMONT."

THE KING TO MR. FOX.

"WINDSOR, *September 1st,* 1783.

"I AM sorry to find, by the private letter of the Duke of Manchester to Mr. Fox, that Mr. Maddison is dead; and the more so, as it appears to have been occasioned by poison, which I should rather think, if so, was accidental, as I cannot conceive that any one could be interested in putting an end to his existence.

"G. R."

DUKE OF MANCHESTER TO MR. FOX.

"PARIS, *September 3rd,* 1783.

"SIR,

"I have just time to say that I signed yesterday the preliminary treaty with the Dutch. I mentioned in my dispatch that I had had a hint that day, that they would propose to me to make it definitive; which, if I had agreed to, all the ideas Mr. Shirley communicated to you must have vanished. Messrs. Boers and Vanderpere had received an alarm from Holland, and came to me in the morning to entreat me not to sign definitively if it was offered. I gave them assurances I would leave them still room to treat with us in a more friendly manner, if their connections in Holland were well inclined. They left me fully satisfied, and I imagine have already sent to their party. I hope you will think I have done well in this? The Comte de Vergennes has lately discovered jealousy about the Dutch, and their proposal to me of signing definitively, which must have originated from him, convinces me of his design. You have now the field more open for what Mr. S. mentions to you, if it is thought a measure to be adopted. Mr. de Brantzen, as well as Berkenrode, seemed easier when they signed, and both showed that they thought themselves now more free and independent of the Court of France. De Brantzen took an opportunity of saying to me, he hoped England would now relax a little, and act more kindly towards them than they could expect while they negotiated through France. He wishes the definitive treaty may not be long deferred. I beg you, therefore, to give me full instructions for further measures as soon as you can. I am going to Versailles to conclude the other treaties, and shall send Mr. Warner with them in the evening on his road to you.

" I am, with great truth, &c.

" MANCHESTER."

SAME TO SAME.

" *September 3rd*, 1783.

" MY DEAR SIR,

" I write this merely to say, that we finished signing our treaties about three o'clock this day, and Mr. Warner proceeded with them immediately to England.

" I am, very truly yours,

" MANCHESTER."

THE KING TO MR. FOX.

"WINDSOR, *September 7th*, 1783.
"7 a.m.

" IT seems extraordinary that France should have so long delayed signing the definitive treaty. The arrival of it must remove any doubts persons might otherwise have harboured on that account. I cannot agree in opinion with the Duke of Manchester that it is desirable to ease the Dutch in the definitive treaty, to regain their affection whilst the French party are the directors; and if M. de Linden is the person fixed on, not Comte Wilderen, for Minister at this Court, any concessions will only encourage them in their Gallican system, from less feeling the inconvenience of their rupture. Whilst, if the treaty is less favourable, those who drew them into the war will become the cause of public hatred, and by subsequent kindnesses they may be perhaps regained; though in states, as well as men, where dislike has once arose, I never expect to see cordiality.

" Nothing can be more avowed than the desertion of the Court of Lisbon; but after Britain has so much lowered herself, can any one be surprised that Courts treat her accordingly ?

" G. R."

EXTRACT FROM A LETTER FROM THE DUKE OF PORTLAND
TO MR. FOX.

"CHISWICK, *September 7th*, 1783.

" I THINK the Duke of Manchester has done well
in getting the Dutch preliminaries signed in the
manner and at the time he contended for. I forgot
to mention on Friday that the King expressed his
indifference upon political subjects to be such, *since
the vote respecting the American War*, that he did not
feel the least anxiety for the arrival of the definitive
treaty, or had been sensible of any upon account of
any of the delays which have retarded its conclusion.
Lord N. told me that he spoke of the Russian
manifesto with much ill-humour and resentment, and
intimated some degree of apprehension of being
drawn into taking a part with the Empress ; but upon
Lord North's submitting to him the impolicy of
joining France in opposition to Russia, he very
readily concurred in it, and said that would be going
a great deal too far."

DUKE OF MANCHESTER TO MR. FOX.

[ABSTRACT.]

" PARIS, *September 7th*, 1783.

" REPORTS the satisfaction of Messrs. Boers and
Vanderpere at the signature of the preliminaries, their
expectation of its salutary effect in Holland, their hopes
that the English party may be restored to their superiority,—think much depends on the part taken by
England. The French party at present strong—much

prudence required to bring back men's minds, and to counteract it.   An English person should be sent authorised to hold friendly language.   The French party entire masters of the government ; but, though nothing can be done instantly, the demonstration of kindness from England would gradually effect much. ' I expect the Dutch ambassadors will press forward the definitive treaty ; this they (meaning Messrs. Boers and Vanderpere) are afraid of.'   I must beg you to write to me on this head.   M. Vanderpere wishes much that Mr. Shirley should be sent over to Holland ; he thinks him a man likely to conciliate, &c.   He has promised to write to M. de Lynde, who is the person in whom the Stadtholder confides, and is employed by that prince to signify his ideas to him.   There follows news from Mr. Oaks of a mysterious journey of King of France to Compiegne, to meet the Emperor or some distinguished person, and determine a private treaty with King of Prussia."

MR. FOX TO THE DUKE OF MANCHESTER.

"*September* 12*th*, 1783.

" MY DEAR LORD,

    " I have just received your Grace's private letter of the 7th, containing Mr. Oaks' extraordinary intelligence.   There are so many mails due, that we are totally without news from the Continent, and consequently I am wholly without means of judging of the probability of what he says, by comparing it with what one hears from other parts.   With regard

to the man himself, I know little of him, but that
Mr. Stephens of the Admiralty told me his intelligence from his friend had often proved useful.   He
appears to me to be very credulous, which is always a
bad circumstance, as it makes him liable to be imposed
upon.   With respect to the Dutch business, I very
much agree with your Grace's letter in general, and
will endeavour to engage Mr. Shirley to go into
Holland ; but the great difficulty appears to me to be
this :—What mark of returning confidence can the
States-General give us sufficiently unequivocal to
justify us in making any concessions to them in the
definitive treaty ?   On the other hand, what steps
can this country take (objectionable concessions in
the definitive treaty excepted) which will tend to
strengthen our friends in Holland ?   Nobody can
wish more than I do the revival of the old friendship
between the two countries, but I will fairly own, that
while the tide continues to run against the Prince of
Orange as it now does, I cannot be sanguine.   However, I promise you that I will act with the same zeal
as if I was.

" It will be very material to know what credit ought
to be given to the ideas, generally spreading, of an
alliance between France and Prussia.   I do not yet
believe it to be far advanced.   No symptoms certainly
appear of it in this place ; but whether either the
French Ambassador or the Austrian Minister here
are much trusted by their Courts I doubt.   The
accounts brought by Captain Warner of the attention
that is paying to the French army, and of the bad

state of their navy, are both, in my opinion, very good for us. Every particle of intelligence that can be gathered, relative to what part France will take in this Eastern business, is infinitely interesting. I rather incline to think now that, after trying all that intrigue can do in vain, she will leave the Turks to their fate. But I do not find this to be the general opinion. If it were not for the unaccountable levity of the Court of Petersburg, I should think that the present circumstances must furnish us with some opportunity of forming a league to balance the family compact, and in this article of a continental alliance, as a balance to the house of Bourbon, consists, as your Grace knows, the whole of my foreign politics. And I am very happy to find that *every one* of the present Ministers agree with me in this respect. Some * have their partialities to the Emperor, as I own I have to the King of Prussia, but between these two the circumstances of the time will decide too forcibly to admit of the operation of either of these biasses.

" I am, &c.,

" C. J. FOX."

EXTRACT FROM A LETTER OF THE DUKE OF MANCHESTER
TO MR. FOX.

" PARIS, *September 11th,* 1783.

" THE persons mentioned by the Duke of Portland and yourself (for successors to Mr. Maddison) are, I doubt not, all very proper. One person only

---

* Lord Stormont probably.

(Mr. Gibbon) has, I am told, rendered himself obnoxious here by an expression in his book, in which he talks of the French sceptre slumbering in the hands of an Arcadius or Honorius. The King formerly took notice of the expression."

MR. FOX TO SIR JOHN STEPNEY.

"St. James's, *September 12th*, 1783.

" Dear Sir John,

" There are so many mails due, that we are in total want of information from the Continent. Everybody is full of impatience to see what conduct the different Courts of Europe will hold in the scene that is now opening; and you may easily suppose that yours is not the least looked to. I have no doubt of hearing from you as often as you have anything material to communicate. I expect a great number of false reports, idle stories, and loose conjectures, from all quarters, but everything now is interesting. All ideas of change here seem to have vanished; but as there are no solid grounds to form conjectures upon, they come and vanish according to caprice, and nothing else." [Then follows cypher (thus interpreted) : The business in my despatch is very material; and the answer to it, or rather the steps taken in consequence of it, may be a touchstone to the French bent where you are. I write these few words, only that you may know how necessary it is for you, not only to execute your commission with zeal, but to pay particular attention to the *manner* in which your request is received, and the effect it produces.]

" I am, my dear Sir John, &c.

"C. J. FOX."

EXTRACT FROM A LETTER FROM DUKE OF MANCHESTER TO MR. FOX.

"*September* 19*th*, 1783.

" I HAVE every reason to believe that the supposed treaty between France and Prussia does not yet exist.

" I believe there was once an idea of sending a joint fleet with Spain, to dispute the entrance of the Mediterranean with any Russian fleet, but that project is, I fancy, laid aside as too dangerous an experiment.

" I talked likewise with Messrs. Vanderpere and Boers upon the subject of the nomination of Mr. Lynden, who will strive all in their power to prevent it. Boers said England should refuse to receive him. I have likewise hinted to the Dutch Ambassadors the dislike of the proposed appointment as an impolitic measure, and will do it further.

" I am, &c.,

"MANCHESTER."

THE KING TO MR. FOX.

" QUEEN's HOUSE, *September* 24*th*, 1783.

" IF there is the least remains of decency in the Dutch, after the strong representations against Mr. Lynden's nomination, this cannot take place ;

but should passion prevail, I quite agree with Mr. Boers that from hence he must be refused.

"G. R."

THE KING TO MR. FOX.

"Windsor, *September* 27th, 1783.

" I enclose the letter I have written to the Prince of Orange, as also one to Prince Lewis, who would be hurt if on such an occasion I did call [" *not* " probably omitted] for his opinion also.   General O'Hara had best go to the Greffier and open himself fully, but explaining to him that it is as to a friend of the Stadtholder, not in his official capacity, and get his opinion as to the least public way of conveying my two letters.   I own I am gloomy on the subject from an opinion of the Prince's natural want of vigour, which I fear will make him at last lose all the efficacy of the station, and the name without the reality can neither be creditable for himself, nor of utility to the public.

"G. R."

MR. FOX TO THE KING.

" St. James's, *September* 28th, 1783.

" Mr. Fox humbly begs leave to acknowledge the honour of your Majesty's commands of yesterday. He has taken the liberty of sending your Majesty a copy of his private letter to General O'Hara, as well as of the paper enclosed in it ; and of his letter to

Mr. Greffier Fagel, in order that your Majesty may be the better able to judge whether what was intended by your Majesty has been carried into execution conformably to your Majesty's ideas. Mr. Storer is setting out, and is strictly charged to deliver the packet for General O'Hara with his own hands."

SAME TO SAME.

"WINDSOR, *September 28th*, 1783.

"THE letter to General O'Hara, the paper enclosed in it, and the one to the Greffier, contain all that occurs to me as necessary to be wrote on the present occasion."

LORD NORTH TO MR. FOX.

"LOWER GROSVENOR STREET, *September 27th*, 1783.

" DEAR SIR,

" The cause of the delay of which M. del Campo complains is, I take it, that it was neither known at my office when the ratifications were sent, nor that the orders for restitution ought to have accompanied the ratifications. The business, however, is now in such forwardness, that you will have the orders for evacuating East Florida, and for appointing commissioners to settle the district for cutting logwood on Monday morning, together with the necessary passports. I wish you would *look over these papers before they go to the King,* especially the order respecting the logwood letters. The draughts will be sent to you to-morrow. *My private letter* to the Governor of Jamaica is a matter of considerable nicety, and I own myself a good deal perplexed as to the manner of writing it.

" With great truth, dear Sir, very sincerely yours,

" NORTH."

IRISH AFFAIRS.

[The most important event that occurred in Ireland during the Coalition Administration was the convention of delegates from the armed Volunteers' associations, which met at Dublin on the 10th of November, under the guidance of Lord Bristol, Bishop of Derry, and of the celebrated Mr. Flood and others, for the purpose of preparing and introducing into the House of Commons a measure of Parliamentary Reform. This attempt to overawe and intimidate the Legislature was resisted by the House of Commons, and defeated by a large majority. The correspondence of Mr. Fox at this critical period with Lord Northington, Lord Lieutenant, and with General Burgoyne, Commander-in-Chief in Ireland, well deserve attention from his biographer, as evidence of his firmness and decision in repelling a proposition, to the principles of which he was not averse, because it was brought forward in a manner he thought dangerous to the peace and future stability of the country. The greater part of it has been already published,* but in a collection of materials for a Life of Mr. Fox it cannot be omitted.]

* Life of Mr. Grattan, by his Son, vol. iii.

MR. FOX TO LORD NORTHINGTON.

"St. James's Place, *November 1st,* 1783.

" Dear Northington,

" I believe it is a better excuse, and I am sure it is a truer one, for having so long postponed my letter to you, to say that it is owing to my idleness rather than my business. The few moments of idleness one has just before the opening of the most terrific session of Parliament that ever was held, are too valuable to be employed in anything that looks so very like business as writing a letter. I was ten days at Newmarket, Norfolk, &c. which came under the description of perfect idleness, and since my return I have put off writing from day to day in order to be more perfectly master of those topics upon which I mean to write to you, and which are of infinite import-ance not only to the credit of our Administration, but to the well-being of the country. And, first with respect to the Volunteers and their delegates; I want words to express to you how *critical* in the genuine sense of the word I conceive the present moment to be. Unless they dissolve in a reasonable time, Govern-ment, and even the name of it, must be at an end; this, I think, will hardly be disputed. Now it appears to me that upon the event of the present session of your Parliament, this question will entirely depend. If they are treated as they ought to be, if you show *firmness,* and that firmness is seconded by the aristo-cracy and Parliament, I look to their dissolution as a certain and not very distant event. If otherwise,

I reckon their government, or rather their anarchy, as firmly established, as such a thing is capable of being; but your Government certainly as completely annihilated. If you ask me what I mean by firmness, I have no scruple in saying, that I mean it in the strictest sense, and understand by it a determination not to be swayed in any the slightest degree by the Volunteers, nor even to attend to any petition that may come from them. This sounds violent, but I am clear it is right, for if *they* can pretend with any plausibility that they have carried any one point, it will be a motive for their continuing in their present state, and they will argue thus :—'We carried this this year; let us go on as we have done, and we shall carry some other point in the next.' Immense concessions were made in the Duke of Portland's time, and those concessions were declared by an almost unanimous House of Commons to be sufficient. The account must be considered as having been closed on the day of that vote, and should never again be opened on any pretence whatever. It is true that the Bill we passed here last year does not agree with my system, but you know the history of that Bill, and the stage in which it was when we came in ; otherwise I am satisfied it never would have been passed, at least I am sure it would not without the strongest opposition from the Duke of Portland and me. It is possible that I may be told that these are fine *words*, but that to act up to them is impossible. It may be so, but every information I have had from Ireland leads me to think that the spirit and firmness of the aristocracy will depend entirely upon the degree shown of those qualities in the Castle. Recollect that this is a crisis. Peace is the natural period to the Volunteers; and if they are encouraged to subsist for any considerable time after this period, all is gone, and our connection with Ireland is worse than none at all. I have so high an opinion of Grattan's integrity and love of his country, that I cannot persuade myself that he can see the present situation in any other light than that in which I do. Volunteers, and soon possibly Volunteers without property, will be the only government in Ireland, unless they are faced this year in a manful manner; and there is no man in conscience and honour so much bound to face them as Grattan himself. He has employed a dangerous instrument for honourable purposes; now that those purposes are answered, fully answered, by his own declaration in the vote before alluded to, is he not peculiarly bound to take care that so dangerous a weapon should no longer remain in unskilful, or perhaps wicked hands, to be employed for objects as bad as his were just and honourable? England justly relied much on his opinion that they would be satisfactory, in making the concessions in 1782, and he is therefore bound to England for the Irish part of the bargain, which was nothing more than to be satisfied. I heard with great satisfaction from Serjeant Adair that Grattan, though a friend to the Parliamentary reform, would take a wise distinction upon the manner in which it comes to the consideration of Parliament, and oppose it steadily upon that ground, but from what the Duke of Portland read me from Pelham's letter, I do not think this appears quite so certain. I know your natural inclination is to firmness, perhaps much more than mine is, and therefore, I hope all I have said upon the subject is superfluous; but I am so perfectly convinced that this is the crisis of the fate of Ireland that I cannot help dwelling upon it. The Volunteers never were, depend upon it, so considerable as they were represented: their having chosen a madman for their head, of whose honesty too there is no opinion, and their having laid their chief stress upon a point upon which there is so much real difference of opinion in both countries, and which militates as much against the interests of the prevailing influences in Parliament, are circumstances which must have weakened them. If they are resisted I am satisfied they will be defeated, and I cannot bring myself to think that much is risked in the trial, for if they are suffered to carry their points by timidity and acquiescence, it is as much over with English Government, in my judgment, as if they had carried them by force. All other points appear to me to be trifling in comparison of this great one of the Volunteers, but I will trouble you with a few observations upon some others. In regard to annual sessions, I own I do not think them very material, and in some respects, perhaps, I see some advantages arising to Government from them. You must have misunderstood Lord North, if you considered yourself as precluded either from consenting to them, or even from proposing them by your friends in Parliament. The

propriety of such a measure was meant to be left to
your discretion, but it was the mentioning of them in
the speech that was objected to, and I own I concurred
in this objection; but if I had imagined that you
thought this form of proposing them to be as material
as I now suspect you did, I should have been of
another opinion. I wish, therefore, for the future,
when you write for instructions on material points,
that you or Pelham would write a private letter to
the Duke of Portland or me, letting us know how far
you consider each point as important to your plans
and arrangements; if we had conceived that you
considered the mention of this point in the speech to
be of this nature, I have no doubt but your instructions would have been agreeable to your wishes.
With respect to some other points which have been
discussed among us to-day, perhaps the same observation will hold. I own I think the production of Pinto's
paper to the House formally, a very exceptionable
measure; but if you upon the spot judge it necessary,
my opinion will alter. However, I must say that it
would be a very dangerous precedent, and tend very
much to embarrass persons in my situation in all future
negotiations. You will understand, however, that my
objection is entirely to the formal production of it. I
have none whatever to Pelham's informing the House
correctly of all that has passed, and even reading
Pinto's memorial as part of his speech if he choose it.
My objection is, to the grounding of a proceeding
upon a memorial of a foreign Minister, which, in my
opinion, ought never to be done, except in the cases

of going to war, or of censuring a Minister. However, this may be given up to a very pressing
conveniency, though certainly it ought not to be done.
But no conveniency in my opinion would justify
the laying before the Irish Parliament the Definitive
Treaties, Preliminaries, &c. If they are once produced,
who can say that they shall not be discussed; that
Addresses shall not be moved upon them; and that
the opinions of the two kingdoms, upon the conduct
of the Ministers who made them, may not be diametrically opposite? The responsibility of Ministers here
can only be to the British Parliament, and to lay
treaties before an Assembly to whom we are not
responsible, would only be an idle compliment at
best, but might be in the end productive of some of
the worst consequences, which are to be feared from
the very peculiar relation in which the two kingdoms
now stand one to the other. What you propose about
beer is so reasonable that there can be no objection of
a public nature, but the intention which there is in
the Treasury of laying a very heavy tax upon that
article (which by the way ought not to be mentioned),
makes one wish, if possible, to avoid doing anything
which our brewers will complain of. The prudence of
listening to this objection will depend upon the degree
of advantage you expect from the measure you propose,
and of this you must be the judge. I hope, my dear
Northington, that you will not consider this long
letter as meant to blame your conduct, but, I think,
I owe it as much to my friendship for you as to the
public, to give you fairly my opinion and advice in

your most arduous situation, and I will fairly own
that there is one principle which seems to run through
your different despatches which a little alarms me ;
it is this :—You seem to think, as if it were absolutely
necessary at the outset of your Government to do
something that may appear to be obtaining boons,
however trifling, for Ireland ; and what I confess I
like still less is, to see that this is in some measure
grounded upon the ampleness of former concessions.
Now I see this in quite a different light, and reason,
that because those concessions were so ample no
further ones are necessary. If because the Duke of
Portland gave much, you are to give something, consider how this reasoning will apply to your successor.
I repeat it again, the account must be considered as
having been closed in 1782. Ireland has no right to
expect from any Lord-Lieutenant to carry any more
points for her. Convenient and proper regulations
will always be adopted for their own sakes, and stand
upon their own ground ; but boons, gifts, and compliments, Ireland has no right to expect. She has
more to fear from us than we from her. Her linen
trade, which is her staple, depends entirely upon the
protection of this country. I do not mean by saying
this that menace ought to be used, but neither ought
we, in our present situation, to pay her too much
court.

    " This country is reduced low enough, God knows,
but depend upon it we shall be tired if, year after
year, we are to hear of granting something new, or
acquiescing in something new, for the sake of pleasing

Ireland. I am sure you must feel as I do upon this subject, but, situated as you are, among Irishmen who, next to a job for themselves, love nothing so well as a job for their country, and hardly ever seeing any one who talks to you soundly on our side of the question, it is next to impossible but you must fall insensibly into Irish ideas more than we do, who see the reverse of the picture, and who, of course, are much more sensible to the reproaches of this country than of that. Ireland appears to me now to be like one of her most eminent jobbers, who, after having obtained the Prime Serjeantry, the Secretaryship of State, and twenty other great places, insisted upon the Lord-Lieutenant's adding a major's half-pay to the rest of his emoluments. It would be most unconscionable, after this very long letter, to trouble you with anything of a private nature, so that I will defer till my next letter the few things I have to say of that sort. I hear many of our friends disapprove of the idea of advancing Scott and Fitzgibbon. You know I am no enemy to coalitions, but all I say is, take care when you are giving great things to oblige those to whom you give them, and that you do not strengthen an enemy instead of gaining a friend. I repeat it again, my dear Northington, that if there should appear in this long and hastily-written letter some shades of dissatisfaction, I hope you will attribute it to the earnest manner in which I am used to write and speak, and to the sincerity and openness which I owe to you. I have no doubt but you will have done what is best, but the times are so very critical, that I cannot help speaking anxiously and eagerly upon points which must, in my judgment, decide the future happiness of both kingdoms. I am very sincerely, my dear Northington,

"Yours ever,

"C. J. FOX.

"I congratulate you upon the excellent accounts I hear of Pelham from all quarters."

EXTRACTS FROM A LETTER OF MR. FOX TO LORD
NORTHINGTON.

"November 7th, 1783.

"I TROUBLED you so long last week upon public affairs, that I will spare you this time, after having just told you that I continue, or rather grow stronger, in the sentiments which I then expressed, and mentioning one only point more, which I forgot in my last letter. This point is the 'Regium Donum' to the dissenting clergy, which ought to be increased by Government, and upon the subject of which I have long expected some application in your public despatches.

"You have enough to do without thinking of English politics. Our India measure will come on soon after the meeting. It will be a vigorous and a hazardous one, and if we get that well over, I have very little apprehension about anything else here.

"We are all anxious to know what has been the end of the affair between Flood and Grattan. I should

really think it a great national misfortune if anything
was to happen to the latter.

" Yours ever sincerely,

" C. J. FOX."

[Lord Northington having written to Mr. Fox, that
he had recommended Mr. Dickson for the bishopric
of Down, Mr. Fox replied as follows :—]

SAME TO SAME.

" *November* 14*th*, 1783.

" I do not lose a moment, my dear Northington, in
thanking you most cordially for your letter of the 10th.
It never can be in any man's power to confer an obligation upon me that will give me so much pleasure as
you have done in this instance, and I am sure, now
that you have had an opportunity of renewing your
old acquaintance with him, that it must give you
infinite satisfaction to serve such a man as Dickson.
He may depend upon my doing everything to ensure
your kind intentions to him having their full effect.

" We shall be impatient to hear further accounts of
your delegates, and in the mean time I am infinitely
pleased to hear that the Bishop of Derry is disappointed in his hopes from the populace, and feel much
disposed to be sanguine upon your affairs in general,
provided always that a proper spirit is shown, and that
Grattan acts as he ought.

" Yours ever most sincerely,

" C. J. FOX.

" P.S. Our India business, upon which all depends,

comes on Tuesday, and on that day se'nnight, or thereabouts, the great contest about it upon the second reading will, in my opinion, be the most important question to us that is ever likely to come on.   I mention this to you, both because I know that at a distance the comparative importance of questions is generally not immediately understood, and because if you do not want him very much, I wish you would send us over Luttrell.   As to Burgoyne, I fear it can scarcely be done with propriety."

LORD NORTHINGTON TO MR. FOX.

"DUBLIN CASTLE, November 17th, 1783.

" MY DEAR FOX,

" Many thanks to you for your long and interesting letter of the 1st of this month.   The frank communication of your sentiments afforded me real pleasure, as I look upon it as a very convincing proof of your regard and friendship for me.   I am highly anxious to cultivate those sentiments, and in order so to do, will make a suitable return to your last, by a most unreserved and open declaration of my opinions to you.   This situation is certainly of the most troublesome and arduous, and I require every assistance which your understanding, knowledge, and experience can give me.   I therefore most earnestly entreat you, whenever you think matters are not going in the manner you would wish, that you would send me an early notice of it, that I may have opportunity of changing my measures in time, or of satisfying you and the Duke of Portland, by my reasons, for my adherence to my own plan. You must, however, be disposed to make great allowances. Government, although strong, cannot do always here as it would wish. People are not yet brought to act well together. The late concussion of parties leaves some points which, each party being pledged, are still objects of contention. The country at large is unsettled, much disorder prevailing, and consequently difficulties hourly arise in one shape or another. The Duke of Portland and yourself will perhaps think me remiss in my communications, yet no blame should be laid to me, as it has been owing to the quick succession of things in the meeting, and the daily expectation I entertained of being able to give some very authentic and agreeable intelligence to you. But first to the Volunteers, which seems to occupy your attention in England.

" I agree in opinion with you, that nothing could happen more disgraceful to a Government, or which, at first view, carries with it more the appearance of danger and mischief than the meeting of the present Convention; its continuance and the objects of its consideration, I have looked on with infinite concern and anxiety, and have watched its motions and proceedings with the utmost attention and care. I am not disposed, however, to be equally apprehensive with yourself as to the consequences which it may produce. It is composed of such an heterogeneous set; their characters, principles, and views so different, that its resolutions are not likely to be such as will create material embarrassment or distress to Government.

I am thoroughly disposed to meet with firmness, and oppose with resolution, whenever Government can properly act; but that period, in my opinion, is not yet arrived. If you consider the consequence and credit these Volunteers have obtained; that at the time those great concessions were made in the Duke of Portland's administration, the Address of the two Houses of Parliament was carried up between rows of Volunteers under arms: That our friend Richard, then Secretary, in an interruption of a debate, acquainting the House of the Duke of Portland's waiting for them, assigned, as an additional apology, that there was a number of worthy and respectable men then under arms to do honour to the business of that day: That they have received three times the thanks of Parliament for their good conduct. When you consider the pains which have been used, with so much industry and success, to create fresh discontent among the Volunteers—the court which Lord Temple paid them—the bill which passed the English Parliament to quiet those alarms, and which they consider as obtained by their exertions. After a mature consideration of these matters, you will not be surprised that the idea of Government's interference to prevent this meeting, met with no advocates to support it, nor any then hardy enough to avow the recommendation of it. As it was, therefore, inexpedient to attempt to do what was not likely to be attended with any salutary effects, the next step was to try, by means of our friends in this assembly, to perplex its proceedings, and create confusion in their delibe-

rations, in order, if possible, to bring their meeting
into contempt, and to create a necessity of its dissolving itself. These methods have had a considerable
effect ; they are strangely embarrassed by a multi-
plicity of plans, and are much alarmed by the Roman
Catholics claiming a right to vote (a wish which the
more respectable of that persuasion disavow and
disapprove of), and many have already returned to
their homes disgusted. Another desirable step was
to involve them, if possible, in a dispute with the
House of Commons, and to create a necessity of a
declaration from that House to support the dignity
of Parliament, and to maintain its rights. It was
imagined a favourable opportunity would have presented itself upon the Down petition, which, however,
by a reconciliation between the parties, has been
avoided.

" It is with pleasure, I can assure you, that few men
entertain any apprehensions of mischief arising from
this meeting. Friends of all denominations, new and
old, agree that no consequences are to be feared.
That it will end in confusion, and contempt will
attend its fall. The measure now in contemplation is
that of sending the plan which may be agreed upon
to the different counties, to have meetings of freeholders called, and to instruct the members to vote
for it. If it once gets into such hands, there will be
no future occasions for conventional meetings.
Mr. Flood has shown much disinclination to attend
these meetings, but has been frequently summoned.
The advice he has given, being frequently called upon

to do so, was to take up every plan which had been delivered, to strike out every exceptionable part of each, mix the whole together, and so let it go down to the counties—a mass of information for the counties to deliberate upon. He declared his reverence for the old constitution, that it could not be touched without infinite hazard, and, if he had not been pressed, would have avoided giving any plan or assistance *to them*.

" November 18th. I have been interrupted since Monday, and have not had an opportunity of resuming my letter until now.

" Nothing is more true than that the House of Commons passed an almost unanimous vote of satisfaction at the close of the last session. Yet it is equally true, that satisfaction was of short duration, and that new dissatisfactions succeeded almost immediately. These were pretty universal; so that in the contemplation of the public at large, and in some measure of Parliament, that vote is nearly obsolete. In their opinions, many things remained still to be arranged; and particular objects of regulation, which the friends of Government had pledged themselves to when in Opposition, were supposed and understood by them to be reserved for a settlement at a period which would afford more leisure than the conclusion of an end of a session. It must be an object with Administration here, to bring the revenue and expense to meet, so as to prevent what can never be justifiable, an increase of debt during a peace. To effect this, additional duties must be laid upon taxable objects, in the manner least burthensome to the country. As this country is open to the trade of Great Britain, it is scarcely possible to fix upon anything, as an object of regulation, which does not in a greater or less degree affect some article of British trade : such is the beer regulation, which I have found it necessary to adopt, upon the representation of the advantages which might accrue to the country in promoting the use of beer instead of spirit, and from those which I expect to derive to my administration. Such too is the sugar duty, which, trifling as it is to both countries, is an object of great consequence to me, as most of the Duke of Portland's friends have pledged themselves to it. Lord North's instructions are so positive on that head, that I have resisted hitherto their wishes, and nothing but extreme necessity will justify a concession. It is a matter of some surprise to me that the Duke of Portland, who could not be ignorant how pledged his friends were ; and who, according to their report, had held out to them a settlement of the duty at twelve shillings, should not make it a point in the Cabinet that it should be acceded to.

"I cannot think that it was the intention of the Cabinet to give me a discretionary power with regard to annual sessions, nor that the expressions used by Lord North in his despatch did by any means convey such a meaning. 'The *innumerable* inconveniences of annual sessions of Parliament must be obvious to your Excellency, and how much they outweigh the advantages expected from them. As to the pretence

used by the supporters of provincial meetings, it is
so mere a pretence, that it cannot be considered as a
reason for any alteration of consequence.   His
Majesty's servants wish, therefore, that the grants of
money may be made as usual for two years, unless
your Excellency, upon the fullest and most mature
inquiry, is perfectly convinced that they cannot be
obtained in the usual manner,' &c. &c.

" A more decisive opinion of the impropriety of
the measure cannot be given, and the direction is
positive to resist, as far as resistance can be useful to
defeat it.   His Lordship states no one of the inconveniences, which were to overbalance the advantages
to this country of a speedy distribution of justice,
early opportunity of following England in her commercial regulations before an opposition could form
itself against them, and the reasonable expectation of
putting an end to these strange, unwarrantable
meetings, the idle projects of minds unemployed
except every other year.   As far as I am able to
judge, my opinion is that Ireland will be most easily
governed by annual meetings.   It will knit more
firmly together the supporters of Government, marshal
the phalanx more readily.   You will not have to be
making bargains for the support of a particular
sessions, after which every man is usually left at
liberty, and is to renew his agreement again; but it
will be a steady and fixed support, not liable to change,
and more to be depended on.   Your sentiments
with regard to Pinto's paper and the production
of the treaties are unanswerable.   I shall there-

fore take care that your ideas on this head are
followed.

" ' Convenient and proper regulations will always be
adopted for their own sakes, and stand upon their
own ground; but boons, gifts, and compliments
Ireland has no right to expect.' I will agree with
you on your own statement. As to boons, gifts, and
compliments, I do not suppose you rank under that
head regulations which of necessity arise out of the new
situation of Ireland, I mean the establishment of an
admiralty court, and post-office, and annual sessions,
all objects which the new constitution of Ireland
comprehends within it. Such measures then I must
understand to be ranked under that head, as even
recommended to Government for their consideration,
in my first and second despatch, as public—I mean
parliamentary matters. I mentioned many, in order
that some might be acceded to, and that Government
at home might make their choice.

" The sugar refinery was one; an object so much at
heart that my predictions have been verified, and the
desertion of every man of the Duke of Portland's
friends has made it necessary for us to acquiesce in.
This I refused to do until the very hour of debate,
but was constrained upon an almost certainty of
being beat.

" The silk and woollen manufactories in a system of
equalisation; that is, reducing the duty in England
upon Irish woollen to the duty here upon English.
There never can exist a competition, at least not for
this country, owing to the superior skill, diligence,

and capital of England.   Upon a non-importation
agreement which lasted a considerable time, this was
clearly proved. The effects produced were an increase
of price and worse materials.   The enormous duty,
therefore, is nothing but a name to defend the English
woollens against an attack which will never be made.
Whose then was the boon to be given here?   The
Navigation Act was meant to undergo consideration in
England, as we were led to believe.   It was therefore
recommended to Administration to take that part of
it into their consideration at the same time, which
particularly affects Ireland.   As I have enlarged upon
this head much, in my despatch secret and confidential
of the 24th of last month, and may have occasion to
trouble you again, I will not enter any further upon
it now.

" The duty upon iron exported was proposed simply
to bring it upon an equality according to the calculation of the duties paid in England upon the import-
ation of bar-iron.   If it was found erroneous, the wish
was to establish such as might bear a fair proportion
upon *the grounds and idea of the original compact.*   I
do not see much concession or any great boon accorded
to Ireland by such a measure.

" I must revert to my old idea, that is, that the
trade to Ireland being open for England, any regulations she may find it expedient to make must
interfere with English trade, and I cannot help
observing, that the old notions seem to govern even
now the King's councils, and that a strong jealousy
exists about any trifling advantage likely to be gained

by Ireland. Upon the Portuguese business I shall write soon more fully. I wish you would tell me whether you would like to have an Address from both houses on this subject, desiring the King to interpose afresh ; or should it be taken up in the Committee and some retaliating taxes laid ; or will you not disapprove if both steps are taken ? It cannot be allowed for a moment, I apprehend, that Ireland is not included in that treaty called the Methuen Treaty. Many of our friends, you hear, disapprove of the proposed arrangements for Scott and Fitzgibbon. Are they of this or your side of the water ? If on my side, I can contradict it thus far. Grattan was consulted, and was content to act with Fitzgibbon, and has no objection to Scott being Prime Serjeant. The Attorney-General likewise approves of Fitzgibbon. He stands fairest in rank, abilities, and professional knowledge. It is proposed he should take the lead in the House of Commons. Scott's appointment to the Prime Serjeantry has been warmly urged by Conolly and Mr. Loftus. These two are considerable friends of yours and the Duke of Portland's. Have those who disapprove suggested any other persons ? Is it an easy task, in the present state of the House of Commons, to find sufficient men for these situations ?

" To trouble you thus long at a time when you are engaged on subjects of such vast importance, appears unreasonable. I wish to clear myself of any ideas you may entertain that I am unnecessarily giving way to the demands of this country, either through inattention, or from an affectation of popularity. I am not the sort of man, if I know myself at all, to put any value on so trifling an acquisition. If I was, the example of my predecessor would furnish me with a sufficient check. It was acquired by him to a great degree, and vanished in an instant.

" I have a most difficult task. The country is full of disorder, madness, and inconsistency, deriving much of its inclination to disquiet and vexation from a notion of the instability of Government at home, and the influence of a *secret hand* attempting to undermine Government here ; I mean a secret hand from a high quarter. I will more particularly state this matter to you in my next.

" In addition to all this, I must confess it is a very wrong measure of English Government to make this country the first step in politics, as it usually has been; and I am sure, men of abilities, knowledge of business, and experience, ought to be employed here, both in the capacity of Lord Lieutenant and Secretary, not gentlemen taken wild from Brookes's to make their *dénouement* in public life. I feel very forcibly the truth of this observation in my own instance, and wish heartily it was better supplied. However, as I am in this predicament, I will not shrink from the collar, and will manage as well as I can. I depend upon assistance from yourself and the Duke of Portland, and particularly for *support in the objects* I recommend. I wish you at a leisure hour to hint to the Duke of Portland, that I hope soon for an answer to the subjects I wrote to him upon some time ago.

" Thank Hare most kindly for me for his account of the debates. I hope he will continue them. The matter you mentioned to me came on this day. I will send you an account by the next post.

" You will, I hope, excuse this sad scrawl, and the hurry in which I have writ. I am so pestered at this time, that I scarcely can command a moment's leisure, which you will readily discover, as this is the third day since this letter was begun.

" Believe me to be, my dear Fox,

" With great truth and regard,

" Ever sincerely yours, &c.

" NORTHINGTON."

LORD NORTHINGTON TO MR. FOX.*

" DUBLIN CASTLE, *November* 30*th*, 1783.

" MY DEAR FOX,

" The opportunity which I have waited for with so much anxiety and impatience has at last presented itself, and I have seized it with eagerness ; and I flatter myself that it has been so managed as to be the production of the most salutary consequences. This Committee of Convention having finished their plan, instructed Mr. Flood and Mr. Brownlow, two of its principal members, to introduce it into Parliament. They did not choose to venture upon their original idea of petitioning Parliament, but introduced it as a proposition of their own. By my friends employed

---

* Published in Memoirs of Mr. Grattan, by his Son, vol. iii. 156—158, but with several omissions, both as to words and sentiments.

amongst them to give me all possible intelligence, I
was apprised, late of the Friday, of their intention of
introducing it the next day in the House; and I
immediately determined to call as considerable and
as full a meeting as possible of those, without any
exceptions, who had declared in disapprobation, to me
personally, or through other means, of this Conventional Assembly. Accordingly, a full assembly of
great property and consequence appeared. It was
proposed by Government to meet the question in the
most decided manner, and to bring to issue the
contest between Parliament and this motley assembly
usurping its rights. This idea of Government met
with a very considerable support; great heartiness
showed itself in the principal men of consequence and
fortune, and a decisive spirit of opposition to the present
unwarrantable encroachments appeared with every man
attached to the Administration, and even from those
who, upon former points, had shown a disposition to
be adverse. The idea started from Government was
to oppose *the leave* for bringing in a bill for the
Reform of Parliament in the first step, upon the
ground of *the plan originating in an assembly unconstitutional and illegal*, and meant to awe and control
the Legislature. This bold mode of treating it was
certainly the most proper; at the same time, it was
subject to a defection of those who had been instructed
on this idea of reform, or those who were still anxious
to retain some small degree of popularity amongst
the Volunteers. To have met it indirectly would have
given us at least fourteen votes more than we had to

number. Grattan, having pledged himself to the
idea of a Reform of Parliament, could not feel the
distinction between the refusal of leave on the ground
of its having come from an exceptionable quarter, and
the absolute denial of receiving any plan of Reform.
He voted against us, and spoke; but his speech
evidently showed that he meant us no harm; and
upon the question of the resolution to support Parliament, he voted with us. The resolutions are gone
to the Lords, who will concur with them, except, it is
said, Lord Mountmorris, Lord Aldborough, and Lord
Charlemont. It is the universal opinion, that this
day has given a most complete defeat to the Volunteers and to their Conventional Assembly. Some of
most consideration have been with me, to declare,
that under the circumstances of being pledged at
contested elections, and others fettered by instructions,
they were obliged to oppose me, but that their pledge
is now at an end; they have voted to introduce it into
the House, that has failed; they are now ready to
receive my instructions as to the means of preventing
any future discontents or disquietudes in their different counties. Among the foremost of them is
O'Neill.

" I feel great satisfaction at the contemplation of
having postponed the taking any vigorous exertions
until the Assembly had showed itself to be such as to
alarm moderate men, and to acquire no small degree
of odium. If, in consequence of the wishes on your
side of the water, I had opposed this meeting by
active measures at an earlier period, I should have

had the prejudices, the opinions, and the affections of all men to have combated against. The degree of esteem these gentlemen were held in by the folly of this country, no man can have an adequate idea of that has not been an eye-witness thereof. It would have been urged, how rash to oppose with the power of Government that which must prove ridiculous, confused, and perplexed, and will end in contempt. It is inciting a civil war. Have they not constantly behaved themselves with propriety and good order? Have you not thanked them lately? How then can you entertain a suspicion of them until their conduct, in some degree, shall justify it. Although persons of every description think that nothing more will come of this meeting, I am not of opinion that a matter of this sort can settle itself immediately. Government is, however, now embarked; it has waited with a proper degree of moderation and temper; it has now shown itself with spirit, decision, and resolution; and, at all events, it is determined not to yield. Such is my purpose; and, therefore, you will have quiet and order in the country; or if it is fit in future to concede, you will send me a successor. Neither Flood nor Mr. Brownlow dare avow that they acted by instructions from this Assembly. Our Attorney-General acted with great ability, firmness, and decision. Such likewise was the conduct of our Prime Serjeant, who, upon a former occasion, from mere ignorance of Parliament, brought us into a considerable scrape. Fitzgibbon acquitted himself astonishingly; as did Daly, Forster, and almost every

man on the side of Government. Pole voted and
spoke in support of the resolutions, both at the
meeting in the morning, and in the House of
Commons, although his brother, Lord Mornington,
approved only of resisting the introduction of the
bill.

"I just now learn that it is in the contemplation
of Flood to carry over an Address as the deputed
Ambassador of the Delegates to the King, expressive
of their loyalty, or as a sort of counter-declaration
to the resolution of Parliament, and that he is to
set off to-morrow night; if that is the case, Luttrell
means to accompany him in order to prevent any
false statement in the English House of Commons
of what has passed here. If this business goes
off, as I sanguinely hope it may, and the Address
should go to the King, an answer of temper and
firmness at the same time would highly suit the
present state of things. Such as a retrospective
compliment to the conduct of the Volunteers, and
disapprobation of their present meeting, an hope,
expectation, or advice of their disbanding themselves.
I shall, however, be able more fully to write upon
this subject after to-morrow. If, however, the business should be likely to have a fair issue, I submit to
you, whether it will be unreasonable in me to hope
that I may receive some notification of the King's
approbation of my conduct. It will be at all times
pleasant, but particularly so, when it is supposed
here that it is likely you will be turned out by the
failure of the East India Bill in the House of Lords.

"I have written this in the greatest hurry, after a dinner of forty members of the House of Commons. If parts are unintelligible, either from the hand-writing, or as complete nonsense, I must rely upon your excuse, for you must know that after a great Irish dinner, it is not the time for sense or precision.

"Adieu, my dear Fox, believe me, most truly,

"Affectionately yours,

"NORTHINGTON."

GENERAL BURGOYNE TO MR. FOX.

"*October* 31*st*, 1783.

[After stating various reasons why he does not obey the call he had received to the opening of Parliament, he goes on to say :—]

"Add to this the apprehensions that timid and melancholy speculators entertain upon the meeting of the Convention of Delegates the 10th of next month. I have not myself any idea of serious commotion, but we have strengthened the garrison of Dublin, and it might be thought wrong in the Commander-in-Chief to be absent. You have doubtless the fullest infor-mation of the proceedings and language of the Bishop of Derry, and of the mode in which the friends of Government mean to meet the question of Parlia-mentary reform, if urged otherwise than by application to Parliament.

"I take for granted you are far from discounte-nancing the abstract question of Parliamentary re-form *here* as well as in England; but I am impatient for your sentiments upon the prosecution of this national object, however desirable in itself, upon the principles of the Dungannon meeting, and under the influence of an armed force. Much difference of opinion also prevails upon the conduct that respectable characters, lovers of the Constitution, and of the good order of the State, ought to hold on the 10th November, they themselves being Delegates chosen such in their absence and without their consent. Ought they to appear and to debate against the illegality of the meeting, thinking it such? Or ought they entirely to deprive it of their sanction by their absence? Conolly, who is one of the body, is clearly for the latter measure."

SAME TO SAME.

"*November 8th,* 1783.

" MY DEAR CHARLES,

"When I acknowledge the receipt of yours, expressing an expectation of seeing me at the meeting, you will not doubt that the reasons must be cogent indeed that prevent my presenting myself to you, instead of this letter. But with all my anxiety from public and private motives to join you, I cannot but own that the pressure of business immediately upon my station ought to detain me here some little (I hope very little) time. The staff and the whole arrangement of the military establishment comes before the Committee of Supply on Monday or Tuesday next; and though it is not probable that, not being a member, I should be called upon by the House for explanations, it is thought advisable by all the defenders of Government measures, that I should be present for the purpose of their consulting me personally, should occasion so require. The consultations of the Delegates begin the same time, and were any disturbances to arise among the populace, Lord Northington, I know, would wish for my presence. When I mention this, I have the utmost satisfaction in adding my fullest confidence that nothing unpleasing to Government is to be apprehended. The Bishop of Derry found very little encouragement in his progress, and was received in Dublin with gaping coldness at the best, and in some streets with derision. There is great alarm, much discord of opinion, and some evident despair among the parties; and the general opinion is, that after various discussions, among which many will be very wild, they will throw the business for the present back again upon county meetings. I hear to-day that the Bishop talks of leaving Dublin before the end of the week.

" Besides the calls upon my presence, which I have already mentioned, the troops are daily arriving, and till they are all arrived the reduction of the other cannot be finally carried into effect; but these circumstances will have a short period, and I conclude I shall be at liberty to attend your call in a fortnight without inconvenience to the public service, or risk of personal censure. But let me know by a single line whether my journey need then be pressed, or whether I may take a little more latitude, should any circumstance of business, not essential, but merely of regular

course, make me incline to see it over.   Should India
affairs come early before you, I have a natural desire
to be present, however little I can flatter myself with
being of use to you.

" Lord Northington has just told me, the apprehensions respecting the Volunteers are strong in London.
I find from others that reports have been circulated
of insults offered to the regiments landed in the
north.   It is so much the reverse, that every regiment is full of acknowledgment for the cordiality of
their reception.   Both men and officers have received
free quarter from the inhabitants in many places, and
perfect civility in all.

" Believe me ever most faithfully yours,

"J. BURGOYNE."

SAME TO SAME.

" *November* 17, 1783.

" MORE thanks to you than I can express, my
dearest Charles, for your letter of the 7th.   My
friendship was highly gratified by so great a mark of
your confidence, and my pride was not less so at
finding that my sentiments had exactly tallied with
yours upon every circumstance of Irish affairs.

" I had yesterday a very long conversation with
Lord Northington upon the subject, in which he
treated me in the most confidential manner, and communicated to me all you had written to him relative
to this strange crisis.   I neither doubt his conformity
of opinion nor his spirit, but I believe the true
reasons for not yet taking up the matter in Parliament

have been, first, the backwardness of those who ought
to have taken the lead in the House; next, the weak
state of military force, till very lately; and lastly, the
opinion that the meeting of the Delegates had appearances of such diversity of sentiments and jarring
interests, as would effectuate its own speedy dissolution; and should it not, it was thought to be still in
time for Parliament to come forward with a declaration in whatever manner the Convention proceeded.
I believe Lord Northington and Pelham, and a great
and respectable majority of both Houses, to be firm
with you in the argument you urge with such irresistible
force; that the requests of persons in arms, and under
the various circumstances of the Volunteer Delegates,
however humble they may be, or to whatever branch
of the State they may be addressed, cannot be taken
into consideration.

" The above is my opinion of the reasons that in
fact have operated; I give none upon the point
whether they ought to have done so, or whether the
more vigorous measure should at all events have been
pushed in the first instance.

" Now for the state of things actually subsisting:
Lord Bristol is certainly disappointed and mortified;
there is no popularity in his favour; he has few or
no visitants; he could not obtain the chair in the
Sub-Committee; nor, even among the most desperate
of his party, can there be discerned any spirit that can
flatter a conspirator. The embarrassments and the
confusion in debate augment daily. Flood has been
forced by importunity that would receive no denial,

to appear in his robes of flannel ; but when pressed
for assistance he wrapped himself up still more closely
in caution and obscurity and half sentences. He
acknowledged his favourable wishes to Parliamentary
reform, and the having given great attention to it as
an abstract and theoretical question ; but declared he
had never seen a plan of reform from Mr. Locke's time
to the present that was not objectionable. No one
can suppose his designs friendly to Government, but
whatever they may be, they do not at present tend
to encourage the violent party.

"A greater embarrassment yet has arisen in the
Convention, which you will see in print, viz. the interference (but upon different principles) of the Catholics.
By the mouth of Lord Kenmare, they relinquish their
pretensions to suffrages at elections ; by the mouth
of Sir Patrick Bellew they assert them. I wish they
did so more soundly, for I am clearly of opinion that
every alarm of the increase of Catholic interest and
prevalence beyond the present limits, which give them
in the general opinion all the share of rights necessary
for their happiness, and consistent with the safety of
their Protestant fellow-subjects ; every idea, I think,
of an extension of their claims, excites new jealousy
and dread of the Volunteers, and cements and ani-
mates the real friends of the Constitution, and surely
with reason ; for, upon the very principle of free and
conscientious suffrage, nothing can be more impossible
than a Protestant representation chosen by Catholic
electors. Can any man give the Catholics a right of
voting, and doubt of the subversion of the Church

Establishment as a natural, if not an immediate, consequence ?   The very basis of the Brunswick throne, the Protestant interest of Europe, is threatened. You will pardon this digression from the matters of fact I was now relating, for I could not help it.

" The report of the House is, that the Committee have determined upon a plan, in which the Catholics are excluded, and which will be ready to be laid before the Convention on Friday next ; and common opinion is, that either the Convention will break up in confusion, or that they will tread back their former steps, refer the plan back to the people at large, and petition Parliament, and instruct members from county meetings in brown coats.   I found Ogle, who dined with me yesterday, sanguine in this expectation; and he, and all others, who advised silence in Parliament till a petition came forward, plume themselves upon the prudence of that measure, and think that Parliament is now out of the scrape.

" Another curious circumstance has, nevertheless, arisen, that may, in a few days, produce a decisive explanation between Parliament and Delegates.

" The Election Committee upon the Down petition have reported it frivolous and vexatious.   The House have sentenced Stewart to pay costs, and, meaning to censure the other petitioners at the bar, have ordered them to attend in custody.   Some of these petitioners are Delegates, and I hear will resist, and that they will be supported in so doing by Brownlow.   Some people suppose that they will set up privilege as representatives against the authority of the *old* House of Commons ; I scarcely believe they will be so wild as that ; but I think it very likely they will take up the old ground of the printers in London, and deny the power of the Commons to attack the persons of subjects at large.

" Since writing the above, I have had a private interview with Pelham, to whom I communicated great part of your letter. He agrees in every sentiment ; and I sincerely believe both he and his chief are men of very true spirit. He confirms everything I had supposed, relative to the deficiency of true spirit in those they have to deal with. It is even more deficient than true honesty in this country, and that is saying a great deal. Men of the best sense, of the highest character, of the greatest zeal in the cause of good government, are affected by the idlest breath of popularity, and cannot bear to be clouded even by the vapour of a minute. Upon the whole, the utmost hopes I can give you are, that, if contrary to the present expectation, a petition should come from the Convention to Parliament, it will be treated (however humbly it may be conceived or preferred) in the manner you desire. I think it also probable, that the affair of the Down petitioners may produce some vigour in the House, and lead to declaratory resolutions upon the dignity and authority of Parliament ; but if you look for any spontaneous proceedings in Parliament upon the subject of the Convention, I think you will be mistaken.

" In regard to all the common measures of Government, the strength will be found ample and respectable, except, I fear, in one instance, viz., the sugar business. So many men, attached to the Castle in other matters, think themselves so pledged in this to the other side, that it will be well if the question be not lost.

" Northington and Pelham, who both treat me with unbounded confidence, wish so much for my continuance here just at present, that I ought not to quit them immediately, unless I receive another call from you. I trust, however, I shall still be able, without impropriety, to join you before the holidays. In the meantime, it shall be the use of the confidence I enjoy to inculcate and enforce your opinions; confident that, in so doing, I am effectually serving them and the country. I dare say Northington will write to you in respect to the Luttrells' going over, as he himself will to Lord North. He certainly at present is of great use here. Whenever Flood goes over, I shall do my best to detach Luttrell after him. He has attacked him here with success, and in your House will be of service, at least of that of the sword-fish, who gets under the whale's belly, and pricks him up, to enable an adversary of greater power to knock him down again.

" I make no apology for the length of this.

" Believe me, my dearest Charles,

" Inviolably yours,

"J. BURGOYNE."

[The following letters from Mr. Fox and from Mr. Fitzpatrick to Lord Ossory deserve insertion, because they touch on various incidents that occurred during the Coalition Administration, and express the unreserved feelings of the Ministers at the time they were written.]

MR. FOX TO LORD OSSORY.

"St. James's, 18th April.

" Dear Ossory,

" I do assure you that I do not treat other people as I have done you, nor should I even have taken the liberty of treating you so, if I had not been in hopes before this time of answering your letter in the pleasantest manner. But the fact is, that I have not yet had time to think of the arrangement about Consuls, nor even about Foreign Ministers. You may depend upon my taking the first opportunity I can of attending to your recommendation, and I suppose such a one must soon offer. With regard to things in general, I think they go on very well; but, perhaps, you reckon me, and justly too, a sanguine person. In both the skirmishes we have had, one in the House of Lords upon the Irish Bill, and one in the House of Commons upon the Loan, we had, without partiality, very considerable advantage. The indecency of Lord Thurlow's opposition is disapproved even by his friends; and the popularity of Lord John's character made the insinuations thrown out (though at the same time disclaimed) by Pitt, thought uncandid and injudicious. Whether Opposition will be strong remains to be seen, but that it is determined and virulent there is no doubt. The

King continues to behave with every degree of civility,
and sometimes even with cordiality; *cependant il faut
voir.*   My love to Henry, and tell him that his friend
must wait a little, though I do not think his application unreasonable.   Remember me to Lady Ossory,
and believe me,

" My dear Ossory, yours ever sincerely,

"C. J. FOX."

MR. FITZPATRICK TO LORD OSSORY.

" 26*th July,* 1783.

" DEAR BROTHER,

" The situation of the Ministry is just what it
was.   They are supposed to be as well at Court as
any other set of men, and that is nothing to boast of.
No peerages, no marks of real support, but civility
enough.   It is said that he told Lord Weymouth
he liked them just as well as anything else he could
look to.   I have got a villa near Hampstead, and
lead a *vie champétre.*   Adieu.   Pray remember me
to Lady O.

" Yours, &c.

"R. F."

MR. FOX TO LORD OSSORY.

"WIMBLEDON, 12*th August,* 1783.

" DEAR OSSORY,

" I beg your pardon for not having written to
you sooner.   I would certainly do anything in my
father's affairs that I can do with propriety; but what
that is, I do not know.   My brother (administrator

de bonis to his father the first Lord Holland's will)
will be here by the beginning of October, and not
before. With respect to Peerages, the Duke of
Portland did again mention them to the King, just
before the prorogation, and was refused in a very
civil, but, as it appeared to me, very determined
manner. I own I do not think this refusal indicates
so much as some people are willing to imagine; but
of this I am clear, that it is not a subject on which we
ought to quarrel. If ever there was a situation in
which it was becoming to bear all that can be borne,
without absolute dishonour, or immediate detriment
to the country, I think ours is that situation; and
perhaps I have the more confidence in my opinion in
this matter, as it is not on that side upon which I am
most likely to err. Pray make my best respects to
Lady Ossory, and tell her that Mr. Becker shall have
his consulship whenever the new ones are appointed,
though, by his conversation, it seemed to me to be
doubtful whether he would accept it; but, if he does
not, that is not my fault.

"There is no news of any consequence. His
Majesty continues just as he was, very civil, but no
more. Many people think there is to be a change
before the meeting of Parliament, but I do not.
Opinions are much divided whether there will be a
war between Russia and Turkey; and, still more,
whether that war, if it take place, will have any
influence on the affairs of this country. I must not
tell you what I think of it, *mais je ne m'endors point.*
I hear nothing can be so cried up as Shelburne is at

Paris, nor so cried down as we are. I missed Lord Holland by accident when he went from Eton ; pray give my love to him. I hardly ever see anything of Richard except when I meet him at Court, he is so completely shut up in his villa, which I have not yet seen ; when I do see him he croaks as usual. I hope you will read Carlisle's tragedy, and think, as I do, that it has great merit. If one could strike out a hundred or two of metaphors, it would really be a most excellent play.

"Adieu, &c."

[On the report of Lord Ashburton's death, who had received a grant of the Duchy of Lancaster for life, Mr. Fox wrote instantly to the Duke of Portland to recommend Lord Derby for the place, and had the following answer.]

"CHISWICK, *Monday Night, August 25th*, 1783.

" MY DEAR FOX,

" Lord Ashburton is certainly dead ; for Baring sent me an account of it on Saturday, which he desired might be communicated to the King. I hesitated a little whether his request should not be immediately complied with, and Derby proposed ; but a moment's recollection decided me in favour of an audience, and I hope to send a messenger to Knowsley before I leave town on Wednesday."

[This would hardly have deserved notice were it not for a letter of Lord Loughborough to Mr. Fox, which shows that the abolition of the Duchy had been under consideration.]

LORD LOUGHBOROUGH TO MR. FOX.

" My dear Sir,

" Lord Derby's appointment gives great satisfaction in this part of the world, where the choice of
a Chancellor of the Duchy is a very interesting point;
and his acceptance of it, without any charge to the
public, ought to make it everywhere a popular
measure. Though there are a few abuses in the
management of the Duchy, which a Chancellor with
proper information might easily correct, and some
unnecessary charge in the establishment, I am persuaded that the abolition of the Duchy would give
great alarm, and occasion much dissatisfaction amongst
those who hold their estates under it; and I believe
the immediate appointment of a Chancellor is the
more acceptable, that it tends to quiet any apprehensions of such a revolution."

[None of the political adherents of Lord Shelburne
remained so long in office after the change of Government as Mr. Dundas. He had been Lord Advocate
under Lord North, and a warm supporter of the
American War; but having in some measure
separated from that nobleman towards the close of
his Administration, he retained his office under Lord
Rockingham, and remained in possession of it, with
other appointments, under Lord Shelburne. It was
not till the middle of August that he was turned out
by the Duke of Portland, and his long continuance in
office after his friends were dismissed, seems to have

created an opinion in Scotland that he was supported from a quarter which the Ministers could not resist.]

" I have seen George North," says the Duke of Portland to Mr. Fox, " who has undertaken for the Lord Advocate's dismission being expedited this evening." " By a letter I have received here from Scotland," writes Lord Loughborough from Buxton, " I am perfectly convinced that the more vigour Administration exerts there, the stronger its influence will be. It began to be seriously credited that it was not permitted to them to remove any person protected by Dundas ; and though I am sorry for the loss of Campbell's ability and plain good sense, which are not easily replaced, his removal, I am certain, will give double the effect to the removal of Dundas."

[One of the most serious obstacles to the formation of the Coalition Administration had been the refusal of Mr. Fox to allow Lord Thurlow to remain Lord Chancellor ; and an attempt of Lord Thurlow's friends to have the Tellership, which had been granted to him in reversion, exempted from the Exchequer Regulation Bill, had been resisted, and with difficulty defeated by the new Ministers. An overture was nevertheless made during the summer, on the part of his friends, to have him reinstated as Chancellor, which seems to have been entertained, and even taken into serious consideration, by Mr. Fox and the Duke of Portland, as appears from the following letter of Lord Loughborough, who was consulted about it.]

SAME TO SAME.

" My dear Sir,

" To prevent any possibility of misunderstanding upon the subject of our conversation yesterday, I shall state to you in the fullest and, as to myself, the most binding manner, the exact state of my sentiments.

" When you told me the full extent of the message conveyed to you by Mr. Rigby, it was so unexpected, that my answer was the unpremeditated and genuine expression of my thoughts. On my way from your house to the Duke of Portland's, I considered it a little more, and repeated there, in more general terms, my ready acquiescence in any proposition that might strengthen his Administration. Yesterday I met the subject fully prepared: my sentiments had not varied, and were formed upon this short and plain consideration; that when I agreed to act in the Commission, I told you I meant to be united with you; and that, I understand, implies an acquiescence in any proper situation that the advantage of a common cause requires. I did not at that moment foresee a probability of Lord Thurlow's accession to the same cause; nor can I say what effect that consideration might have had on my mind at that time. But if the course of events produces it now, my situation shall be no obstacle to it.

" I am not sure that I shall give you an impartial opinion on the expediency of a union with him; but you must allow me to state my reasons for and against, on which you will judge.

" The accession of Lord Thurlow gives you, in the first place, the use of his abilities. It secures Lord Weymouth, and it must attract Lord Gower. It presents an appearance of influence in the closet, and you are offered a proof of it by the disposal of some peerages. The advantage of the last point seems to me very questionable; for his influence, though employed for you, is not your influence; and peerages which the Administration could only obtain by his aid, will not add to the reputation of their strength. The three first points are the fair amount of the acquisition, and they make it considerable enough to deserve a very high price. This will be to be fully replaced. You then bring into your Cabinet a temper which you have never yet tried in business, and which hitherto has been mostly employed to perplex and to censure the measures of those he acted with. You gain a powerful and, of course, a formidable ally; but are you clear that you will gain a hearty and cordial friend ?

" On these grounds you must decide if I were not in existence; and in deliberating on them, I desire you to remember that I am, no further than as my existence saves you from a necessity of submitting to any disadvantageous terms.

" If the result of the deliberation is a wish to restore the Seals to Lord Thurlow, I have no aversion to return to my former situation; not that I prefer, as Mr. Rigby supposes, the Common Law Courts. My ambition is to be at the head of my profession, but it is not that sort of ambition which would either sacrifice myself or endanger my friends in the pursuit. You asked me with much kindness, whether I should not feel mortified at the preference, from the rivalship that has subsisted between Lord Thurlow and me; I have already experienced how far that can go when Lord North and Lord Suffolk left me only the second choice. It would not affect me very strongly, nor at all, if Lord Thurlow were capable of an handsome return to civility. But he never has; nor if we lived one hundred years, never would forgive the preference once meant for me. This, however, is too childish an emotion to sway my general conduct, and I cheerfully give you my most explicit assent to any course you may think most conducive to the full establishment of the Administration. I give it without reserve or qualification, for I act with too much confidence to desire to guard against a removal that should express any appearance of disregard to me.

" One caution it is necessary to mention on account of other people, which might not perhaps occur to you. Some care must be taken before you give a power not easily controlled, that Wallace, Lee, Mansfield, and the King's Counsel you have made, be not left totally exposed. Experience suggests and justifies the reflection that they may suffer by it, and a neglect of this sort would affect the credit of the Administration with a very considerable profession.

" I ever am, my dear Sir,

" Your most faithful and obedient servant,

" LOUGHBOROUGH."

[It was perhaps in reference to the proceedings in this overture that the following letter was written by the Duke of Portland to Mr. Fox.]

DUKE OF PORTLAND TO MR. FOX.

" Thursday morning, 9 *o'clock.*

" CHARLES TOWNSHEND told me yesterday that Rigby had invited himself to dine at Weymouth's purposely to meet Thurlow, and call upon him for an explanation of his conduct. Knowing besides that Weymouth was to see the King, I cannot suppress my curiosity till we meet at Court to learn if any report has been made to you of these conferences. Pray return me Lord Northington's letter, as I imagine the Irish messenger will be despatched to day. I heard yesterday from Windham, who is much alarmed at the idea of the younger Clements * being come over to solicit the peerage for his brother, independent of the conditions agreed upon by Lord N. and the elder Clements. Windham's fears must be preposterous, I think.

" Ever yours, &c.

"P.

" What have you been doing about the Civil List Debt ? I have desired to see Lord John. I am sure the sum voted will not discharge it, at least by what Burke has constantly told me, on *Spears'* information."

* Robert Clements, Esq. was raised to the dignity of Baron Leitrim by letters patent, dated 20th of September, which makes the negotiation with Lord Thurlow to have been in the early part of autumn.

EXTRACT FROM A LETTER OF MR. FOX TO LORD OSSORY.

"ST. ANN'S HILL, *9th September*, 1783.

" NEXT session of Parliament will be a great crisis.
I own I am sanguine about it.   Nothing can go on so
well as we do among ourselves ; but in my particular
situation, it is impossible not to feel every day what
an amazing advantage it would be to the country if it
could ever be in such a state as to promise a permanent Administration in the opinion of Europe.   If
Pitt could be persuaded, (but I despair of it), I am
convinced if he could, he would do more real service
to the country than any man ever did.*   Nothing can,
in my opinion, be so ridiculous as the figure France
will make in this Turkish business.

" Yours ever sincerely,

"C. J. FOX."

SAME TO SAME.

"ST. JAMES'S PLACE, *27th October*, 1873.

" DEAR OSSORY,
" I have a foolish shamefacedness about asking
favours, even of my best friends, which I think rather
grows upon me than goes off, and I am sure there is
nothing else to which I can attribute my not having
spoken to you at Newmarket upon a subject which
Richard had hinted to you before ; I mean the moving
of the Address.   I really shall be much obliged to

* This is remarkable as proving the candour and generosity of Mr. Fox,
and his magnanimous contempt of all jealousy and resentment to his
young rival.—V. H.

you if you will do it. I should almost be afraid of being accused of Crawfordism if I were to tell you how very strongly I feel upon the subject of any marks of public approbation from those with whom I have lived in friendship in private. If you will do it, and the Duke of Devonshire should be prevailed upon to move it in the House of Lords, it will be exactly to my wish. I suppose the seconders should be from the other wing of the army, and consequently I do not much care who they are. If you will undertake it, I will let you know immediately as much of the purport of the speech as can be determined. The principal point in it will certainly be the East India business.

"I am, my dear Ossory,

"Very sincerely yours ever,

"C. J. FOX.

" All our letters from Ireland speak sanguinely."

SAME TO SAME.

"St. James's Place, 5th November, 1783.

" Dear Ossory,

"I am very much obliged to you for your letter, and send you enclosed the King's speech. With regard to any other materials, I scarcely know how to give you any, not from want of topics, but because they are so obvious. In my opinion the more that is said about the East India Company the better; but whether you have read any of the reports, from which matter upon this subject is to be gathered, is more than I know. With respect to what is said about

burthens to be borne for the sake of public credit, it
would certainly have a good grace for a country
gentleman to encourage Ministers to tax for the sake
of it ; but in this you will do as you please. At all
events it would not be amiss to touch upon the
inviolable faith of the country in money matters, and
the security you have that Government will never
listen to the wicked schemes that are every day
recommended of lessening interest, &c. If you say
anything of foreign affairs, and if you agree with me
on the propriety of this country always attending to
them and mixing in them, there will be no harm, I
should think, in saying so. You will observe that
there is nothing said of Ireland by name, though it
may be thought to be alluded to where our *new*
situation is mentioned. I really am at present so
much in doubt whether it will be wise or not to touch
upon a string so delicate, and have not settled my
mind upon the proper manner of doing it, if it is to
be done ; but I will speak to you about this when I
see you. I really do not recollect anything more that
can be of use to you, but I hope you will be in town
time enough to dine with me Sunday, and be at the
meeting here afterwards, and by that time I may be
able to tell you more. The Duke of Devonshire will
not be in town till the moment before the House of
Lords meets, so that he cannot move. I suppose
Fitzwilliam will, unless the Duke of Beaufort does,
in which case Fitzwilliam will second. Flood and
Grattan have been using Billingsgate language to one
another beyond all example. They were taken up

and bound over to the peace upon very great recog-
nisances, but some people imagine they will come
and fight in England.

" Yours most affectionately,

" C. J. FOX."

[Some expressions having crept into the original
draft of the King's speech, which, on reflection, Mr.
Fox thought objectionable, he addressed the following
note to the Duke of Portland :—]

"St. James's Place, Sunday night.
" 9th November, 1783.

" My dear Lord,

" Everybody thinks that the paragraph respecting
the alarming outrages, &c., is not distinctly enough
pointed to the smuggling business, and, from the
strength of the words, may be misconstrued to mean
rebellion, and possibly be applied even to Ireland. I
really think it worth while to have this altered. If
you agree with me, you will send the alteration (with
the reason of it) to the King, and it may be made
time enough for your meeting, and for the Cockpit,*
to-morrow night.

" Yours ever,

" C. J. FOX."

On the 18th of November, Mr Fox introduced the
celebrated and unfortunate India Bill. His speech is
thus noticed in a letter from

---

* It was the usage then for the Minister to read over the speech which
the King was to make to his Parliament, the day before he delivered it;
and the supporters of the Ministers attended in the Cockpit to hear it.
This custom was dropped soon after the French war commenced, in
1794 or 1795.

MR. FITZPATRICK TO LORD OSSORY.

"18th November, 1783.

" CHARLES made a fine speech of two hours
and a quarter, and opened the plan of which you
know the outline.   Pitt threw down the gauntlet of
opposition to the whole system and principles of the
bills, but in the shape of delay, and consequently
moved a call of the House ; this was agreed to for
this day fortnight, but Charles at the same time gave
notice that he should move the second reading of the
Bill for Thursday se'nnight or Thursday next, which
Pitt declared he would oppose, so that a fair trial of
strength is announced for Thursday.   The die is cast,
and Administration is to stand or fall upon the issue
of the question.

                               " Yours,

                                         " R. F."

SAME TO SAME.

"21st November, 1783.

" You were in the right not to come, as we had no
division after a very warm debate, in which Charles
shone as much, if not more, than usual.   Jenkinson
attacked the plan as dangerous to the Crown, by
adding to the influence of Ministers ; and Scott (Lord
Weymouth's lawyer, who would not come into Parliament without the Duke of Portland's approbation),
without giving his opinion upon the measure, was
against us upon the question, as I have no doubt he
will continue to be ; these are strong symptoms of the
opinion of the closet ; and while they may do harm in

some quarters, will do good in others. We appear strong in the House of Commons, though I think it is difficult to foresee the event of the business. * * * The second reading is fixed for Thursday, when they can defer a division no longer, which I am glad of, for I suspect many shabby dogs who want to be pledged by a vote. Rigby, I am told, was very desirous there should be no division; and, in the meantime, is carrying his points with the Treasury for nothing; a very bad, but strong, argument for the measure, is received to-day, in disagreeable despatches from the East Indies. I have not yet heard the particulars, but every thing is as bad as possible. A drawn battle at sea, in which both fleets have suffered, and I hear a total defeat by land; an army lost under General Matthews, and Sir Eyre Coote and Colonel Humberstone both killed; and Tippoo recovering the country he had lost. There will be nothing before Thursday, when I suppose we shall certainly see you.

" Yours affectionately,

" R. F.

" P.S. Erskine was, as you would suppose, a mixture of good and bad; but, in my opinion, promising clearly to be better for the House than Scott."

LORD LOUGHBOROUGH TO MR. FOX.

[Docketed 19*th November*, 1783.]

" *Wednesday*, 4 *o'clock*.

" My dear Sir,

" An idea has been suggested to me that it would tend very much to facilitate the progress of the measure respecting India, if some assurance of dividend were held out to the proprietors, who will be alarmed with an apprehension that they may not be found entitled to any upon a strict investigation of their accounts.

"Their alarm is certainly just, for on every fair principle that authorises a dividend, they are debarred from making any. But it would be very inexpedient to sink the stock entirely, and the strict line will not in the end be drawn against them. A dividend must either be made by connivance, or the public must authorise it; which, in effect, is the same thing as making itself a guarantee to the proprietors for the receipt of a dividend; of the two modes the last is, in my opinion, the best, because it is the fairest.

" If then this must be done finally, whatever advantage may arise from professing it early, is not undeserving attention. At first it occurred to me, that a clause might be inserted in the Bill, empowering the Commissioners to make a dividend during the term of the Act, not less than six, nor more than eight per cent. I have some doubts, however; as this must be stated to be (what in truth it is) an engagement on the part of the public, to secure the payment of money. An objection would not arise to inserting the provision without its being previously resolved in a Committee, or whether it might not be argued as a money clause, and so form a difficulty in the House of Lords.

" The next thing, then, will be to state the proposition as fit to be recommended to the House, and made the subject of a distinct regulation in some other period of the Session, but to state it so early that it may have all the effect it can to compose the fears of the stockholders, and seem to proceed from the attention of Government to their welfare.

" You can better judge how far the idea itself, and any modification of it, may deserve attention, and I have the most perfect faith in the conduct of a business so ably and happily begun.

" I ever am, my dear Sir,

" Yours most entirely,

"LOUGHBOROUGH."

MR. FOX TO LORD OSSORY.

"ST. JAMES'S PLACE, 21st November, 1783.

" DEAR OSSORY,

" I am very glad you did not come up yesterday, as there was no division. Pitt spoke violently and far from well, and Jenkinson came out with as foolish a speech as ever I heard. His appearance will have some bad effects, but I am sure it *has had* some good, and I think the question on the second reading next Thursday, will be to a great degree decisive upon all politics. After having said this, I need not add how much I wish you to be present. I am very confident; but every vote will tell on account of the House of Lords afterwards. If we can beat them, as I hope to do, by a 100 or 150, it will give a most complete blow to the enemy, which they will find it difficult to recover. There is very bad news from

the East Indies, a whole army has been taken by
Tippoo, and it is but a poor comfort that it will help
our question.

" Yours ever sincerely,

"C. J. FOX."

LORD LOUGHBOROUGH TO MR. FOX.

"WESTMINSTER HALL. 10 o'clock.

" MY DEAR SIR,

"Lee, of the House of Commons, has not yet
returned me the amendments which are copying, and
will soon be sent to you. The clause respecting the two
schedules to be made is, in my opinion, not necessary,
unless the want of it should be pressed on the other
side as an objection to the Bill. The schedules
ought to be made, and will be made full as well
without a special direction in the Act. It is only proposed, therefore, as a provisional amendment in case
you find it is called for.

" Piggott's clauses to provide for suits for and
against the Company, and for the use of the seal,
seem unnecessary as the Act is now worded. The
answer to any objection for the want of such clauses
and many others, will be, that the new Directors stand
in the place of the old in all respects. I have sent
you the two additional clauses; the second, I think,
is a very ticklish point. Though it is clearly necessary that the Directors should be Members of Parliament, as much as the Lords of the Treasury and
Admiralty, and the case provided for is merely the

contingency of such alterations as may happen in the persons within five years; you will be teazed with declamations on the Act of Settlement, and all the lawyers against you will maintain that it is clear upon that Act, that the office disqualifies, and you mean to undermine the principles of the Act by creating a shoal of officers by Parliament. I am exceedingly anxious that the objection to my friend Meap should not appear of very great consequence to you, because I shall have otherwise to reproach myself with not having prevented his taking a step that he would not have done if he had not known that I was perfectly indifferent to all Indian politics at the time it happened. If there is any blame in his nomination I am willing to be charged with the whole of it, but I believe his name will not in general be unpopular, and I can answer perfectly to you for his discretion. The protest was a very improper thing. But it is buried; an heap of others equally so; and it is not easy to find eight or ten names clear of all objections.

"I ever am, my dear Sir,

"Yours most entirely,

"LOUGHBOROUGH."

SAME TO SAME.

[Docketed 23rd *November*, 1783.]
"*Sunday, 5 o'clock.*

" MY DEAR SIR,

"Upon reading the Bill, I think it is fairly implied in the second enacting clause, that the Commissioners are to communicate all correspondence to

and from India to the Secretary of State, in the same
manner that the Directors were bound to do, and it
ought not to pass as an omission, at the same time
that there cannot be the least objection to provide for
it explicitly, if the sense or efficacy of the second
enacting clause in this respect is questioned.

" Some handle might be taken to asperse the intention of the Bill, as aiming to withdraw the Commissioners from any dependence on Government, if the
authors of the Bill allowed that such an omission
existed, and I sincerely think the words do not warrant
the objection.   I have received the draft of the second
Bill, and shall employ myself upon it this evening.

" I ever am yours, most entirely,

" LOUGHBOROUGH."

[As the meeting of Parliament drew nigh, Ministers
became anxious about the fate of the India Bill.   In
his letter to Lord Northington, Mr. Fox describes it
as a *vigorous* and *hazardous* measure on which *all
depends*.   On the morning of the day when it was
read for the first time in the House of Commons, Lord
North writes to Mr. Fox :—] "*Influence of the Crown,
and influence of party against Crown and people* are
two of the many topics which will be urged against
your plan.   The latter of the two objections will not
be sounded so high and loudly in the House of Commons, but it may be one of the most fatal objections
to your measure.   It certainly ought to be obviated
as much as possible."

[Mr. Fox has been blamed for his imprudence in bringing forward his India Bill before his Ministry was firmly established, and before the anger of the King for the violence done to him at its first formation had been at all appeased or even softened. He was himself aware of the peril he incurred, and while the Bill was still pending, and in his opinion with great probability of success, he wrote to a most intimate friend what may be considered as an explanation and vindication of his precipitancy :] " They are endeavouring to make a great cry against us, and will, I am afraid, succeed in making us very unpopular in the city. However, I know I am right, and must bear the consequences, though I dislike unpopularity as much as any man. Indeed, it is no hypocrisy in me to say, that the consciousness of having always acted upon principle in public matters, and my determination always to do so, is the great comfort of my life. I know I never did act more upon principle than at this moment, when they are abusing me so. If I had considered nothing but keeping my power, it was the safest way to leave things as they are, or to propose some trifling alteration, and I am not at all ignorant of the political danger which I run by this bold measure ; but whether I succeed or no, I shall always be glad that I attempted, because I know I have done no more than I was bound to do, in risking my power and that of my friends when the happiness of so many millions is at stake. I write very gravely, because the amazing abuse which is heaped upon me makes me feel so. I have the weakness of disliking abuse, but

that weakness shall never prevent me from doing what
I think right.   Do not fancy from all this that I am
out of spirits, or even that I am much alarmed for the
success of our scheme.   On the contrary, I am very
sanguine ; but the reflection of how much depends
at the moment upon me, is enough to make any man
who has any feeling serious.   But as there is no reason
why I should make you so, we will talk of other
things."

MR. FITZPATRICK TO LORD OSSORY.

" *Monday, December* 15*th*, 1783.

" LORD TEMPLE had a long audience on Thursday
last, and is said to have come out declaring himself
authorised to say that the King disapproved of the
Bill, as unconstitutional, and subversive of the rights
of the Crown, and that he should consider all who
voted for it as his enemies.   Lord Temple has not
dared to avow this, but continues to insinuate it.
The Bishops waver, and *the Thanes fly from us;*
in my opinion, the Bill will not pass ; the Lords are
now sitting, and the debate will certainly be too late
to send you an account of the division ; the proxies
of the King's friends are arrived against the Bill.
The public is full of alarm and astonishment at the
treachery as well as the imprudence of this unconstitutional interference.   No body guesses what will
be the consequence of a conduct that is generally
compared to that of Charles the First in 1641.   I
hope you will come to town, for it will be certainly

impossible to send you satisfactory accounts, and some measures must, of course, be immediately taken in the House of Commons. I consider the Ministry as over.

" Yours affectionately,

" R. F."

SAME TO SAME.

" December 16th, 1783,
" Tuesday morning, 3 o'clock.

" ADMINISTRATION were beat by eight. The Commons do not meet till Wednesday, when it is agreed they must not acquiesce tamely. We shall depend upon seeing you; the left wing of the Coalition is stout and in good spirits. The Prince of Wales voted in the minority. We shall certainly have a question on Wednesday.

" Yours,

" R. F."

[When the India Bill was thrown out, Mr. Fox gave vent to his first feelings of disappointment in the following short note :] " I am too much hurried to write to you an account of our misfortune. We are beat in the House of Lords by such treachery on the part of the King, and such meanness on the part of his *friends* in the House of Lords, as one could not expect either from him or them. I will write to you more in a day or two. We are not yet out, but I suppose we shall be to-morrow. However, we are so strong, that nobody can undertake, without madness; and, if they do, I think we shall destroy them almost as soon as they are formed."

MR. FITZPATRICK TO LORD OSSORY.

"*Thursday morning*, 1 *o'clock*.

" DEAR BROTHER,

" Though you deserve to hear no news, I just write to inform you that Charles and Lord North have just received their dismission. We expect a dissolution, but are sanguine enough to hope for a majority in the new Parliament. Charles has written to the Duke of Bedford, and hopes he will come to town, as I take it for granted you will.

" Yours affectionately,

"R. F."

[The following note from Mr. Charles Townshend, afterwards Lord Bayning, has been preserved among Mr. Fox's papers. It is inserted here as contemporary written evidence of the King's private interference to influence the votes of individual peers, while the India Bill was pending in the House of Lords. It is dated on Sunday evening, and must have been written on the 14th of December, the day before the first division in the Lords on the Bill.]

" STANHOPE STREET, *Sunday evening.*

" DEAR SIR,

" I called at your house this morning, and not finding you at home, I desired Lord North to tell you that Bishop Butler is safe, and that Lord Onslow gave me his proxy to-day in favour of the Bill. Fearing that Lady Onslow's illness might prevent him from supporting it in person, I have sent to Lord Bagot to desire him to take it. It is true that Lord Onslow did receive an intimation by message that the King is against the bill, but it did not come from Lord Temple, or from any person high in credit either at St. James's or anywhere else. Lord North not having seen you this morning, you are troubled with this note from

"Dear Sir,

"Yours most sincerely,

"CHARLES TOWNSHEND."

[During the Christmas recess that followed, there seems to have been, from some quarter or other, the suggestion of a possible coalition between him and Mr. Pitt; for, on the 30th of December, Mr. Fox writes to say:] "You are certainly right in wishing me not to join Pitt; but, as to the other coalition, even those who disapproved of it formerly are now come over to it, from the very honourable manner in which Lord North has conducted himself, and from the heartiness with which his friends and ours have acted together upon this occasion."

[On the 22nd and 26th of December Mr. Fox wrote to Lord Northington as follows.]

MR. FOX TO LORD NORTHINGTON.

"BROOKS's, *Monday night,*
22nd December, 1783.

"MY DEAR NORTHINGTON,

"You will easily forgive me for not having written during all this strange confusion, when I assure you that I could have told you no more than any of your other correspondents. But I now think it necessary to dispatch a servant to you, to let you know that Lord Temple has this day resigned. What will follow is not yet known, but I think there can be very little doubt but our Administration will again be established. I lose no time in sending you this intelligence, because it may prevent measures you would otherwise be taking. The confusion of the enemy is beyond all description, and the triumph of our friends proportionable. I own I am one of those who rather am sorry that the thing was not brought to a decision by a dissolution, because the blame will now be laid on Temple's cowardice, and not upon the real impracticability of the attempt. I am too much hurried to write any more. We have carried an excellent Address to-day without a division, and shall go up with it on Wednesday.

" Yours ever sincerely,

" C. J. FOX."

SAME TO SAME.

" BROOKS'S, December 26th, 1783.

" MY DEAR NORTHINGTON,

" You will not be surprised that I have not time to write to you fully by Pelham's messenger. I am quite clear you should take no step towards resignation (except, perhaps, notifying your intention conditionally) till you hear the event of the 12th of January. I have no doubt but it will be the most

decisive victory on our side that ever happened in
Parliament. If I am right in this, you will, I am
sure, agree with me that it is desirable you should
take no step till you hear the event.

" Yours ever sincerely,

"C. J. FOX.

" P.S. I neither quit your house nor dismiss one
servant till I see the event of the 12th.

" Pelham suggests a doubt what answer you can
give to Lord Sydney's letter. I think the best would
be the true one, that you wait for the 12th of January,
and you may, if you please, add, that it is by my
advice that you do so. When Pitt asked me at Court
for a longer adjournment, I gave him as one of my
reasons for refusing him, my wish to prevent an
unnecessary change in Ireland, upon which he himself
suggested that I might ask it of you as a favour to
stay till Parliament here should have met. To this
I made no answer, because I would not be engaged
to *him;* but my opinion is clearly for your doing
nothing at present."

[Though Lord Northington declined to comply with
Mr. Fox's request that he would take no immediate
step towards resignation, he remained at his post till
the arrival of the Duke of Rutland as Lord Lieutenant, in February, 1784. His last letter to Mr. Fox
concludes with these words :—]

" For God's sake steer clear of the quicksands of
St. Albans. A coalition such as they propose, with

so strong an aversion in a certain quarter, can be productive only of certain ruin and destruction to you. A formidable Opposition is surely more preferable and safe than power by such an union acquired." *

* I give here, from the " Memoirs of the Court and Cabinets of George III.," the portraits of Lord North and Mr. Fox, as painted by the King. They are less unfair than might have been expected.

[Extract of a letter from Mr. W. Grenville to Lord Temple, dated March 28, 1783 :]

" While I was reading these letters, he went over with me a great variety of topics, chiefly the same as in the two former conversations, and very particularly upon the characters of Lord North and Fox, whom I think he described very justly, though certainly not in the most flattering colours. The first, he said, was a man composed entirely of negative qualities, and actuated, in every instance, by a desire of present ease at the risk of any future difficulty. This he instanced in the American war, and in the riots of 1780, of which he gave me a very long detail. As to Fox, he allowed that he was a man of parts, quickness, and great eloquence; but that he wanted application, and consequently the fundamental knowledge necessary for business, and above all, was totally destitute of discretion and sound judgment."— *Court and Cabinets of George III.,* vol. i. p. 203.

BOOK THE FOURTH.

PART THE FOURTH.

* WE have seen that, at the end of the year 1783, Mr. Fox entertained a confident hope that, on the 12th of January, he should succeed in displacing the intrusive Ministers, and restoring the Administration dismissed in so abrupt a manner by the King.

Unfortunately, Mr. Fox had made this a struggle for life and death between the prerogative of the Crown and the privilege of the House of Commons. "Only think, Sir," said Dr. Johnson, "it was a struggle between George the Third's sceptre and Mr. Fox's tongue."

Dr. Johnson hardly exaggerates the importance, although he does not rightly appreciate the character, of this struggle. Had Mr. Fox succeeded, not Mr. Fox's tongue, but the majority of the existing House of Commons, would have ruled England.

On the 12th of January, Mr. Fox laid down the principles on which he asked the support of the majority. He asserted that the Crown did not possess the prerogative of dissolving Parliament in the middle of a session. He quoted a pamphlet of

Lord Somers in support of his opinion. In order
to carry this doctrine into practical effect, he now
proposed to go into committee on the state of the
nation, " that they might prevent their dissolution."
" But nothing had yet happened," continued Mr. Fox,
quoting his opponents, " to make the dissolution of
the Parliament necessary! No! What did that
signify? Let us go into the committee, and make
it impossible. Let us preserve the beauty of our
Constitution ; of that happy practicable equilibrium
which has all the efficacy of monarchy, and all the
liberty of republicanism, moderating the despotism of
the one, and the licentiousness of the other ; that
which was in theory proved to be fallacious, but
which has been, since the Revolution, so pure and so
effectual."

The motion of Mr. Fox was carried by a majority
of 39.

At nearly three o'clock in the morning, the House
resolved itself into a committee : and Mr. Fox moved
two resolutions ; one declaring, that any person
issuing money for the public service, without the
sanction of an Appropriation Act, would be guilty of
a high crime and misdemeanour ; the other, deferring
the second reading of the Mutiny Bill till Monday,
the 23rd of February. Other resolutions were then
moved and carried. The first of these, proposed by
Lord Surrey, affirmed, " That in the present situation
of his Majesty's dominions, it was peculiarly necessary
that there should be an Administration which had
the confidence of that House and the public." Another

resolution, likewise moved by Lord Surrey, declared that the late changes in the King's Councils had been preceded by rumours that the name of the King had been unconstitutionally used. At seven o'clock in the morning, after a violent debate, this motion was carried by 296 to 54.

Such then was the position of the contending parties. It can hardly be denied that the conduct of the King, in using his own personal influence against the measure of his own Government, was not constitutional nor his manner of doing so upright. It follows that Mr. Pitt and his colleagues, who accepted office upon the success of this intrigue, placed themselves in an unconstitutional position.

On the other hand, the conduct of Mr. Fox and the majority of the House of Commons was wanting in dignity, and in adherence to the spirit of the Constitution.

Their first act had been to place on record a resolution against the King's behaviour while Mr. Fox and Lord North were still in his service.

Their second act had been to move resolutions not to censure the new Ministers for accepting office, in which they would have been perfectly right, but to endeavour to secure themselves against a dissolution. They thus virtually declared that they must themselves decide in the dispute between the Crown and the House of Commons. Such an assumption was obviously inconsistent with their own declaration, that it was necessary the Administration should have the confidence not only of Parliament, but of " the public."

The attempt of Mr. Fox to show that the Crown
had not the prerogative of dissolving Parliament in
the middle of a session, had neither law nor precedent
in its support.   The authority of Lord Somers, even
if it went the whole length of the dictum of Mr. Fox,
could only be available against the abuse of the prerogative by repeated dissolutions, with a view to the
discontinuance of Parliament.   But the practice, as
well as the theory, of our mixed Government shows,
that when two of the powers of the State cannot
agree, and the business of the State is stopt, the
only appeal is to the people at large.   Thus when,
in the reign of Queen Anne, the House of Lords and
the House of Commons fulmined resolutions at each
other, a dissolution cleared the air, and restored
serenity.   If no case had occurred since the Revolution of a quarrel between the Crown and the House
of Commons, the cause is to be sought in the prudence
with which every Sovereign, who had reigned since
that event, had wielded his constitutional authority.
If George the Third had been wanting in that
prudence, it did not follow that he was debarred
his right of appealing to the people.   Any other
doctrine would invest the House of Commons,
elected for the ordinary business of the State, with
a supreme power over every branch of it.   This
supreme power must vest somewhere ; according to
our Constitution, it vests in the common assent of the
realm, signified by the persons duly qualified to elect
the members of the House of Commons. *

* Of course I do not mean that the House of Commons when elected

The right course for Mr. Fox to pursue, therefore, on the rejection of the India Bill was, first, to tender his resignation ; secondly, To move resolutions against the use of secret influence ; thirdly, To give the Crown every facility for dissolving Parliament.

Had he taken this course, it is most probable that in a new Parliament a majority would have been found to disapprove of the violent steps by which the King had baffled the House of Commons. The India Bill, if again introduced, would not then have been liable to the poisonous influence of an intrigue.

In the mode adopted by Mr. Fox, these fair prospects were sacrificed to the hope of immediate success. For the second time, Mr. Fox took a course which success alone could justify. He placed the whole question at issue upon the permanence, the steadiness, and the popularity of the majority of the House of Commons. In all these respects he was liable to disappointment. A popular body was likely to hesitate in its course, and to fluctuate in its attachments. The fear of extreme counsels ; the dread of weakening authority ; the hope of reconciling adverse parties by moderation ; the corrupt influence of the rewards of the Crown ; all these motives were sure to sap the majority in its foundations. Its popularity was no less fleeting. The question would be asked, How was this majority composed on which were said to rest the hopes of popular liberty ? What were the objects for which they placed at hazard the peace of the realm,

have not every power to alter laws which those laws assign to them. But when they differ from the Crown, it is for the people to decide the suit.

and the authority of the Monarch ?   The answers to these questions were sure to be framed with perverse skill, and to be barbed with fatal dexterity.   It would be said that the majority was composed in part of the men who had led the country to loss and disgrace during the American War ; and, in part, of the men who had promised to bring them to punishment for that misconduct.   It would be said that the object for which these two hostile parties had combined, was to erect a power neither elected by the people, nor removable by the Crown ; in whose store all the treasures of India were to be thrown, for the purpose of maintaining the sway of an oligarchy, unknown to the Constitution, and hateful to the nation.

Such were the dangers rashly incurred by Mr. Fox ; such were the perils by which he was over-whelmed.   Yet it is impossible not to admire the wonderful resource, the untiring energy, the various eloquence, the manly courage, with which he con-ducted this extraordinary campaign.   No less mar-vellous is the ascendancy which he maintained over Lord North and the mixed forces he commanded in his repeated assaults on the personal authority of the Sovereign, and his maintenance of the popular power represented by the House of Commons.

On the other hand, due praise must be given to the boldness, calmness, and perseverance of Mr. Pitt. He committed a great fault in accepting office as the price of an unworthy intrigue.   He thus became " the child and the champion" of that secret influence which his father had denounced.   But having accepted a post he ought to have declined, he raised and dignified the position he had assumed. When urged by a neutral body to unite with Mr. Fox, he refused to do so on any but "fair and equal" terms. He said truly and honourably that he would not march out of his post with a halter round his neck, change his armour, and meanly beg to be re-admitted as a volunteer in the army of the enemy. He yielded however so far, that he was ready to meet the Duke of Portland to consider the formation of a new Ministry. Difficulties in words and forms arose, upon the use of the term "equal," the substitution of the word "equitable," and the proposal that the Duke of Portland should receive a direct message from the King. But it was clear that the real differences lay much deeper ; and that while the King would only have admitted Mr. Fox in order to overthrow him at a more convenient time, Mr. Fox would not have consented to enter office without a preponderance which would have afforded sufficient security against the enmity of the Court.

The contest may be said to have lasted from the 29th of December, when the first hostile motion was made, till the 25th of March, when Parliament was dissolved.*

[Of this great struggle between the Crown and the House of Commons, few memorials were found among the papers left by Mr. Fox. The following deserve insertion, as containing the particulars of the last fruitless attempt to form a coalition of parties before the abandonment of the contest.]

A written message from the King, delivered by Lord Sydney to the Duke of Portland, on 15th February, 1784 :—

"QUEEN'S HOUSE, *February* 15*th*, 1784.

"THE wish I entertain of seeing the present divisions healed by the formation of a new Administration, on a wide basis, and on a fair and equal footing, induces me to send Lord Sydney to acquaint the Duke of Portland of my desire, that the Duke of Portland and Mr. Pitt may meet to confer on a plan for that purpose to be laid before me. I shall be ready to consider any proposal which they may be enabled to bring me in consequence.

"G. R."

DUKE OF PORTLAND'S REPLY TO LORD SYDNEY.

"*Sunday evening*, *February* 15*th*, 1784.

"MY LORD,

"I have in consequence of the indulgence signified to me by your Lordship given myself time fully to consider the communication which I had the honour of receiving from you.

"I am highly sensible of his Majesty's goodness in wishing to put an end to the present divisions, and no man can be better disposed to an humble obedience to his Majesty's gracious orders, to take any step in my power towards forming an extended and united

Administration on a wide and solid basis. But your Lordship is too well apprised of my unalterable opinion that the confidence of the House of Commons is indispensably necessary to any arrangement which can promise quiet to the country, or energy to His Majesty's government, not to perceive the impossibility of my conferring with Mr. Pitt upon any plan of ministerial settlement, until he shall have signified to the House in some way or other his inclination to comply with their wishes. I do assure your Lordship with very great sincerity, that all obstacles to the restoration of a general good understanding among all parties, are exceedingly disagreeable to me, but you are satisfied that this is no difficulty raised upon the occasion, but that I have been constantly uniform in the same sentiment.

" I must beg leave to add, that before I can take any step towards any arrangement, it will be indispensably necessary for his Majesty's service that I should receive the same proofs of his Majesty's confidence, as your Lordship will remember I thought necessary on a former occasion, and which I then obtained. I have rarely, if ever, known anything but an increase of difficulties to have been the consequence of any other mode of proceeding. These I would, by all means, avoid. Your Lordship will, therefore, lay me with the most profound and dutiful respect at his Majesty's feet, assuring him of my entire devotion to his service, and that I shall humbly obey his orders, whenever his Majesty is pleased to call upon me personally to attend him ; and that if

his Majesty commands me, I shall most dutifully
submit to him such advice, as my unfeigned zeal for
his honour and interest, and for the public service,
may suggest to me, as most likely to promote the
formation of a firm, efficient, extended, and united
Administration.

" I have the honour to be, &c.

" P."

DUKE OF PORTLAND TO MR. FOX.

" Monday evening, February 16th, 1784.

" MY DEAR FOX,

" Mr. Ogilvie has reported to me a conversation
which passed this morning between the Duke of
Richmond and him, to the following purport : that
unless we consented to admit the Chancellor, the
Duke of Richmond, and Lord Gower, together with
Pitt, into the Cabinet, it would be impossible to form
a junction, or any Administration, that would have
the appearance of stability ; for that the King's
partiality to all of them, but particularly to Thurlow,
was so great and so decided, that his Majesty's
confidence could not be obtained by any Ministry of
which the Chancellor was not a part ; and that as
they were the determined supporters of the King
against the encroaching spirit of the Commons, and
were considered to be such by his Majesty, though
he might be satisfied, or might not insist upon all of
them being of the Cabinet, an Administration from
which <i>any</i> of them were excluded, would not be

authorised to expect the cordial support of their
corps. That it was unreasonable in us to expect
even the virtual resignation of the whole, or any of
the present Administration for the purpose of negotiation, as it would be an avowal on their part of the
charge alleged against them by the House of Commons, and be a direct acknowledgment of the unconstitutional principles of which they were accused;
but that if the House was rash, or wicked enough,
to refuse or postpone the supplies to-morrow, one
consequence of which, he asserted, would be your
being execrated, and probably torn to pieces by the
people, *they* would immediately resign, but with
the determination of commencing an immediate and
active opposition; which, being countenanced by the
King, would effectually defeat every measure
attempted to be brought forward in the House of
Lords, and by that means render our Administration
as inefficient as theirs was by our influence in the
House of Commons. He used various arguments
from the abilities of Thurlow and Pitt, from the
King's good opinion of them, and particularly of the
former, and from the integrity, disinterestedness,
and honour of the latter, as well as his (the Duke
of Richmond's) own, to convince Ogilvie of the
reasonableness, the propriety, the policy, and necessity of our adopting his ideas respecting the
composition of a new Administration. Ogilvie
intimated to him that this conversation had the
appearance of a design to make the King independent of Parliament. The Duke did not attempt

to deny or controvert it, and said that he (the Duke
of Richmond) was undoubtedly the King's friend.

" Yours ever,
" P.

" I forgot to mention that he told Ogilvie that the
negotiation opened yesterday *was entirely at an end.*"

SAME TO SAME.

" Tuesday, February 24th, 1784.
" ½ past 5, p.m.

" MY DEAR FOX,

" To satisfy Marsham, who has this moment left
me, I am obliged to importune you with a detail of
the conversation we have had together.

" Marsham, from a misapprehension of what had
passed between him and me and you, and probably
from his great zeal for union, conceiving that all
difficulties in the way of a conference with Pitt would
be got over by my receiving from the King's mouth
the same wishes that his Majesty had expressed in
the written message communicated to me, by his
orders, by Lord Sydney, was in great joy at having
prevailed upon Pitt to obtain, or at least to try to
obtain, the King's consent to honour me with an
audience for that purpose, and is consequently much
hurt at my having declined it, from the impossibility
I was under of discovering any difference between
receiving such a signification from the King in person
and under his hand. Marsham's proposition was,
that the King should send for me to attend him, and
should desire me to confer with Pitt for the purpose

of forming a *new* Administration, but no signification was to be made to the House of a virtual termination of the present Ministry, any otherwise than by a motion to suspend business, because Pitt and I were conferring upon the arrangement of a new one. It appearing to me that the honour of the House of Commons would upon such terms be no more satisfied by my having an audience than by my receiving a message in the King's own writing, and if I was right in declining to comply in the one instance, I should not be less so in the other, I desired Marsham to tell Pitt (who was waiting for him) that I could see no reason to alter my opinion, or to think that the House of Commons ought to be satisfied by the means proposed ; and in that determination Marsham left me, but begged me to communicate it to you without loss of time, as he was convinced you would think otherwise, and wished very earnestly for your coming immediately to town, as from the persuasion he was in respecting your sentiments, he did not doubt of your co-operating with him in disposing me to consider the measure as perfectly satisfactory, and fully adequate to the expectations of the House, and the security of the Constitution, which he insists will be lost by my perseverance in the terms I have repeatedly stated to be necessary.

" I endeavoured to bring to Marsham's recollection the conversation he and I had yesterday morning upon this subject, in which the idea of a conference with Pitt was preceded by the King's permitting me not only to consider the present Administration at

an end, but to presume that he could have no
objection to its being signified in the House of
Commons ; and that it was in consequence of the
King's assent to those propositions that I should
immediately ask his leave to solicit the assistance of the
abilities of such persons as could be useful to Government ; that upon my saying those words, Marsham
interrupted me by supposing the King would imagine
Lord North to be intended, and that I told him
that difficulty should not exist, for that I would particularly mention Mr. Pitt by name. Notwithstanding
this, Marsham says he did not understand what I
said to him in the sense which I contend my words
will only admit, and informs me that Powys intended
to convey the idea of this audience exactly as circum-
scribed, as he has described it to me, as an expedient
by which the honour of the House, as well Mr. Pitt's
and mine, were fully considered and ought to be
satisfied.

"Send me one word by the bearer, unless you
mean to follow him directly.

"Yours ever,

"P.

"I have been frequently interrupted, and it is now
7 o'clock."

SAME TO SAME.

"*Sunday night, February* 29*th*, 1784.

"I HAVE just received the enclosed from Powys, to
whom I gave no encouragement to expect any alteration in the sentiments I expressed to him upon this

subject when we last conversed upon it. He is to
call upon me again to-morrow morning at *ten*,
previous to a meeting at *eleven* at the St. Albans.
I fear it will be impossible for us to have any conversation upon the subject before that time, but as so
far from my seeing any reason to deprecate, the
refusal of a definition, and adherence to the terms of
equality confirms me in my former opinion, I shall
positively decline any conference, and tell Powys that
I consider the negotiation entirely at an end, unless
you signify to me a very decided wish to the
contrary.

"Ever yours,

"PORTLAND."

MR. PITT TO MR. POWYS.

" MR. PITT has all along felt that explanation on all
the particulars, both of measures and arrangements,
with a view to the formation of a new Administration,
would be best obtained by personal and confidential
intercourse. On this idea Mr. Pitt has not attempted
to define in what manner the principles of *equality*
should be applied to all the particulars of arrangements, nor discuss by what precise mode it may
be best carried into effect. But he is so convinced
that it is impossible to form any union except on
that *principle*, that it would be in vain to proceed, if
there is any objection to its being stated in the
outset, that the object for which his Majesty calls on
the Duke of Portland and Mr. Pitt to confer, is the

formation of a new Administration on a wide basis
and on a fair and *equal* footing."

* The general election, as is well known to every
reader, gave a large majority to Mr. Pitt. So decided
was the expression of public opinion that, when in
the new Parliament, Mr. Fox opposed Mr. Pitt's India
Bill, he only obtained a minority of 60 against a
majority of 271.

Important consequences have flowed from this
struggle.

The first of these which shall be mentioned was
one of serious evil. The King, obtaining a triumph
over Mr. Fox and the Whig party, was encouraged
in the indulgence of his own will. Unfortunately his
mind, which was not of a very expansive nature,
retained with adhesive force prejudices of the most
obstinate kind, both as to measures and as to persons.
Thus while in his youth he had embittered and pro-
longed the American war by his ascendancy over Lord
North, and his violent animosity to Lord Chatham,
so in his old age he retarded for a quarter of a
century the conciliation of Ireland by his refusal to take
the advice of Mr. Pitt, and his rooted dislike of Mr. Fox.
Unfortunately also, the prejudices which the Sovereign cherished in his own bosom, were widely diffused
throughout the nation ; so that when he first parted
with, and afterwards conquered Mr. Pitt, he was
followed with such sympathy by his people that for
nearly twenty years after he ceased to rule, the
policy which was recommended by Mr. Pitt and

Lord Grenville, by Mr. Fox and Lord Grey, by Lord Castlereagh and Mr. Canning, by Mr. Grattan and Mr Plunkett, still remained unaccomplished.

Had George III. failed in the struggle against Mr. Fox and Lord North, there can be little doubt that the Union with Ireland would have been accompanied by Catholic Emancipation. For it is to be observed that proudly and resolutely as George III. fought a battle against measures he disapproved and men he disliked, he knew well when concession was inevitable. Thus in 1783 he not only yielded independence to America, but allowed Mr. Fox to be one of his Secretaries of State. Thus again, after the peremptory rejection of Mr. Fox in 1804, he made no objection to him as a Minister, when the death of Mr. Pitt left that great statesman without a rival in the House of Commons.

Another evil consequence of the struggle of 1784 was that it separated for life the two men who were most fitted to guide the destinies of the country. Mr. Fox and Mr. Pitt seemed formed to act together. Mr. Fox had adopted Whig principles from conviction, Mr. Pitt had imbibed them from his illustrious father. Mr. Pitt had in his entrance to public life assisted Mr. Fox and the Rockingham party in their opposition to the American war. Mr. Fox had warmly supported Mr. Pitt in his proposals for a reform in the representation of the people. Both had genius for administration, but in totally different departments. Mr. Fox, with little taste for financial details, was intimately acquainted with the affairs of the Continent of Europe, and with the constitution of his

own country. Mr. Pitt, who had a very superficial
knowledge of foreign affairs, and not much regard
for constitutional learning, had an intuitive genius
for finance and trade, fortified by a study of the
works of Adam Smith, and other eminent authors.
Mr. Fox was before 1784 willing and even desirous
to act with Mr. Pitt.   Had they been in office
together, Mr. Pitt, ten years junior to Mr. Fox in age,
and not yet at least his equal in reputation for parliamentary eloquence, could not have pretended to
other than the second place.   Together they would
have formed the strongest Ministry in ability as well
as in numbers which this country ever saw.

But great as the evils were which flowed from the
dissension and separation of Mr. Fox and Mr. Pitt,
they were neither of the character nor of the permanence which the Whig party believed.   The Court
did not obtain the direction of public affairs.   The
Constitution was not altered in favour of the Crown.

These results did not follow for two very conclusive
reasons.   In the first place, Mr. Pitt was not a man
to bend at the nod of a master, any more than to a
vote of the House of Commons.   Endowed by nature
with great abilities and a strong will, he naturally
sought to convert the popularity he inherited from
the name he bore, and the eloquence he had at command, into a solid reputation, founded on measures
beneficial to his country.   The exhaustion of a costly
war, the abuses of a corrupt Government, the evils of
financial mismanagement, afforded ample scope for
prudence, method, and reformation.

But there was another reason why the Constitution did not receive a permanent injury.

If Mr. Fox had maintained, that a Ministry ought not to continue unless it should acquire the confidence of the House of Commons, and that doctrine had been practically overthrown by the decision of the country ; the Constitution, as it had been understood since the accession of George I., would have been virtually set aside. But the doctrine set up went beyond this, and affirmed that the power of dissolution during a session, or, as Mr. Burke called it, " of penal dissolution," did not belong to the Crown. No advantage would have flowed from the establishment of this opinion ; for had the King taken Mr. Fox back for the remainder of the session, it was not denied that at the end of it he might have sent for Mr. Pitt, and, by his advice, have dissolved the Parliament. On the other side, there was some appearance of assuming for an existing House of Commons, a power beyond that which had been assigned to them, of controlling the Crown by the votes of an ascertained majority.

The precedent of 1784, therefore, establishes this rule of conduct. That if the Ministers chosen by the Crown do not possess the confidence of the House of Commons, they may advise an appeal to the people, with whom rests the ultimate decision. This course has been followed in 1807, in 1831, in 1834, and in 1841. In 1807 and in 1831, the Crown was enabled, as in 1784, to obtain the confidence of the new House of Commons ; in 1834 and in 1841, the

decision was adverse to the existing Ministry. But
in all these cases, a solution of the difficulty was
obtained ; the people themselves decided on the
course to be pursued ; and the progress of Constitutional Government was impeded only for a short
time.*

BOOK THE FIFTH.

—•—

* THE general election of 1784 determined for more
than forty years the question of the government of
England. The unfortunate event of the contest in
America had weakened the rule of the Tory party,
and somewhat shaken the ascendancy of the prerogative. But the dissension between Lord Shelburne
and Mr. Fox, the subsequent coalition with Lord
North, the rise of Mr. Pitt and his junction with the
Duke of Richmond, all these circumstances skilfully
turned to account by the King, gave a complete
triumph to the Crown, and restored to power the
party which, during the American war, supported
every error and upheld every abuse.

It must be owned, that from the moment when
Mr. Pitt determined to separate his fortunes from
those of the Whig party, he played his game with
great vigour and address. He perceived with more
true sagacity than Mr. Fox the extent of aversion
with which the nation regarded the name of Lord
North ; and while he took into his confidence men
who were as responsible as Lord North for the

American policy, and in their hearts more favourable
to it, he sternly refused to sit in the same Cabinet
with the Minister whose name was identified with
oppression, disaster, and disgrace. Mr. Fox, on the
other hand, looking to the kind nature, liberal disposition, and yielding temper of his former foe, had
braved with rash impatience the displeasure of the
Court and the anger of the people.

During the early part of the Coalition Ministry,
Mr. Pitt was guardedly hostile : on the appearance of
the India Bill his opposition was vehement and
decided. His acceptance of office upon the success of
a Court intrigue, was prepared before-hand with much
art and combination, though with little regard to the
spirit of the Constitution.

It has long been known that the King was from
the commencement of the Coalition Ministry bent
upon their overthrow. But the particular steps which
he took for this purpose have only very lately been
revealed to the world. Lord Temple, who was
the chief instrument employed, has left on record
some very interesting details, which I shall give in
his own words. It is worth noticing, before I copy
those words, that Lord Temple was a warm adherent
of the Rockingham party, and that on that Minister's
death he wrote a letter to his brother, Mr. Thomas
Grenville, beginning with declaring his determination
to stand by Lord Rockingham's friends, and ending
with signifying his readiness to accept the office of
Secretary of State, under Lord Shelburne! Ultimately he went as Lord Lieutenant to Ireland, and

resigned on Lord Shelburne's resignation. We may now take his own account of his relations with the King.

"Upon my return to England," he says in his journal, " I was honoured with every public attention from his Majesty, who ostensibly held a language upon my subject, *calculated to raise in the strongest degree the jealousy of his servants.* In the audience which I asked, as a matter of course, after being presented at his levée, he recapitulated all the transactions of that period, with the strongest encomium upon Mr. Pitt, and with much apparent acrimony hinted at Lord Shelburne, whom he stated to have abandoned a situation which was tenable, and particularly so after the popular resentment had been roused. This was naturally attended with strong expressions of resentment and disgust of his Ministers, and of personal abhorrence of Lord North, whom he charged with treachery and ingratitude of the blackest nature. He repeated, *that to such a Ministry he never would give his confidence, and that he would take the first moment for dismissing them."* Lord Temple then discussed with the King the proposal for an allowance of 100,000*l*. to the Prince of Wales. " His Majesty declared himself to be decided to resist this attempt, and to push the consequences to their full extent, and to try the spirit of the Parliament and of the people upon it. I thought it my duty to offer him my humble advice to go on with his Ministers, if possible, in order to throw upon them the ratification of the peace, which they professed to intend to ameliorate, and to give them scope for those mountains of reform, which would inevitably come very short of the expectations of the public. From these public measures, and from their probable dissension, I thought that his Majesty might look forward to a change of his Ministers in the autumn ; and that, as the last resource, a dissolution of this Parliament, chosen by Lord North and occasionally filled by Mr. Fox, might offer him the means of getting rid of the chains which pressed upon him. To all this he assented ; but declared his intention to resist, at all events and hazards, the proposition for this enormous allowance to his Royal Highness, of whose conduct he spoke with much dissatisfaction. He asked what he might look to if, upon this refusal, the Ministry should resign ; and I observed that, not having had the opportunity of consulting my friends, I could only answer that their resignation was a proposition widely differing from their dismissal, and that I did not see the impossibility of accepting his Adminis-tration in such a contingency, provided the supplies and public bills were passed, so as to enable us to prorogue the Parliament. To all this he assented, and declared his intention of endeavouring to gain time, that the business of Parliament might go on ; and agreed with me that such a resignation was improbable, and that it would be advisable not to dismiss them, unless some very particular oppor-tunity presented itself." *

* " Court and Cabinets of George III.," vol. i. p. 303. In a letter of Nov. 6, 1783, Lord Temple says, " I know that Lord Northington is frightened,

Such being the concert established between the King and the leaders of Opposition, it was not difficult to find an opportunity of blackening the Ministry on the India Bill. We have seen how scandalously that wise and just measure was misrepresented ; how a commission for four years was converted in popular estimation into a permanent authority set up against the King. But it has been only very recently shown, that while the King was giving his public sanction to the India Bill, he was secretly plotting its defeat ; and that while his Ministers were allowed to give ostensible advice, other counsellers enjoyed the confidence of the Sovereign. The following is the account given by the Duke of Buckingham of a document hitherto unknown :—

"The opening line, and the note at the foot, are in the hand-writing of Lord Temple ; the body of the memorandum is in a different, and not very legible hand."

"*December 1st,* 1783.

" To begin with stating to his Majesty our sentiments upon the extent of the Bill, viz. :—

" We profess to wish to know whether this Bill appear to his Majesty in this light : a plan to take more than half the royal power, and by that means disable (the King) for the rest of the reign. There

and has uniformly proposed concession on every point, to the fullest extent : *this communication I know directly from the King's mouth,* though not to me but to another person," &c. I need not make any comment.

is nothing else in it which ought to call for this interposition.

" Whether any means can be thought of, short of changing his Ministers, to avoid this evil.

" The refusing the Bill, if it passes the Houses, is a violent means. The changing his Ministers, after the last vote of the Commons, in a less degree might be liable to the same sort of construction.

" An easier way of changing his Government would be, by taking some opportunity of doing it; when, in the progress of it, it shall have received more discountenance than hitherto.

" This must be expected to happen in the Lords in a greater degree than it can be hoped for in the Commons.

" But a sufficient degree of it may not occur in the Lords, if those whose duty to his Majesty would excite them to appear, are not acquainted with his wishes, and that, in a manner, which would make it impossible to pretend a doubt of it, in case they were so disposed.

" By these means, the discountenance might be hoped to raise difficulties so high, as to throw it (out), and leave his Majesty at perfect liberty to choose whether he will change them or not.

" This is the situation which it is wished his Majesty should find himself in.

" Delivered by Lord Thurlow, Dec. 1st, 1783.

" NUGENT TEMPLE." *

This document is probably in the hand-writing

---

* " Court and Cabinets of George III.," vol. i. p. 288.

of Lord Thurlow. It proves beyond a doubt the
authenticity of the celebrated paper, to the effect,
that " His Majesty allows Earl Temple to say, that
whoever voted for the India Bill was not only not his
friend, but would be considered by him as an enemy ;
and if these words were not strong enough, Earl
Temple might use whatever words he might deem
stronger, and more to the purpose." It proves,
moreover, that this course of proceeding, tainted, as
it was, with duplicity, and the breach of constitutional
duty, was advised by Lord Thurlow and Lord Temple.
It was probably known to Mr. Pitt.

It must be granted, however, that Mr. Pitt,
having taken this course, joined to great boldness,
sagacity, and discretion. By patience and perseverance
he wearied out a foe who was more ardent than
measured in his attacks ; and while he bore his
defeats with calmness, the country, saturate with
calumny, began to resent the attempt of the Coalition
party as the cabal of a domineering aristocracy. The
old servants of the Crown, the young favourite of
the people ; Government influence, the name of the
Sovereign ; the cry against coalition, the belief that
the India Bill was a measure to perpetuate Whig
influence ; all these things worked together, and
pervaded town and county. Thus the dissolution of
Parliament, when it came, swept like a storm over
the parties of Lord North and Mr. Fox : the Minister
of the American war, and its great opponent, were
reduced together to a minority unpopular as Lord
North, and powerless as Mr. Fox.

One of the first measures of Mr. Pitt's Administration was necessarily an India Bill. Avoiding the rocks upon which his rivals had struck, he neither deprived the Company of the government of India, nor erected a body, whose independence of the Crown might give umbrage both to the King and to the country. The administration and the trade were left in the hands of the Company, while a control and superintendence were placed in a board named by the Crown, and removable with the Ministers of the day.

It was easy for Mr. Fox, with his vast powers of reasoning, long exercised on this subject, to prove that these two authorities must be always in conflict ; that, with two supreme heads confronted, confusion must ensue, and that the abuses of the Indian Government must be perpetuated under so strange and anomalous a system.

The experience of seventy years, however, has blunted arguments which could not be logically refuted. The real supremacy of the Ministers of the Crown, usually kept in the back ground, but always ready to be exerted, has kept in check the administration of the Company, and placed the affairs of India under that guarantee of ministerial responsibility by which all things in Great Britain are ordered and controlled. The Directors of the East India Company have not ventured to connive at acts which a minister of the Crown would not sanction; and a minister of the Crown would not sanction acts which he could not defend in Parliament. Thus silently, but effectually, the spirit of the British Constitution has pervaded India, and the most absolute despotism has been qualified and tempered by the genius of representative government.

In giving to the India Bill of Mr. Pitt, however, all the credit which can possibly be due to it, we must not lose sight of another and more powerful cause of the improvement which has taken place in the morality of our governors of India. Lord Clive and Mr. Hastings, invested with an irregular power ; contending every month for the existence of a British settlement, without any military means of adequate proportion ; sought by complicated intrigue, by insincere alliances, by acts of violence at one moment, and of treachery at another, to rear and to consolidate a sovereignty of London merchants. In the words of Erskine they sought to "support an empire, which Heaven never gave, by means which it never can sanction."

This course of cupidity and fraud, of robbery and oppression, was brought to a close by the impeachment of Warren Hastings. The mind of Mr. Burke comprehended the vast extent of the question, and his genius animated the heavy mass of materials which his industry had enabled him to master. He enlisted in this cause the powerful reasoning of Fox and the brilliant fancy of Sheridan. After a time he succeeded in gaining the support of Mr. Pitt, and armed against the former governor of India the great battery of parliamentary impeachment. Whether the Minister was convinced by the evidence which threw so full a light on the misdeeds of Warren

Hastings, or whether he was glad to protect himself from the ambition of a rival by acceding to a prosecution against him,* the effect was no less certain. For years Mr. Burke persevered in his great task. Neither the dilatory plea of a dissolution of Parliament, nor the appalling earthquake of the French Revolution (to none more appalling than to him), ever distracted his attention from his great Indian enterprise. The speeches delivered by him in Westminster Hall are great monuments of industry and eloquence ; they surpass in power those of Cicero when denouncing the crimes of Verres. Finally, although the impeachment ended in an acquittal, its results were memorable and beneficial. Never has the great object of punishment, the prevention of crime, been attained more completely than by this trial. The Lords and Commons

---

* This last interpretation, which has hitherto been a vague rumour, derives much support from some passages in the Rockingham Correspondence. The most striking of these occur in a letter of Lord Bulkeley to Lord Buckingham :

" P.S. It is said that the King abuses Dundas to those about him very much, in a language that is very much copied by those whom we all know by the term of ' King's friends ;' and there are some who pretend to say that his loss of ground at Buckingham House has been owing to the part he took against Hastings, in which he has the reputation of having engaged Pitt to concur. *　*　*

" On one of the adjourned questions on Hastings's trial in the House of Lords, Lord Maitland, standing next to Dundas, asked him what he thought would be the result of the inquiry ; to which he replied in these words: ' I don't care what is done with him, for you and your friends in Opposition have done our business, by keeping him out of the Board of Control.' Lord Maitland on this called up Colonel Fitzpatrick and Dudley Long, in whose presence Dundas actually repeated his words, and they, of course, trumpeted them all over town, and they have occasioned much conversation and much abuse of Dundas, in addition to their former abuse on the part of Hastings's friends. The folly of such language, especially to three violent Oppositionists, was very absurd, weak, and ill-judged, but the fact is certain."

of England, assembled in Westminster Hall, in the
presence of the Judges, the Bar, the aristocracy
and the public, heard the whole record of Indian
transactions unrolled before them, and the acts of
our agents brought to the test of English law and
Christian morality.   No palliation, no plea of necessity could alter the character of those acts ; and no
man who could aspire to civil or judicial authority
in India, would ever dare to repeat conduct which
during seven years of a solemn process, before an
august tribunal, had been denounced as wicked,
oppressive, perfidious, rapacious, and cruel.   The
conscience of mankind was brought in presence of
negotiations, treaties, usurpations, conquests, veiled
in the haze of an obscure distance, and covered by
the jungle of strange manners, and uncouth phrase-
ology.   The sentence was pronounced, not by the
Peers, but by the universal opinion of right and
wrong.   Mr. Hastings was acquitted, but tyranny,
deceit, and injustice were condemned.   India was
saved from abominations disgraceful to the English
name, and the hands of Cornwallis, Minto, Bentinck,
and Auckland, have swayed an empire where Cheyt
Sing was despoiled and Nuncomar was executed.

Thus, after the rejection of the India Bill, and
amid the rout of the Whig party, Mr. Burke and
Mr. Fox succeeded in their great object of saving
the Indian people from rapine and fraud.

The other public transactions which occurred
between 1784 and 1793 are chiefly,—the financial
system established by Mr. Pitt—the commercial treaty

with France of 1786—the invasion of Holland in
1787—and the Regency question in 1788.

However unjustifiable may have been the conduct
of Mr. Pitt in making himself the instrument of a
Court intrigue, candour must allow that his subsequent
administration during peace was marked by large
public views, was founded on sound principles, and
led to happy results.

The financial administration of Lord North had
been a mere series of shifts and expedients to supply
the wants of years of war and misfortune. Amid
the losses of the empire the old corrupt practices
had flourished unchecked, if not increased under that
indolent and easy Minister. Mr. Pitt with a vigorous
hand pruned the luxuriance of prodigality, and grafted
on the ancient system the new maxims he had learnt
in the school of Adam Smith. A reduction of the
tea duties checked smuggling and increased consump-
tion ; a prudent economy enabled the Minister to set
apart a million a year as a sinking fund for the
redemption of the National Debt.

This excellent measure, at first absurdly cried up,
has since suffered in general estimation, from two
circumstances. First, there was a pretension of a new
discovery in the principle that the sinking fund was
to be allowed to increase at compound interest. It
was clear that such increase of the sum set apart to
pay off debt could only increase so long as the
nation should be willing to bear taxes for the purpose
of relieving their posterity. Such a sacrifice could
not be expected to last very long, or to be persisted

in to a very large amount. For instance, when the interest of the debt should be reduced to five millions yearly, and the sinking fund amount to ten millions yearly, it was to be expected that the impatience of taxation would prevent the further diminution of the debt at the expense of the existing generation. But, secondly, it was gravely propounded that when the debt should be increased by borrowing, the sinking fund might with great public benefit continue its operations ; as if a loan of thirty millions, of which ten were to be devoted to the sinking fund, could be a more profitable policy, than a loan of twenty millions without any sinking fund at all. But it was absurdly supposed that the price of the funds was kept up by the fallacious sinking fund, and at all events while the nation lost by the large amount of loan pressing on the market, the stock-jobbers profited by the delusion.*

While the financial measures of Mr. Pitt created for him a just popularity with the mercantile classes, a treaty with France, based on sound commercial principles, made him odious to the manufacturers. Mr. Fox unwisely and inconsiderately joined in the ignorant, but popular clamour, and even countenanced the barbarous and hateful doctrine, that the French were our natural enemies.

The treaty took effect ; its provisions were very beneficial to both countries ; the French improved their hardwares and their pottery ; the English their silks and ribbands ; but the war soon put an end to

---

* See the excellent work of Mr. Hamilton, a professor of Aberdeen, and a pamphlet of Lord Grenville, upon this subject.

this beneficial intercourse. By this time Mr. Fox had taken juster views of the national policy towards France ; and while Mr. Pitt held up the governing party of France to odium, he attempted, but in vain, to establish between two great nations the relations of friendship and goodwill.

The mental disorder which in 1788 afflicted the King, gave rise to a singular and deplorable contest. Mr. Pitt, as the guardian of the rights of the Crown, Mr. Fox, as the champion of the rights of the People, the Prince of Wales, as a dutiful son, the Queen, as an affectionate mother, seem all to have deserted their proper posts, and given but too much reason for censure.

The temporary incapacity of the Sovereign was a situation not provided for in the Constitution. A few precedents of the middle ages only exhibited the dominion of force, and the prevalence of that party which had the most followers and the strongest army. But the examples of the Parliaments which restored Charles II. and placed William upon the Throne, furnished analogies which should not have been over-looked. The existence of a Parliament, legally elected and legally summoned, gave an advantage to the statesmen in 1788 over those who had to supply the void of the Commonwealth in 1660, and provide for the vacancy of the Throne in 1688.

According to these analogies, the Parliament should first have inquired by whom the royal prerogative should be exercised during the temporary incapacity of their lawful possessor. This inquiry could not be long, nor its result doubtful : the Prince of Wales was then twenty-six years of age, and fully qualified to hold the sceptre which had fallen from the hands of his father. The ordinary control of the House of Commons would have prevented any flagrant abuse of the powers of Government ; and it was not to be supposed that the Prince of Wales would attempt so monstrous an act as the usurpation of the Crown, when the King, his father, should be sufficiently recovered to resume his royal functions. The violence of party, however, and the suspicions which were entertained of the intentions both of Mr. Fox and Mr. Pitt, precluded this fair and reasonable settlement.

On the 10th of December, Parliament being assembled, Mr. Pitt moved, in the House of Commons, for a committee to search for precedents, " in the case of the personal exercise of the royal authority being prevented or interrupted, by infancy, sickness, infirmity, or otherwise, with a view to provide for the same." Mr. Fox immediately rose, and having denied that there was any precedent applicable to the case, proceeded to say—" The circumstances to be provided for did not depend on their deliberations as a House of Parliament ; it rested elsewhere. There was then a person in the kingdom different from any other person that any existing precedents could refer to—an heir-apparent, of full age and capacity to exercise the royal power. It behoved them, therefore, to waste not a moment unnecessarily, but to proceed with all becoming speed and diligence to restore the sovereign power and the

exercise of the royal authority." He went on, after
referring to the law and Constitution, to say, "that
he had not in his mind a doubt, and he should think
himself culpable if he did not take the first opportunity of declaring it, that in the present condition
of his Majesty, his Royal Highness the Prince of
Wales had as clear, as express a right to exercise the
power of sovereignty, during the period of the illness
and incapacity with which it had pleased God to
afflict his Majesty, as in the case of his Majesty's
having undergone a natural demise."

Mr. Pitt was on his side equally rash, and, indeed,
still more unjustifiable ; for he had just moved for
precedents to inquire what had been done in similar
cases. He now declared, that—" To assert an
inherent right in the Prince of Wales to assume the
government, is virtually to revive those exploded
ideas of the divine and indefeasible authority of
princes, which have so justly sunk into contempt and
almost into oblivion. Kings and princes derive their
power from the people; and to the people alone, through
the organ of their representatives, does it appertain
to decide in cases for which the Constitution has
made no specific or positive provision." Not content
with thus asserting the doctrine of the sovereignty
of the people, he proceeded to point it still more
directly to the present case, by declaring, "that
the Prince of Wales had no more right to exercise
the powers of government than any other person in
the realm." It is said that during the delivery of
Mr. Fox's speech, Mr. Pitt slapped his thigh, and

exclaimed with triumph—"I'll un-whig the gentleman for the rest of his life!"

There can be little doubt that both these declarations were unsound in doctrine and unwise in
policy. In a Constitution so regularly poised as ours,
it would have been the height of imprudence for the
Prince of Wales to have assumed the rights of
sovereignty until the Houses of Parliament had
ascertained the incapacity of the reigning King, and
acknowledged the necessity of their being exercised
by the Prince of Wales. On the other hand it would
have been dangerous in the extreme for the Houses
of Parliament to have travelled out of the road of
hereditary succession, and have sought elsewhere than
in the person of the next heir to the throne a depo-
sitary of the royal power. The doctrine of Mr. Fox,
the popular leader, went far to set aside the constitutional authority of Parliament, while that of
Mr. Pitt, the organ of the Crown, tended to shake
the stability of the monarchy, and to peril the great
rule of hereditary succession. In the peculiar
position of Mr. Fox it was moreover unwise in him
to show any impatience to wrest the royal authority
from the temporary grasp of his rival : in the
abnormal situation of Mr. Pitt, it was highly indis-
creet to snatch at a temporary advantage over his
opponent, at the expense of his duty to the Royal
Prerogative, confided for the moment to his care and
affection.

Both these great men seem to have felt that they
had gone too far, and in their subsequent speeches

Mr. Fox returned to his habits of close reasoning, and Mr. Pitt to the use of dignified declamation. Each regained accordingly the position that became him : Mr. Fox that of a constitutional statesman, Mr. Pitt that of a loyal and enlightened Minister of the Crown.

On the subject of restrictions I do not wish to enter at length. The very proposal to exact them led to the creation of the absurd phantom of a royal assent given by the Houses of Parliament to their own act, by a fiction of their own creation ; to the avowal and proclamation that the King's son was not to be trusted with the interests of the monarchy and the care of his father ; in short, to theories absurd in reason, and conclusions shocking to feeling. The general doctrines of Mr. Fox upon this subject are stated by him, with his usual force, in his historical work, in a passage on the Exclusion Bill. He composed this passage one day in his garden at St. Anne's, and having written it down when he came in, gave it to Mr. Adam, saying, " Here is a justification of our conduct on the Regency Bill." The chief part of this passage is as follows :—

" The Whigs, who consider the powers of the Crown as a trust for the people, a doctrine which the Tories themselves, when pushed in argument, will sometimes admit, naturally think it their duty rather to change the manager of the trust than impair the subject of it ; while others, who consider them as the right or property of the King, will as naturally act as they would do in the case of any other property, and consent to the loss or annihilation of any part of it, for the purpose of preserving the remainder to him whom they style the rightful owner."

It has been objected to this doctrine that it excludes the consideration of such reforms as may reduce the powers of the Crown, where hurtful, or excessive. But if such powers exist they ought to be curtailed, whether under a King or a Regent; and the argument, both on the Whig and Tory side, proceeds on the supposition that the prerogative is such as ought to be retained, whether under a King or under a Regent.

While permanent restrictions were thus opposed to sound constitutional principle, there was apparent reason for limiting, for a short period, the exercise of those powers of the Crown which are not absolutely necessary for the efficient discharge of its duties, and which might be exerted in so unwarrantable a manner as to cripple the subsequent use of the prerogative. Thus the creation of twenty peers in six months might produce an inconvenience, if at the end of that time the former sovereign, the former ministry, and the former policy should be restored.

All reasonable restrictions, however, might have been imposed by Act of Parliament, with the Royal Assent given by the Regent acting on behalf of the Crown.

The conduct of the Prince of Wales and Duke of York, during the period of the King's illness, was the subject of much adverse comment. I should have been disposed to allow these unhappy dissensions to pass without notice from me, had not the recent publication of the "Court and Cabinets of George the Third" revived the censures so freely expressed on the behaviour of the Princes. It seems to me necessary to place before the reader of these volumes the other side of the question ; and I have therefore inserted a letter and memorial written in the name of the Prince of Wales by Sir Gilbert Elliot, which are found among Mr. Fox's papers. The letter was certainly never sent, but the memorial appears to have been delivered.

In the Appendix I have placed a letter of Sir Robert Adair, relating to the vulgar accusation, that he was sent by Mr. Fox in 1790 to thwart at St. Petersburg the negotiations of Mr. Pitt.*

[During this period few manuscript memorials of Mr. Fox have been found among his papers. The scraps that have been preserved, relate to the West-minster election—to the Irish propositions—to the commercial treaty with France—to the revolution in Holland—to the Russian armament—to the impeach-ment of Hastings ; and to the Slave Trade. Those which relate to the Prince of Wales and to the Regency are more voluminous and more valuable.]

According to the unanimous voice of his friends and contemporaries none of the published speeches of Mr. Fox gives such a just and lively picture of the style and character of his eloquence as his speech on the Westminster scrutiny, that mean and odious device of the pettifogging genius of Kenyon, ungene-rously adopted by Mr. Pitt. Mr. Fox's speech on this occasion was reported with great care by one of his most devoted partisans, and afterwards corrected by several of his most intimate friends. Of the election itself, a dull and bulky account has been published in quarto ; but to some it may be more interesting to read the following hasty scraps, written by Mr. Fox whilst it was going on, as showing in what temper of mind he viewed the different stages of its progress. The polling began on the 1st of April and continued to the 18th of May, when instead of returning the two candidates highest on the poll, the High Bailiff granted a scrutiny, for which he was afterwards fined in the sum of 2000*l.*, by the verdict of a jury, in the Court of Common Pleas.

" April 3rd.—Plenty of bad news from all quarters, but I think I feel that misfortunes, when they come thick, have the effect rather of rousing my spirits than sinking them.

" April 5th. The thing is far from being over, and I have still hopes ; but their beating me two days following, looks ugly—bad news from other places. I think there is no chance of the poll being over 'till the end of this week.

" April 6th. Our sanguine friends still hope, not I, but I must not give it up for several days. Sawbridge is chosen for the City.

" April 7th. Worse and worse, but I am afraid I must not give it up, though there is very little chance indeed.

" April 8th. I must not give it up, though I wish it. Indeed I feel that I ought not, while there is a bare possibility. Bad news from York, and alarms about poor Andrew St. John in Bedfordshire. I have serious thoughts, if I am beaten here, of not coming into Parliament at all.

" April 9th. The poll to-day was for one hour only, and we had six majority. If Sir Cecil does not beat me much to-morrow, which I think he will not do, I must go on, though much against my inclination. We have certainly a chance, but a small one.

" April 20th. I have gained thirty-two to-day, so that we are all in spirits again. If it will do, it is very well; but if it does not, I shall be very sorry for this advantage, as it will be the means of making it last a long time. St. John has carried his Bedford-shire election by *one* vote."

" April 27th. I gained forty-eight upon them to-day, and am now, as you see, twenty a-head. My opinion is that it will be over Saturday next or Monday ; but my friends think otherwise. I really believe we are quite sure here ; but there may be a scrutiny, which will be troublesome beyond measure.

" April 28th. I have gained twenty to-day, which is not so much as we expected, but I cannot think there is any chance of our losing it now.

" April 29th. I gained fifteen to-day ; and as the numbers polled on each side were so small, I begin to have hopes that it will be soon over ; that is, by Monday or Tuesday next.

" April 30th. I have gained thirty to-day, and they polled only twelve, which looks as if they were quite exhausted. However, they talk of persevering, and will do so probably for some days.

" May 1st. I have gained sixteen by the day, and

I really begin to flatter myself that a few days more will finish the business.

" May 3rd. I gained twelve to-day upon very small numbers, but I see less prospect of finishing than I did. No proposal has been made from the other side; and as long as I continue gaining, it is our interest to go on, to prevent a scrutiny. I am quite sure of success ; but I must own I heartily wish it over.

" May 4th. They only polled eleven to-day, and I thirty-three. No proposal for finishing ; nor can I guess when it will be over.

" May 5th. They polled only five to-day, and I thirty-five. One would think it must be soon over, but yet I do not think it will be this week.

" May 7th. We polled only nine to eight to-day, so that I think it must be soon over. I am chosen for Scotch boroughs. Whether this is good or no, I doubt ; but all my friends think so, and I always think their judgment better than my own, with respect to what regards *myself* in political matters."

Such was the slow and tiresome march of popular elections in those days. Riot, drinking, debauchery, and corruption, followed the camp of the opposing parties.

1785.

The unpopularity Mr. Fox had incurred by the Coalition and India Bill had been most painful to him ; and though at no time of his life was he ever deterred by the fear of popular clamour from pursuing the course that, to his judgment, seemed the right one, it was with no small pleasure he enjoyed the first return of the popularity he had lost. His opposition to Mr. Pitt's Irish propositions, which were equally unacceptable to English manufacturers and to Irish patriots, was the first of his public acts which obtained for him that gratification. He foresaw their failure. On the 11th of July he writes to Lord Ossory : " We are going to-day to the last debate of the year. Was there ever a history of folly like this Irish business ? When you are in Ireland you will see the ridicule of this plan to conciliate your countrymen still more strongly." " In September, 1785," says Horace Walpole,* " Charles Fox, Lord Derby, and others of that party, were received (at Manchester) with singular acclamations, and compliments on their opposition to the new taxes and Irish propositions. That town had been the head-quarters of Jacobitism, and as singularly distinguished by the King, who had preferred a guard on himself and palace, in the late war, of a regiment of raw lads raised there for him by Sir Thomas Egerton, who had been rewarded by a peerage." The pleasure this return of popular sympathy gave to Mr. Fox he expresses in a letter, dated Knowsley, September 10th, with almost boyish satisfaction :—

" Our reception at Manchester was the finest thing imaginable, and handsome in all respects. All the principal people came out to meet us, and attended us into the town, with blue and buff cockades, and a

* Manuscript Notes, 1785.

procession as fine, and not unlike, that upon my chairing in Westminster. We dined with 150 people; and Mr. Walker (one of their principal men, who was in London last year on their business), before he gave me as a toast, made them a speech, in which he told them, they knew how prejudiced he had been for Pitt and against the India Bill ; but that in the course of his business in town, he had occasion to know both Pitt and me, and found how much he had been mistaken in both ; that it was the part of honest men, when they found they had been wrong, to set themselves right as soon as possible, &c. ; all which was echoed by the whole room in the most cordial manner. You must allow this was very handsome. The concourse of people to see us was immense ; and I never saw more apparent unanimity than seemed to be in our favour ; and all this in the town of Manchester, which used to be reckoned the worst place for us in the whole country."

To maintain peace, if it could be preserved, without sacrificing national honour, or risking national security, and to leave other nations, without interfering in their domestic concerns, to the free expansion of their natural resources, were the great outlines of the system of foreign policy which Mr. Fox was disposed to cultivate. Regarding the family compact, which united the numerous and powerful branches of the House of Bourbon, as a confederation dangerous to the peace and independence of other nations, and distrusting the restless and intriguing spirit that had for ages directed the Councils of France, his jealousy of that power was the leading feature of his European politics. During the American War he had witnessed the peril to which England had been exposed by her neglect of continental alliances, and therefore on his accession to office, in 1782, his first objects had been to detach Holland from France, to conciliate the Northern powers, and to form connexions in Germany and Russia that might counterbalance the exorbitant power of the House of Bourbon.

The family connexions and strict alliance between the courts of Versailles and Vienna forbad any immediate attempt to detach the Emperor of Germany from his brother-in-law. But knowing the many grounds of rivality and enmity between France and Austria, some of which had declared themselves in the recent affair of the Scheldt, Mr. Fox looked forward to the rupture of their alliance at some future period, and he was therefore averse to any measures not called for by an obvious necessity, that tended still further to alienate from England the Emperor of Germany, her ancient ally. The accession of the Elector of Hanover, in 1785, to the German Confederation had therefore his decided disapprobation.

" Foreign affairs," he writes, in November, 1785, to Mr. Fitzpatrick, " must be attended to. The Elector of Hanover taking a step which precludes England from any possible connexion with the Imperial Courts ; France riveting the Dutch still more to her, preserving the Emperor and King of Prussia, and gaining ground even with Russia, without losing her influence with the Porte, and secured by the conduct of the Elector of Hanover against the only alliance that can ever make us formidable to her ; Portugal connected with Spain ; a French port in the Baltic—a circumstance rendered ten times more formidable upon a supposition of Russia being upon distant terms with us in case of a war ; all these things together appear to me circumstances of alarm beyond any that have ever existed, and I question much whether France has not gained more since the peace than during the war. In short, unless some of these things can be undone, there seems to be little left for England but to join the train and to become one of the followers of the House of Bourbon, which would be almost as dangerous as it would be disgraceful. I am sure this was Shelburne's system. I had been persuaded by Sir James Harris that it was not Pitt's, but there are several circumstances that look like it, and indeed it may be a doubt whether the German League leaves him the choice of any other. The worst of all is, that I am far from sure whether the country in general would not like a good understanding with France (from the vain hopes of a durable peace) better than anything. I am sure that any Minister who can like it must not only be insensible to the interests of his country, but to any feelings of personal pride ; for, depend upon it, whenever you are in such a situation the French will make you feel it enough. I understand they have had more Cabinets within this fortnight than are usual in a twelvemonth, and that the couriers both from abroad and from Ireland have been in proportion. What can be coming from Ireland I cannot guess. The signing of the definitive treaty between the Emperor and the Dutch, and of the alliance between France and Holland, might occasion many of the couriers, but not the Cabinets, as I hardly suppose these events (especially the latter) are notified in form to Great Britain so as to require an answer. You must see from all this the necessity of drawing the public attention to foreign affairs, however difficult it may be, and especially as there is not one instance in the whole reign where the mischief of the King's acting separately from his Ministers can be made so plain to the commonest understanding, as this of the German League.

"St. Ann's Hill, *Wednesday.*

MR. FOX TO COLONEL FITZPATRICK.

"St. Ann's Hill, *Sunday, November* [*or December*], 1785.

" Dear Dick,

" We mean to be in town on Wednesday, to see the 'Country Girl.' We shall dine at four, and I hope, if I do not see you before, that you will dine with us. The best, would be for you to come down Tuesday, and we might go to town together Wednesday in chaise or on horseback, according to the weather. I dare say Burgoyne would come with you if you were to propose it to him, if Jack will not.

" I will bring your Eclogue with me. I cannot think as you do of the insignificancy of newspapers, though

I think that others overrate their importance. I am clear, too, that *paragraphs* alone will not do. Subjects of importance should be first treated gravely in letters or pamphlets, or, best of all perhaps, in series of letters, and afterwards the paragraphs do very well as an accompaniment. It is not till a subject has been so much discussed as to become almost threadbare, that *paragraphs,* which consist principally in allusions, can be generally understood. Secret Influence, Indian Government, and now Irish Propositions, are all fit subjects, therefore, for paragraphs ; but foreign politics must first be treated in some serious and plain way, and must be much explained to the public, before any paragraphs alluding to them can be understood by one in a thousand. The Pig is not quite gone. Colonel Byron, thank God, is. He stayed one night, and was much less intolerable than I expected. I think Hume's History of Charles I. the most mischievous book that ever was written. It is written with more art than any other part of his works—infinitely—and is, I think, in that view a masterpiece. I do not think any answer to it, or comment upon it, would do much good, or at least not so much as another history of the times written with his art, or even with the half of it, in the opposite view. Adieu.

"Yours most affectionately."

The following extract from a letter written to a friend at Paris on the 24th of January, 1787, shows the feelings that induced Mr. Fox to oppose *in limine* the proposal of a more intimate connection with France :—

"I went to the House of Commons just after I finished my letter, and, upon the whole, it was thought by others as well as by myself better that I should speak, and not let the thing go off quite silently, which, if I had not spoken, it would have done. I spoke pretty strongly against French connexions and France, and Pitt made as bad a speech in answer as could be wished. There was no more debate, and no division ; so that I was time enough to go to dinner at Derby's, where everybody seemed to think I had done right. I know the French well enough to know, that, though they are very civil, and such of them as hear me may say I speak well upon these subjects, yet that they will make it the fashion some way or other to run me down ; so that if you should hear me spoken of differently from what you wish, you must not mind it. It may be ridiculous vanity in me to think that they will take any notice of me ; but I know how attentive they are to these things, and how very adverse they were to me as a Minister, particularly on account of the friendship which they thought I was cultivating with Russia."

[The successful interposition of England and Prussia in support of the Stadtholder against the French party in Holland, and the consequent renewal of our ancient alliance with the United Provinces, were too much in accordance with Mr. Fox's continental system not to meet with his hearty concurrence.

His approbation of them was expressed with his usual warmth in Parliament. It revived his hopes of a return to our old system of policy, instead of the new-fangled doctrines of confidence in the moderate and pacific views of the Bourbon courts. It was therefore with no small regret that he heard of a demand made by the King of Prussia, to be reimbursed by the Dutch, for the expenses of his expedition into Holland before his troops evacuated the country.]

"This demand," he observes, in a private letter, "is so distressing and violent a measure, that, if adhered to, it must ruin the Prince of Orange's interest in Holland, and consequently ours, as we shall be considered as the introducer of a plunderer; and I understand our Ministers have declared their disapprobation of the measure. The Princess of Orange has stopped the execution of it for a moment; but if she has not interest enough with her brother to persuade him to give it up, all that has been done will be of no use, and the French interest probably revive in Holland."

[The confidence which the Prince of Wales had reposed in Mr. Fox, before and during the Coalition Administration, continued for many years unabated, and it was met by Mr. Fox with warm and affectionate attachment. Of the sincerity of his regard for his Royal Highness he gave an unequivocal proof, by venturing, uncalled and unsolicited, to interpose in private with his advice in a matter of the utmost delicacy, where he had reason to apprehend that,

under the influence of violent passion for a lady, the
Prince was about to act in a manner prejudicial to
all his future prospects. Mrs. Fitzherbert, the lady
alluded to, was a widow, and had been twice married.
Her family and connections were respectable, and her
character irreproachable ; but she was a Roman
Catholic, firm in her religion and above changing it
from worldly motives. She was of great beauty and
distinguished manners. So early as summer, 1784, the
Prince had been desperately in love with her, and to
escape from his importunities she had gone abroad.
She came back to England in December, 1785. The
Prince, who had kept up a constant correspondence
with her while she was on the Continent, renewed his
attentions to her on her return, and as they seemed
to be more favourably received than they had been
before, a report prevailed that he intended to marry
her, though a Roman Catholic. Mr. Fox thereupon
wrote to him a most friendly and sensible letter, of
which a draft was found among his papers in his own
handwriting :]

" December 10th, 1785.

" SIR,

    " I hope your Royal Highness does me the
justice to believe that it is with the utmost reluctance
that I trouble you with my opinion unasked at any
time, much more so upon a subject where it may not
be agreeable to your wishes. I am sure nothing
could ever make me take this liberty but the conde-
scension you have honoured me with upon so many
occasions, and the zealous and grateful attachment

which I feel for your Royal Highness, and which makes me run the risk even of displeasing you, for the purpose of doing you real service.

" I was told just before I left town yesterday, that Mrs. Fitzherbert was arrived, and if I had heard only this, I should have felt most unfeigned joy at an event which I knew would contribute so much to your Royal Highness's satisfaction ; but I was told at the same time, that from a variety of circumstances, which had been observed and put together, there was reason to suppose, that you were going to take the very desperate step (pardon the expression) of marrying her at this moment. If such an idea be really in your mind, and it is not too late, for God's sake let me call your attention to some considerations, which my attachment to your Royal Highness, and the real concern that I take in whatever relates to your interest, have suggested to me, and which may possibly have the more weight with you when you perceive that Mrs. Fitzherbert is equally interested in most of them with yourself. In the first place, you are aware that a marriage with a Catholic throws the Prince contracting such marriage out of the succession of the Crown. Now, what change may have happened in Mrs. F.'s sentiments upon religious matters, I know not, but I do not understand that any public profession of change has been made ; and surely, Sir, this is not a matter to be trifled with, and your Royal Highness must excuse the freedom with which I write. If there be a doubt about her previous conversion, consider the circum-

stances in which *you* stand : the King not feeling for
you as a father ought ; the Duke of York professedly
his favourite, and likely to be married to the King's
wishes ; the nation full of its old prejudices against
Catholics, and justly dreading all disputes about
succession. In all these circumstances your enemies
might take such advantages of any doubt of this
nature as I shudder to think of, and though your
generosity might think no sacrifice too great to be
made to a person whom you love so entirely, consider
what her reflections must be in such an event, and
how impossible it would be for her ever to forgive
herself. I have stated this danger upon the supposition that the marriage could be a real one, but your
Royal Highness knows as well as I that according to
the present laws of the country it can not, and I need
not point out to your good sense what a source of
uneasiness it must be to you, to her, and above all
to the nation, to have it a matter of dispute and
discussion whether the Prince of Wales is or is not
married. All speculations upon the feelings of the
public are uncertain, but I doubt whether an uncertainty of this kind, by keeping men's minds in
perpetual agitation upon a matter of this moment,
might not cause a greater ferment than any other
possible situation. If there should be children from
the marriage, I need not say how much the uneasiness as well of yourselves as of the nation must be
aggravated. If anything could add to the weight of
these considerations, it is the impossibility of remedying
the mischiefs I have alluded to. For, if your Royal

Highness should think proper, when you are twenty-
five years old, to notify to Parliament your intention
to marry (by which means alone a *legal* marriage can
be contracted), in what manner can it be notified ?
If the previous marriage is mentioned or owned, will
it not be said that you have set at defiance the laws
of your country, and that you now come to Parliament for a sanction to what you have already done
in contempt of it ?   If there are children, will it not
be said that we must look for future applications
to legitimate them, and consequently be liable to
disputes for the succession between the eldest son—
and the eldest son after the legal marriage ? And will
not the entire annulling of the whole marriage be
suggested as the most secure way of preventing all
such disputes ?   If the marriage is not mentioned to
Parliament, but yet is known to have been solemnised,
as it certainly will be known if it takes place, these
are the consequences : *first*, that any child born in
the interim is immediately illegitimated ; and *next*,
that arguments will be drawn from the circumstance
of the concealed marriage against the public one.
It will be said that a woman who has lived with you
as your wife without being so, is not fit to be Queen
of England ; and thus the very thing that is done for
the sake of her reputation will be used against it :
and what would make this worse would be that the
marriage being known (though not officially communicated to Parliament) it would be impossible to
deny the assertion.   *   *   * If, in consequence of
your notification, steps should be taken in Parliament,

and an Act passed (which considering the present
state of the power of King and Ministry is more than
probable) to prevent your marriage, you will be
reduced to the most difficult of all dilemmas with
respect to the footing upon which your marriage is
to stand for the future, and your children will be born
to pretensions which must make their situation
unhappy, if not dangerous. These situations appear
to me, of all others, the most to be pitied, and the
more so, because the more indications the persons
born in such circumstances give of spirit, talents, or
anything that is good, the more they will be suspected
and oppressed, and the more will they regret the
being deprived of what they must naturally think
themselves entitled to. I could mention many other
considerations upon this business, if I did not think
those I have stated of so much importance that
smaller ones would divert your attention from them,
rather than add to their weight. That I have written
with a freedom which on any other occasion would
be unbecoming, I readily confess, and nothing would
have induced me to do it but a deep sense of my
duty to a Prince, who has honoured me with so much
of his confidence, and who would have but an ill
return for all his favours and goodness to me, if I
were to avoid speaking *truth to him, however disagreeable at so critical a juncture.*

" The sum of my humble advice, nay, of my earnest
entreaties, to your Royal Highness, is this, that you
would not think of marrying till you can marry
legally. When that time comes, you must judge

for yourself : and, no doubt, you will take into consideration both what is due to private honour and your public station. In the meanwhile, a mock marriage, for it can be no other, is neither honourable for any of the parties, nor, with respect to your Royal Highness, even safe. This appears so clear to me, that, if I were Mrs. Fitzherbert's father or brother, I would advise her not by any means to agree to it.

*   *   *   *   *

It is high time I should finish this very long, and, perhaps, your Royal Highness may think, ill-timed letter ; but, such as it is, it is dictated by pure zeal and attachment to your Royal Highness. With respect to Mrs. F., she is a person with whom I have scarcely the honour of being acquainted ; but I hear from everybody that her character is irreproachable, and her manners most amiable. Your Royal Highness knows, too, that I have not the same objection in my mind to intermarriages with Princes and subjects which many have ; but, under the present circumstances, marriage appears to me to be the most desperate measure for all the parties concerned that their worst enemies could have suggested."

To this letter the Prince of Wales returned next day the following answer :—

" CARLTON HOUSE, December 11th, 1785.
" Sunday morning, 2 o'clock.

" MY DEAR CHARLES,

" Your letter of last night afforded me more true satisfaction than I can find words to express, as it is an additional proof to me, w^h* I assure you I did not want, of y^r having y^t true regard and affection for me, w^h it is not only ye wish but ye ambition of my life to merit. Make yourself easy, my dear friend ; believe me the world will now soon be convinced y^t there not only is, but never was, any ground for these reports, w^h of late have been so malevolently circulated.† I have not seen you since the apostacy of Eden. I think it ought to have ye same effect upon all our friends y^t it has upon me ; I mean the linking us closer to each other ; and I believe you will easily believe these to be my sentiments, for you are perfectly well acquainted with my ways of thinking upon these sort of subjects. When I say, my ways of thinking, I think I had better say, my old maxim, w^h I ever intend to adhere to ; I mean y^t of swimming or sinking with my friends. I have not time to add much more, except just to say, y^t I believe I shall

* His Royal Highness always used these and other abbrevia-tions.—V. H.

† [The assurance given by his Royal Highness, that there was no ground *at that time* for the report of his marriage with Mrs. Fitzherbert, was possibly true, for the marriage did not take place till ten days after-wards. This letter was written on the 11th of December, and the marriage was not solemnised till the 21st. It was performed in private by a clergy-man of the Church of England, in the manner prescribed by the Common Prayer-book ; and the certificate, dated the 21st of December, 1785, was attested by two witnesses. The transaction was concealed as well from Mr. Fox as from the public ; and, though it was early suspected, and at length very generally believed, that some ceremony of marriage had passed between Mrs. Fitzherbert and his Royal Highness, these parti-culars were not known to any but the parties concerned till after his death.]—I. A.

It will be perceived how quickly the Prince, after his denial, flies to another subject.—J. R.

meet you at dinner at Bushy on Tuesday, and to
desire you to believe me at all times,

" My dear Charles,

" Most affectionately yours,

"GEORGE P."

[In July, 1786, the Prince having become embarrassed in his circumstances, and having applied in
vain to his father for relief, broke up his establishment, and having set apart 40,000*l.* a-year for the
payment of his debts, he resolved to live on the
remainder of his allowance as a private gentleman.
The following letter seems to imply that Mr. Fox
had been consulted, and had approved of this determination.*]

PRINCE OF WALES TO MR. FOX.

"BRIGHTON, *July* 19*th*, 1786.

" MY DEAR CHARLES,

" I am more obliged to you than I can possibly
express for the contents of ye letter I yesterday
received from you, and am more and more convinced
of the necessity of pursuing that plan w^h, I assure
you, I never should have adopted, had I not intended
to have gone thr° with it. With regard to the
other plan you mention, I approve most highly of it,

---

* The Prince showed me this letter. As well as I remember it contained
great commendation of the resolution the Prince had taken, and urged the
necessity of adhering to it. But it did not, according to my recollection,
contain any reference to previous communications on the subject, though
such had probably taken place. What the other plan was to which the
letter refers, I do not remember.—*Note by the late Lord Grey.*

but shall not touch upon it at all at present, as I
mean to be in London for a few hours on Monday
next, when I hope to have the pleasure of seeing
you, and of discussing the matter fully at length.
At twelve o'clock, I shall be ready to receive you at
Carlton House. I will not trespass any further upon
y^r patience at present, but conclude, with assuring
you, that no one can feel more sensibly every mark of
y^r friendship and regard, than

" Your sincerely affectionate,

" GEORGE P."

[The Prince continued to live in retirement till the
spring of 1787, when it was thought by some of his
friends that an application should be made to Parliament for the payment of his debts and some addition
to his income. On this intention being announced,
it was met by a cold and somewhat menacing
resistance on the part of the Minister, and in one of
the preliminary discussions, Mr. Rolle, member for
Devonshire, (since raised to the peerage by the
Crown, and consigned to immortality by the wits)
rose and declared that if such a motion was made, he
would move the previous question upon it, because
the question itself "involved matter by which the
Constitution, both in Church and State, might be
essentially affected." These mysterious words were
understood to allude to a supposed private marriage
of the Prince of Wales with Mrs. Fitzherbert, which
had been asserted or insinuated in the newspapers.
and had not been contradicted. Mr. Fox, who had

not been in the House when the member for Devonshire
made these remarks, took the opportunity of a suc-
ceeding debate to treat the report alluded to as a
vile calumny, and " to deny it *in toto*, in point of fact,
as well as law.   The fact not only never could have
happened legally, but never did happen in any way
whatsoever, and had from the beginning been a
base and malicious falsehood."   On being further
questioned, Mr. Fox declared that " he had direct
authority for what he had said."]

[That Mr. Fox was ignorant of the marriage that
had been contracted in secret, and that he had direct
authority from the Prince of Wales to make the
assertion which he did, no one who knew him can
doubt.   It was not in his character either to assert
what he knew to be false, or to claim an authority
he did not possess.   Had it been otherwise, had the
denial or assertion been made without authority, it
cannot be supposed that the Prince would not, in
private at least, have disavowed the authority on
which he pretended to speak.   No such disavowal is
ever pretended to have been made ; and a private
letter, written by him that very evening to Mr. Fox,
while it alludes to the anger of Mrs. Fitzherbert at
what had passed in the House of Commons, does not
assert or insinuate that the declaration made in
public by Mr. Fox was not warranted by the
assurances given to him in private by his Royal
Highness.]

"April 30th, 1787.

" Monday night, 12 *o'clock.*

" MY DEAR CHARLES,

"I beg to see you for five minutes to-morrow, after I have seen Marsham and Powys, whom I beg you will desire to be at Carlton House *at one o'clock to-morrow.* When I see you I will relate to you what has passed between *my friend and me* relative to yᵉ seeing *you.* I feel more comfortable by Sheridan's and Grey's account of what has passed to-day.* I have had a distant insinuation that some sort of message or terms are also to be proposed to me to-morrow. If you come a little after two you will be sure to find me.

" Ever affectionately yours,

"GEORGE P."

[Another letter, written ten days afterwards, shows the anxiety of the Prince about his negotiation with the Minister, and his earnest desire that Mr. Fox would remain in town while it was pending ; but it contains no censure, complaint, or disavowal of what Mr. Fox had said some days before in the House of Commons.]

---

* I do not recollect having given him any account that would satisfy him. On the contrary, in a long conversation which I had with him, in which he was dreadfully agitated, the object was to get me to say something in Parliament for the satisfaction of Mrs. Fitzherbert, which might take off the effect of Fox's declaration. I expressly told him how prejudicial a continuance of the discussion must be to him, and positively refused to do what he desired. He put an end to the conversation abruptly by saying, " Well, if nobody else will, Sheridan must."—*Note by Lord Grey.*

PRINCE OF WALES TO MR. FOX.

"CARLTON HOUSE, *May* 10*th*, 1787.

" MY DEAR CHARLES,

" No answer is come as yet from Pitt, excepting y^t he was to see ye King to-night, and w^d endeavour to get everything settled if he c^d. Some sort of an answer I shall certainly have this evening, when he quits the Queen's House, w^h I will communicate to you as soon as possible after I have received it. His own statement y^t he has made out, as expenses for every year from the time I came of age, is thirty thousand pounds a quarter; consequently annually an hundred and twenty thousand pounds; ye moment I get a copy of y^m I will transmit it to you for y^r inspection. In ye meantime I beg you will not think of going to Newmarket till you have heard again from me; how late it may be I cannot answer for. Adieu, my dear friend. Pray excuse haste.

" Ever yours,

"G. P."

[These remarks have become necessary in consequence of facts having since come to light which were then unknown. It is now ascertained beyond a doubt, that, notwithstanding the declaration of Mr. Fox in Parliament, the Prince of Wales was at that time secretly married to Mrs. Fitzherbert.* The marriage, as formerly stated in a note, was performed by a clergyman of the Church of England, and attested

---

* He confessed it to me in the interview which I have mentioned.— *Note by Lord Grey.*

by two witnesses.   It was no doubt an illegal marriage ; but as a religious ceremony it was duly
solemnised.   The House of Commons was therefore
imposed upon by the declaration made in the name
of the Prince ; but the imposition was not practised
by Mr. Fox, who had himself been deceived.]

[That the assurances given to Mr. Fox by his
Royal Highness were concealed from Mrs. Fitzherbert, or grossly misrepresented to her, is
exceedingly probable.   Her permanent resentment
to Mr. Fox is a proof that the truth was unknown
to her.]

MR. FOX TO MR. FITZPATRICK.

"St. Ann's Hill, *Friday, August*, 1787.

" Dear Dick,

" I have seen Coutts, who is very handsomely
willing to lend me 5000*l*., but says he should lend it
with much more pleasure, and would even go farther,
if either by means of you or your brother there were
hopes of exonerating me altogether.   I have therefore desired Macartney to state the things to Ossory ;
but I am sure you will agree with me that the chance
of success will be greater in proportion as the assistance asked is less, and therefore I should be very
glad to deduct this 600*l*. from the sum I have
mentioned.

" I have told you, my dear Dick, what I think
reasonable ; but if you think otherwise, I am sure
I do not consider (and I am sure you do not) any

difference of opinions about such *rascal counters*, of any consequence.

> " Yours most affectionately.

> "C. J. FOX."

SAME TO SAME.

> "St. James's Street, *November 7th*, 1787.

" Dear Dick,

" I am desired to tell you that it is thought right there should be a great show of Whigs at Lord Mayor's, on Friday, and they have insisted on my coming to town on purpose ; though I am just going home after so long an absence, which is rather hard. You will have a ticket sent you.

" I wish to know what the permanent augmentation of the Army is to be, for if it is to be as I hear, we must resist it *à toute outrance,* and endeavour to get an attendance before Christmas.

> " Yours affectionately,

> "C. J. FOX."

[Among the documents on the subject of the Regency is one apparently in the handwriting of Lord Loughborough, docketed " Materials for a Pamphlet." It contains the grounds of the opinion entertained by that noble Lord and adopted by Mr. Fox, " that from the moment the two Houses of Parliament declared the King unable to exercise his royal authority, a right to exercise that authority attached to the Prince of Wales," but that it was a right of which he could not take possession, use or act upon, " till it was adjudicated to him by the two Houses of Parliament."]

[However erroneous we may think this or any other doctrine that attributes to any individual, or to any constituted authority existing in the State, a strict or legal right to claim or to dispose of the royal authority, while the King is alive, but incapable of exercising it, the assertion of this doctrine on the present occasion led to such important consequences, that the legal and constitutional views, on which it was placed and defended by its original author, cannot fail to deserve being recorded.]

MATERIALS FOR A PAMPHLET.

At the conference of the Lords and Commons in the Convention Parliament, 1689, the Lords maintained the distinction between a right and the exercise of a right.* Several cases were put, among which was included that actually in question.

On the part of the Commons it was not necessary to *deny* the reality of the distinction, inasmuch as their vote repelled its application; they having resolved that the throne was vacant, the right itself was gone. They could not *admit* the distinction, because they must have been pressed with its conclusion in favour of the lineal successor, and it was their purpose to distance from the discussion the pretensions of the Prince of Wales. They judiciously *avoided it*. But it is manifest in the

---

* " Distinguendum quoque non minus in *imperio* quam dominio jus ab usu juris, sive actus primus ab actu secundo; nam sicut rex infans jus habet sed imperium exercere non potest, sic et *furiosus* et captivus," &c., &c.—Grotius, " De Jure Belli et Pacis."

N.B. Grotius makes no distinction between incapacity by infancy, and incapacity by lunacy. In the nature of the thing there is, however, a very obvious distinction, and very pointed to the present question.

construction of the argument on both sides—from the direct assertion of the principle on the one side, and the indirect admission of the other, implied from their alluding to its consequences, that both parties were agreed, " That were the Throne *full of the right*, and the case were such as to separate the *right* from the *exercise of it*, the administration of the kingly power would attach in the successor, and that *ex necessitate*, in conformity to, and maintenance of the maxim that the King never dies."

Objection.

The maxim of law which prevails in common descents is opposed to this reasoning. *Nemo est hæres viventis.* The heir cannot take in the life of the ancestor *as heir*. The Prince of Wales, therefore, *as heir*, has no more right than any other person in these realms. For this is even not the case of a civil death. It is certainly true that this is not the case of a civil death. The civil death recognised in the books upon which the heir could take during the natural life of the ancestor, was by *profession* in the times of popery.

The law of this country, however, never considered *lunacy*, or even *idiotism*, as such a civil death as to entitle the heir. Originally, the lord claims the custody of the lands as a sort of temporary escheat. Afterwards, the king took, probably as universal occupant of a property derelict, so long as the idiot or lunatic lived. The right of the heir did not accrue till his natural death. The statute 17 Ed. II., cap. 10, declares, " That the King shall provide for the custody, &c., of lunatics." This custody is by special commission entrusted to the Chancellor. who has an equitable *discretion* in the appointment of the committee of the estate, as well as of the person ; so that it is certain that in general the heir has no claim by *law*.

Answer to Objection.

The objection proceeds upon a supposition of an exact analogy between common descents and the descents of the Crown, which is not the case. The subjects are different. There is certainly an analogy between them; but there are also material exceptions to this analogy—exceptions which are necessitated by the peculiar nature and constitution of the subject in which they prevail.

The peculiar nature of the subject will appear from this definition of it.

The King is a *body politic* or *corporation sole,* the succession on which is, so far, and so far only, governed by the rules which prevail in common descents, as is consistent with the nature of such a Constitution.

The definition may be illustrated by a very material exception to the above supposed analogy.

Among the females, the Crown descends to the eldest daughter and her issue.

In *conformity* to the common law she takes, though a female. In *conformity,* also, to the common law, she takes by right of primogeniture; but, in derogation of the common law, she takes in exclusion of females in the same degree, and this from a necessity created by the constitution of the royal body politic.

Another very material distinction, which is also a derivation from the nature of this constitution, or body politic, is this :—

That though in common descents, upon the death of the ancestor, an entry on the part of the heir is necessary to complete his title, so that if he die without entry made, his heir shall not be entitled, but the heir of the person last seised; yet, in the case of the Crown, it vests in the heir *ex instanti,* without interval, or any act on his part; and that, from necessity, to preserve the perpetuity of the body politic.

These distinctions, at the same time that they furnish a general answer to an argument which proceeds upon a supposed analogy between the succession to the Crown and the succession to real estates in general, suggest further observations upon the point in question.

1. It is asked where the doctrine contended for is to be found—in what precedent? What book case? What authority? it may be answered, in no one of these sources, for the very obvious reason that the case itself is novel. But, if it can be found in the law by which the royal body politic is constituted, it can want none of these sanctions; for it is from that law that the eldest female derives her title. 2. It is to be observed that the heir to the crown does not take *merely as heir* in the general legal sense of the word, for the eldest female is not the heir in that sense; strictly speaking the heir to the crown takes by *succession;* a word peculiarly appropriated to the mode by which a corporation is continued. The general position, " Nemo est hæres viventis," need not be impeached —it may be admitted that no man can take as *heir* in the lifetime of his ancestor, and yet it will not follow that the Prince of Wales cannot take as immediate *successor.* This leads to the very point in question.

Position.

" That on the declared incapacity of his Majesty, a right attaches in the Prince of Wales to exercise the royal authority with all its functions for the time such incapacity exists."

This must be law—if it follows of necessity from the law of the constitution of the royal body politic; and it must follow of necessity, if the reverse of the position be destructive of such constitution.

It is to be observed, we are speaking not of the natural individual; but of a being the creature of politic institution for the great purposes of civil government. The distinctive character of it, and that which it was formed to sustain, is its perpetuity. That this character may be supported, there must be no interval in its duration. Hence the maxim that " the King never dies," and hence it is, that upon the death of the natural person the king survives in his successor.

There is therefore, it is to be observed, an *indissoluble continuity* between the person actually occupying the throne, and his successor; for without this *indissoluble continuity* the perpetuity of the body politic could not be sustained.

From *this* position, the position above stated follows of necessity.

This position was established in law to preserve the perpetuity of the crown. The throne must ever be full. It must be full not only of the right, but of the power to exercise the right; for otherwise it would be ineffective to the very purpose for which this body politic was constituted, *i. e.*, that of government. Now, as upon the dissolution of the natural person, the heir succeeds, to sustain both the right and power to exercise the right; so, upon the incapacity* of the natural person by the suspension of his

---

* " It will be asked, whether this reasoning would hold in case of incapacity by infancy, and whether the heir in such case would have a right to succeed to sustain the power of which the infant King was incapable? I answer, certainly not. In construction of law the King never is a minor. And though the subject can avoid grants made during infancy, the King cannot."—Co. Litt. 43.

And in the nature of the thing there is an obvious difference between incapacity by infancy and incapacity by lunacy. In the case of infancy there is a *persona*, a moral agent; and in the case of lunacy there is none. The acts of an infant may have discretion; the acts of a lunatic cannot. Hence, though by the general law an infant may in some cases be civilly or criminally answerable for his acts, a lunatic cannot be either in any case.

In the case of an infant king, the Regent does not take by succession, but by appointment.

moral agency, the heir must succeed to sustain the exercise of the right; and both from the same necessity, namely, to preserve the throne from being vacant.

The above reasoning explains what is meant by the heir-apparent and successor being a *joint person* with the reigning king.

The charter* of Edward the Third to his son and heir-apparent, the Duke of Cornwall, recognises him, " ut ipsum qui reputatione juris censetur eadem persona nobiscum."

The prince, by the common law, is reputed as the same person with the king, and so declared.†

It is also from this continuity of person that it has been held, that if the prince, as Prince of Wales, hath judgment to recover, and afterwards the crown descendeth unto him, he, as king, shall sue out execution.

It is also in this pre-eminent character that the law invests him with dignities and prerogatives, above all other subjects; for, as the above statute expresses it, " Coruscat radiis Regis patris sui et censetur una persona cum ipso Rege."

His proper title since the Union is, Magnæ Britanniæ Princeps. His crown is distinguished by its similarity to the imperial crown.

The compassing his death was, by the common law, before the Statute 25th Edward the Third, treason.‡

Statutes which concern him, are such acts whereof the Judges and all the realm must take cognisance as general statutes. By the resolution of all the Judges,§ he is expressly excepted from all other subjects in various statutes: the Statute of Liveries; that concerning the Retainer of Chaplains, &c. &c.

He had the prerogative of purveyance.

In the case of a king incapable from lunacy, the *persona* is gone *pro tempore*; it is extinguished. The Regent may take by succession.

* Selden's " Titles of Honour," 595.

† Stat. temp. H. 6; Co. Rep. 8, 28.

‡ Lord Coke, *ibid.*   § *Ibid.*

The inapplicability of the argument arising from a supposed analogy between the case of common and that of royal descents has been endeavoured to be shown. It has also been attempted to deduce the position proposed as a direct consequence from the constitution of the royal body politic.

Let the indirect argument be tried, and let it be examined whether the reverse of this position be not impossible, the constitution established as it is.

In the first place it is clear (and this the very objection admits) that the conjuncture operates to a separation of the right and the exercise of the right.

2. The exercise of the right must vest somewhere, for neither by the law of the country, the law of reason, nor the law of God, can it remain with the lunatic.

3. If it is to vest, it must either vest in the heir and successor, or in the people by its representatives.

4. It cannot vest in the people in any case short of an actual dissolution of the government.

5. But the dissolution of the government cannot be pretended while the crown is full of the right,* and there is a parliament regularly convened. It cannot vest in the people, but by *devolution*. Now there can be no *devolution* (or escheat) while there remains a right of succession.

6. It cannot vest in the people; therefore it must vest in the successor.

If it should appear that nothing short of a dissolution of government, and a consequent devolution or escheat of the kingly power should vest it in the people; and if it should appear that the present case does not amount to a dissolution of the government; it may be asked by what authority the two Houses can take upon themselves the disposition of it. If there is anything of sense in the *cantilena* of Westminster Hall,

---

* N.B. The argument on both sides in the conference of the Convention. Parliament admitted this.

"cujus est dare, ejus est disponere," certainly it must be true that "cujus non est dare, non est ejus disponere."

How can they propose a reduction of a subject which is not in their power?

The law of the land has established the course of descent. Parliament regularly constituted has directed it, and has by statute (Anne) enacted its penalties upon those who shall deny or contrive to interrupt the course of succession as established.

The constitution has prescribed the limits to which a body so collected shall proceed, and no further. They have a *judicial* declaratory power, certainly not a *legislative* declaratory power, that the event has taken place in which the law must take its course, certainly no more.

[The following extract from a confidential letter of Mr. Fox, written (15th December) on the day before a majority of the House of Commons decided in favour of the resolutions proposed by Mr. Pitt, shows at once his uncertainty as to the issue of the approaching contest; his sanguine expectation of coming soon into office; his satisfaction with the conduct of the Prince of Wales and Duke of York; and the firm opinion, which he ever after maintained, that in appointing a Regent, the royal authority ought to be transferred to him without limitation or reservation]:—

"We shall have several hard fights in the House of Commons this week and next, in some of which I fear we shall be beat; but whether we are or not, I think it certain that in about a fortnight we shall come in. If we carry our questions, we shall come in in a more creditable and triumphant way, but at

any rate the Prince must be Regent, and of consequence the Ministry must be changed.   The manner
in which the Prince has behaved through the whole,
has been the most steady, the most friendly, and
the handsomest that can be conceived.   You know
when he sets his mind to a thing he can do it well,
and in this instance he has done it most thoroughly.
The Duke of York, who is steadiness itself, has
undoubtedly contributed to help him to his good
resolutions, and seems as warmly our friend as the
Prince himself.   In short, with regard to Princes,
everything is easy and pleasant, much beyond what I
could form any idea of.   In regard to other things I
am rather afraid they will get some cry against
the Prince for grasping, as they call it, at too much
power ; but I am sure I cannot in conscience advise
him to give up anything that is really necessary to
his Government, or indeed to claim anything else as
Regent, but the full power of a King, to which he
is certainly entitled.   The King himself (notwithstanding the reports which you may possibly hear)
is certainly worse, and perfectly mad.   I believe
the chance of his recovery is very small indeed,
but I do not think there is any probability of his
dying."

1789.

[During the latter part of the discussions on
the Regency Bill, Mr. Fox was at Bath on account of
his health, which had suffered severely in consequence of the rapid journey he made from Bologna to

England, on receiving intelligence of the King's illness. From Bath he corresponded with his friends in London on the progress of the Bill]:—

MR. FOX TO MR. FITZPATRICK.

"BATH, *February* 17*th*, 1789.

"DEAR DICK,

"You have heard before this of our triumphant majority in the House of Lords in Ireland, but I think one of the best parts of the news is the Address having been put off till yesterday, which seems to remove all apprehension of the difficulty which you mention in your letter, and which in effect appears to me to be a very serious one. The Delegation cannot leave Dublin till to-morrow ; and as probably it will not be composed of persons who travel like couriers, the Prince will not be able to make an answer till he is actually Regent here. I think this object so material that our friends ought more than ever to avoid anything that tends to delay here.

"If the Bill is passed there can be no difficulty in the Prince's answer, which must be acceptance, with expression of sensibility to the confidence in him. If in spite of my calculations, he should be obliged to make his answer before the Bill has passed—which, by the way, I hardly think possible—it must be couched in some general terms to which the acts he will do in a few days after must give the construction of acceptance. The fact is, our friends have gone too fast in Dublin, but how could they conceive our extreme slowness here ?

"I hope by this time all ideas of the Prince or any of us taking any measure in consequence of the good reports of the King, are at an end ; if they are not, pray do all you can to crush them ; and if it were possible to do anything to cure that habitual spirit of despondency and fear that characterises the Whig party, it would be a good thing, but I suppose that is impossible. I rather think, as you do, that Warren has been frightened ; I am sure, if what I hear is true, that he has not behaved well. Adieu. I leave this place on Thursday, but stay for letters, and therefore if you could let me know by the return of the post, on what day the Regency is like to commence, I should be obliged to you.

" Yours affectionately,

" C. J. FOX."

[When the King's convalescence was declared, the Prince of Wales and Duke of York became anxious for an opportunity to explain and justify to their father the part they had taken during his illness, which they had reason to think would be misrepresented to their prejudice by their enemies. It would seem that their first overture had been made through Lord Thurlow, with whom, at the commencement of the King's illness, they had been in close and confidential communication. A conversation with Lord Thurlow appears to have suggested to the Prince to make some proposition to him, which he desired Mr. Adam to communicate to Mr. Fox ; in reply to which Mr. Fox writes to Mr. Adam on the 22nd of

February, only three days after the King's convalescence had been announced to the House of
Lords.]

" I have no idea that Thurlow can listen to
anything upon the basis you mention. If he does, it
is very well, but you know I have a kind of horror of
negotiations with Thurlow, whatever favourable
appearances they have."

[Their next application was made to their mother.
Certain papers were placed in her hands for the
perusal of the King, and a request conveyed through
her that he would admit them into his presence for
the purpose of vindicating their conduct. This
request having been rejected, on the ground that the
King had resolved to decline all conversation that
might agitate him, the Prince of Wales addressed the
following letter to the Queen, the draft of which is
corrected and the date annexed in the handwriting
of Mr. Fox.]

TO THE QUEEN.

"CARLTON HOUSE, *March 9th*, 1789.

" MADAM,

" The contents of your Majesty's note were
really of too much importance, and of too painful a
nature, for me to return an immediate answer. I have
shown them to my brother, whose sentiments agree
entirely with mine, and who feels as I do the distressing alternative that is offered us, of leaving our
conduct unexplained to the King, or of obtruding
upon him a discussion which may have the effect of

agitating him too much. In this situation, however, we do not hesitate to sacrifice everything to our tenderness for his Majesty, and do not desire he should be further troubled upon our account at present. We have too lively an impression of what they have to answer for, who have brought or suffered others to bring business before the King at a time when all agitation is improper, to be guilty of anything liable to a similar construction. But I trust we shall be permitted to represent to your Majesty a few facts and circumstances relative to the peculiarity of our situation, with the truth of which you are perfectly well acquainted. I conceived myself to have a promise from your Majesty that the papers, which I had sent you, should be given to the King at the first moment of his being in a proper state to attend to business. Relying upon this promise, I thought myself authorised to disbelieve all the reports, which the Ministers had so industriously circulated, of their having laid business before his Majesty, and explained to him what had passed during his illness. But when the Chancellor and Mr. Pitt made their respective declarations in the two Houses of Parliament last Thursday, I could not but suppose there had been some truth in what I had before treated as idle rumour, and wrote to your Majesty in consequence.

" Feeling as my brother and I do for the King's quiet and repose, we consider the answer sent to us as a prohibition with respect to any present explanation of our conduct ; and thus, instead of having the preference, to which we had so just a claim, and which we were induced to expect, we dare not even attempt to counteract the impressions which our enemies, who have daily access to the King, may have given of the part we took in the late important occurrences.   Your Majesty must surely be of opinion that this state of things is neither decent nor just, and that whoever is responsible for what passed at Kew since the King's convalescence, has much indeed to answer for.   I forbear to say anything more upon this painful subject, nor should I have said so much, if I had not thought that I owed to my brother and myself to make your Majesty this true representation of these peculiar hardships of our situation.

"I am, &c."

[The draft of another note to the Queen, in the handwriting of the Prince himself, without date, but manifestly written on this occasion, deserves insertion, because it shows what were his spontaneous feelings and surmises on this extraordinary refusal of a father to listen to the vindication of his children.]

" MADAM,

" The contents of your Majesty's note were really of too much consequence and of too painful a nature for me to return an immediate answer, before I had first seen my brother, and consulted with him whether he saw in the same point of view

and with the same regret what appeared to me a
prohibition on y^t just claim we both conceived we
had on the paternal goodness and affection of
his Majesty, and w^h, we are confident, w^d have
induced his Majesty to have furnished us with the
earliest opportunity of informing him of what had
passed, and of explaining and justifying our own
conduct, if the interested advice of some persons
desirous of sowing dissension between our father and
ourselves, and of concealing the truth from him, had
not interfered. Under this impression, we have
taken the liberty of writing to his Majesty ; and we
wait the result of our letter with ye most anxious
impatience, still confiding y^t, with ye assistance of
your Majesty's gracious and affectionate endeavours,
we may be favoured with the opportunity of communication with him, w^h, tho' denied to us, has
been granted to others, who neither by affection,
duty, or blood, are attached to his Majesty as we
are. With the most respectful submission, I have
ye honour to subscribe myself,

" Madam,

" Your Majesty's, &c."

[It soon became apparent that the Queen's resentment against her sons was not abated by the King's
recovery. The following letter to Mr. Fox from the
Duke of Portland shows how unnecessarily she went
out of her way to make them feel that she considered them as hers and their father's enemies.]

THE DUKE OF PORTLAND TO MR. FOX.

"*March 29th*, 1789.
"*Sunday night*, 11 *o'clock.*

" MY DEAR FOX,

" The Prince and the Duke of York are extremely embarrassed and agitated by a message delivered by the Queen to the latter respecting their coming to the concert, which is to be given at Windsor on Wednesday. The words, as well as I recollect them, were nearly these—'That they would be welcome to the concert, but that she thought it fair to let them know that the entertainment was intended for those who had supported them, ('us' was her word), the King and Queen, on the late occasion.' I own my opinion is clearly for the Princes' taking no notice of the offensive part of the intimation from the Queen for their going to the concert, that no pretence may be taken from their conduct for raising any new difficulty in the way of their access to the King; but they are hurt and offended, and don't relish this advice ; however, they have consented to take no step till to-morrow. I wish to see you at Carlton House at eleven ; for which purpose I send this by a servant to Hockevill, where I am in hopes you will sleep to-night.

" Yours ever,

"P."

[Towards the end of May, a duel was fought between Colonel Lenox and the Duke of York, which had nearly proved fatal to the latter. When intelligence of this affair was communicated to their Majesties, it was received by the Queen with cold indifference, and expressions implying that she thought Colonel Lenox was in the right. Soon after, she gave a ball, to which he was not only invited, but treated with marked attention ; and, to crown all, the King wrote a letter to the Duke of Clarence, expressing his displeasure at the unkindness he had met with from his two elder sons during his illness. Thereupon the Prince was advised to prepare a memorial, and deliver it to his father, as a justification of his own conduct and that of his brother during his Majesty's illness. It was drawn up by Sir Gilbert Elliot, afterwards Earl of Minto. It is a very able paper ; and besides a vindication of the course taken by the party, it contains some interesting details of the King's illness, not generally known.]

MEMORIAL DELIVERED BY THE PRINCE OF WALES TO THE KING.

I owe to your Majesty, at all times, an account of my actions ; but I am most anxious to render that account of myself and my conduct during the unhappy period of your Majesty's illness; because while it was full of delicacy, embarrassment, and difficulty to me, it has been exposed in the same proportion to the malicious or interested misconstruction of others, whom I have reason to think enemies of my honour and welfare, as well as wholly indifferent to those of your Majesty.

My first object is to regain for myself, and my brother the Duke of York, your Majesty's good opinion and affection.

If this point cannot be pursued without falling into a crimination of others (which, indeed, I foresee must be the case), I trust your Majesty will not impute to me, on that account, a desire of intruding officiously into the affairs of your government; but will hold me justified in not sacrificing an object so invaluable as your Majesty's esteem, to any tenderness for those who have never been tender of me, and whose slanders on me, and on every member of our house, have been so systematical, and so interwoven with their actions, that it may be impossible to assert our own honour, without involving a consideration of their conduct. Yet it will be with regret, and it shall therefore be with as much reserve as the occasion can admit of, that I shall represent to your Majesty, in the conduct of those who are honoured with your confidence, what has appeared to me inimical, either to myself, to the Royal Family, to your Majesty, or to your kingdom.

I cannot be supposed desirous of committing myself in personal controversy with any of your Majesty's servants or subjects. But your Majesty will, no doubt, approve of my not declining any matter, however little attracting it may be in itself, which belongs to the important points I have in view.

These are to convince your Majesty, by a concise but faithful account of my conduct, together with the relative events and circumstances, during the late interval, that there has been no action of my life which merits the severe imputation either of personal unkindness to your Majesty or of opposition to the real interests of your Majesty's crown; but, on the contrary, that an affectionate solicitude for your happiness, and an anxious zeal for the rights, security, and honour of your throne, have been among the chief and leading principles which have governed my own and my brother's actions during this arduous and awful period. Permit me, first, to relate those circumstances which are of a private and domestic nature.

The severity of your Majesty's disorder having increased to

an alarming degree, I repaired immediately to Windsor, and
disregarding every other object, applied myself wholly to the
care of a health so valuable, and to the alleviation of your
Majesty's sufferings.   Your Majesty stood at that time
eminently in need of that care and vigilance which natural
and strong affection knows alone how to render.   I felt that
the protection of a parent whom I have always loved, and
whose heart I know has never been estranged from me, was
become my peculiar duty.   That duty I claimed and exercised
as a precious, though melancholy privilege, belonging to my
birth, and conferred on me by nature itself.   I provided what
appeared to me the best means for your recovery ; I observed
the conduct of those who were entrusted with the immediate
attendance on your Majesty ; I referred the plan of management
to your physicians, and superintended the due and punctual
execution of their directions.   In these anxious offices, I had
the consolation of being supported by the constant, unwearied,
and affectionate attendance and counsel of my brother, the
Duke of York.   It is with satisfaction I inform your Majesty
that we desired and received the advice of the Lord Chancellor,
on every material step which we took.   I reflected on the great
personal confidence with which your Majesty had distinguished
Lord Thurlow, and the nature as well as eminence of his
office seemed to point him out as a person who might be
consulted with peculiar propriety in this most critical and
delicate posture of affairs.   In what manner I was able to
discharge these weighty duties, it is not fit that I should be
called upon to speak myself ; I choose rather to refer your
Majesty to the testimony of the Chancellor, and to that of
your Majesty's attendants at that period, who were eye-
witnesses of our conduct.   This only I think it right to say,
that from the hour on which the alarming violence of your
Majesty's illness appeared to require the care which I have
described, until the removal of your Majesty to Kew, neither
myself nor the Duke of York were absent for a day from

Windsor, nor suffered any consideration, even of health, much
less any lighter avocation, to retain us an hour from your
Majesty's chamber, and from the discharge of a duty so dear
to us both.

Next to the care of your Majesty's person, that of your
private and domestic affairs appeared to claim my attention.
While your Majesty and the Queen continued to reside at
Windsor, the money, jewels, and papers, and other effects
belonging to your Majesty, did not seem to require any particular caution for their security. But on the removal of your
Majesty and the Queen to Kew, I considered it as my duty to
provide for the safety of those effects; and I determined at
the same time to do so in such a manner as should be consistent with that scrupulous delicacy which suited the occasion,
and which I felt to be becoming, in a voluntary, although
highly necessary, interference with the affairs of your Majesty
not expressly authorised by your Majesty's orders.

In this view, after mentioning my intentions to the Lord
Chancellor and receiving his approbation, I desired the
attendance of Lord Brudenell, who is keeper of your Majesty's
privy-purse, together with that of Lord Weymouth, whom I
judged to be the person whose presence your Majesty would
the most approve upon such an occasion. I directed them to
take, from your Majesty's drawers at Windsor, the jewels and
the money which were deposited there. An account of each was
taken on the spot, and they were delivered to the custody of
Lord Brudenell, whom I conceived to be the proper officer for
that purpose. Lord Brudenell's receipt was taken at the same
time, specifying both the jewels and the money which were
committed to his charge, and he was directed to deposit these
effects in his office, and be answerable for their safe custody, and
for their production whenever your Majesty should require it.

The situation of the apartments at Windsor in which
these effects were lodged, appeared to me by no means secure,
and the suspicion which might get abroad of their value,

seemed to increase the risk. These circumstances determined me to use the precaution I have described for their
security. Yet I felt it to be a duty of too delicate a nature,
to discharge in my own person, and I selected, to the best of
my judgment for this service, those who I thought would be
most acceptable to your Majesty on such an occasion. The
whole was done in my own presence, but was performed
solely by the hands of Lord Brudenell and Lord Weymouth.
A difficulty occurred concerning your Majesty's papers which
were deposited in the same place. It had been the opinion
of the Lord Chancellor that, for greater security, they should
be removed, and after being properly docketed should be
deposited in some other place. But observing that they
appeared to be arranged with great regularity and method,
and being extremely unwilling that any paper of your Majesty's
should undergo the slightest inspection, or that your Majesty
should even have reason to suspect that they might have been
seen by any one ; I represented these circumstances to the
Chancellor, and, with his consent, determined to leave them
untouched by any hand whatever, exactly in the places and
order in which your Majesty had deposited them. I did not
conceive that papers were in the same danger as money or
jewels ; and I judged that it would be most acceptable to
your Majesty to find your papers exactly as you had left them.
Besides which, I felt an invincible repugnance to permitting,
without your Majesty's order, even that degree of inspection
which was necessary for preserving their arrangement, to any
persons, however confidential I might know them to be with
your Majesty. These were my motives for taking this resolution.
The drawers were accordingly locked and the keys enclosed
in a paper, which was sealed with Lord Weymouth's seal,
as well as with others ; and continued in this manner till it
was restored to your Majesty by my brother, the Duke of
York, as soon as your Majesty's recovery gave us reason to
believe that you would wish to receive it.

I have not troubled your Majesty with the detail of these arrangements in order to claim any positive merit on the occasion. I did my duty and no more. But as this has been the only occasion in my life, in which I have felt an obligation to take on myself the direction of a pecuniary or any similar concern of your Majesty's, I trust only that my conduct in this instance has not been such as to deserve the reproach of personal unkindness towards your Majesty, much less such as to expose me to the dishonourable suspicion of infidelity in trusts of that nature, or to render any degrading and affronting caution more necessary against me than any other person.

With whatever consciousness of rectitude, and, therefore, with whatever satisfaction I may reflect on the discharge of my duty in this instance, yet I have ever since had strong reasons for regretting the necessity I was under to act in it. For it was the first occasion on which I had the misfortune to feel the Queen's displeasure, and to incur her anger.

The measures which I have described for securing your Majesty's effects against the attempts either of theft or curiosity, were no sooner known at Kew, than her Majesty expressed the most marked disapprobation; and, to my extreme astonishment, condescended, at my next interview, to a species and warmth of reproaches, into which nothing could have surprised or betrayed her Majesty, but a degree of passion, which, as I had never witnessed, nor believed to exist, in her Majesty before, so I accounted it the more remarkable on the present occasion, not conceiving in what manner the circumstances were capable of producing so extraordinary an effect.

Without ascribing to this cause the unfortunate indisposition which I have ever since experienced in the Queen's mind, I have to lament it, however, as the period from which I must date the first open demonstration of her anger; and I cannot but be sensible that I have never since recovered with her Majesty any share of that confidence or affection which I once considered it my principal happiness to possess so entirely.

Your Majesty's removal to Kew was directed by a Cabinet Council of your Ministers, who previously assembled at Windsor, and examined your physicians relative to that measure. As soon as that event had taken place, the care of your Majesty fell solely and exclusively into the hands of the Queen. From this period I suddenly found my access to your Majesty prohibited in such a manner, that I was immediately excluded from the satisfaction of seeing your Majesty; and, indeed, almost deprived of the privilege to receive authentic information of your Majesty's health and situation.

I cannot describe to your Majesty, nor is it indeed easy to ascertain the precise means by which this exclusion of myself and of my brother—for it extended to us both—from all personal attendance of dutiful affection on your Majesty, was brought about. We had, indeed, a right, as your sons, and we felt it as such, to as free and unreserved personal admission, and to as full, particular, and confidential information on such a subject, as any other person whatever, until some provision should be made, by a competent authority, for our exclusion. But your Majesty must be sensible, that many considerations, both of affectionate caution, respecting your Majesty's health, and also of personal delicacy, belonging to the peculiar complexion of the times, rendered it impossible for us to assert and insist on this right, invaluable as we deemed it, when opposed by the various devices and pretensions with which the possession of your Majesty's person so abundantly furnished those who wished to remove us from your presence. The consequence was, that notwithstanding all the efforts which the circumstances would allow us to make, we came ultimately to be considered as total strangers in your Majesty's palace, and not only to be debarred from your presence, but from a knowledge even of your Majesty's condition. This exclusion was rendered the more mortifying and irksome to us by our knowledge, that while we were debarred from your presence, many other persons who are neither connected with your Majesty by blood, nor, as we believe, attached to your Majesty by sincere affection, as we are, had free admission whenever they desired it.

It had been the practice of your physicians to send me every day a written account of your Majesty's health, and this communication was naturally somewhat more particular than the public account communicated at St. James's to all the world. It was in fact the only distinction that was made between myself and the rest of your Majesty's subjects. Your Majesty cannot better learn the degree in which it was intended to exclude your sons from intercourse with your Majesty, and knowledge of your situation, than by hearing that an express order was delivered by authority to your Majesty's physicians to refrain from communicating to me any other account of your Majesty's health than that which was transmitted daily to the lord in waiting at St. James's for the information of the public.

I could not, Sir, but feel, in common with my brother, the Duke of York, both grief and mortification at being thus separated and severed, as it were, from your Majesty's person and family. I have had much reason to lament it since, for reasons which may perhaps throw some light on the motive of those who brought it about. For, from the first moment of your Majesty's joyful recovery, your Majesty's ear has, by the banishment of your sons, been exclusively possessed by those who have unfortunately felt either an interest or inclination to misrepresent our conduct, and hurt us in your opinion. I shall for ever account it the greatest calamity of my life, that in the first period of returning health, when your Majesty's mind was yet free from prejudice, your ear untainted by slander, and your heart, as it ever is, (but most peculiarly so in those moments of softness which succeed affliction and disease,) open to impressions of affection, tenderness, and indulgence, I and my brother, who both have ever loved you, and have never justly forfeited our title to your love, were held in exile from your presence, and condemned to silence, while our enemies were labouring, with every advantage of constant intercourse with your Majesty and the impossibility of being answered, to ruin us in your esteem. Not to dwell any longer, however, on this afflicting topic, I must conclude what I had to offer concerning our private or domestic conduct, with observing that, by the means I have described, neither I nor the Duke of York have had any opportunity subsequent to your Majesty's removal to Kew, to evince either duty or unkindness by any act of ours, relative to your Majesty's health or comfort, during the continuance of your illness. Since that period your Majesty has had an opportunity of witnessing our conduct personally, and I leave it without anxiety to your Majesty's equitable judgment, whether any part of our behaviour has been marked with unkindness, or deficient in every demonstration of love and duty which we have been permitted to offer.

In laying before your Majesty an account of those transactions which may be deemed of a public and political nature, it is with the utmost pain that I must recall to my own memory, and perhaps wound your Majesty's feelings, by alluding to the unhappy necessity which appeared to arise out of your severe malady, for supplying by a temporary Government the lamented absence of your Majesty, during the continuance of your illness. But I rely, both on your Majesty's fortitude, and on the ascendancy which the love of justice has in your mind over every weakness of ordinary natures, for your generous approbation of my resolution to postpone the inferior considerations of sensibility and delicacy, to objects which I know your Majesty rates far higher—the honour of your son, the dignity of your family, and the true interests of your crown and people.

Supported by this reflection, I cannot hesitate to set before you a view of the new, anxious, and arduous situation in which your Majesty's indisposition suddenly placed me, as well,

indeed, as the Legislature and the whole nation. Your kingdom and your family were alike deprived of your Majesty's
superintendence and protection, under which they had both
flourished, and while the novelty of these circumstances,
equally calamitous and unprovided for, seemed to open a new
career to speculating or designing men, and to leave no limits
either to ambition or the love of innovation, there fell at
once upon me, in addition to the affliction of witnessing the
sufferings of a beloved father, a train of cares, trusts, and duties
for which I had no preparation, and in which I had never been
exercised.

I am too thoroughly persuaded of the magnanimity as well as
the justice of your Majesty's character to feel the smallest
apprehension that any indisposition can arise in your Majesty's
mind towards me, from the consideration that all men united
without a single exception in the opinion that the temporary
government ought to be placed in my hands. This appeared a
necessary consequence of the relation which I bear to your
Majesty, and I am sure your Majesty will consider it, as you
justly may, as an acknowledgment made to the claim of your
Majesty's blood; not sought by me nor bestowed by Parliament as a thing personal to myself; or as a claim of mine
distinct from, much less adverse to, your Majesty's personal
interests, or those of your crown.

Such were the circumstances which compelled me to take
any part whatever in the affairs of Government. But I cannot
for a moment deny myself the satisfaction of acquainting your
Majesty, and I hope it will remain strongly impressed on your
Majesty's mind throughout, that this necessity was not declared
by me, but was first announced to the world by your Majesty's
Ministers, who took the lead in proposing and bringing forward
every step that has been made for accomplishing this purpose.
While I was permitted to attend on your Majesty, my whole
mind was engaged, and my whole time employed, in the more
interesting cares of private and domestic duty; I refrained

altogether, by system as well as inclination, from every object of a different nature. The only perfectly true and correct account that can be given of the part which I took respecting public measures and the affairs of Government is, that I industriously avoided taking any part at all; I remained from the beginning wholly passive and neutral, until the steps taken by your Majesty's Ministers called me unavoidably from this retirement into action, and rendered it my indispensable duty to your Majesty, your people, and myself, to direct my most serious attention to the consideration of public affairs.

I must once more implore your Majesty to reflect attentively on this circumstance, and allow to it its due weight in the judgment you are to form of my conduct. It is far from my object in this address to defend the wisdom of all I did, or omitted to do, in this trying situation.

I am little concerned in maintaining the ability or even the prudence of my conduct. But I do feel a deep and warm interest in convincing your Majesty that I have been neither an unnatural son nor an undutiful subject, and that your Majesty has been surprised by the misinformation of designing persons into that imputation which cuts me to the quick, and on which I can never reflect without anguish, of unkindness to your Majesty: on this subject, therefore, your Majesty will surely allow that the circumstance I have dwelt on deserves no slight consideration. The part which would have been taken by an unkind son, impatient to clothe himself in the spoils of an absent father, would have been to precipitate, or at least discover some impatience for, the progress of those proceedings which were to invest him with power; to put himself officiously forward; and to take the lead in measures which he was in haste to see accomplished. In looking into my own heart I am conscious that these were not my dispositions, and in reverting to my conduct, I am happy that I may assert with confidence it does not bear the character or the most distant indication of such a frame of mind. Instead of any impatient precipitation, I persevered so strictly in this resolution of inaction that I abstained, longer perhaps than in such critical and important circumstances I might seem justified in doing, even from consulting and advising with those friends in whose wisdom and integrity I place the greatest confidence. Nor was this conduct an accidental indulgence of indolence and inattention, but it was the result of a deliberate judgment, dictated by those dutiful and affectionate feelings for your Majesty which sprung from the occasion. I must be permitted to claim, with the greater confidence, the full effect of this determination on your Majesty's mind, as it was not adopted without opposition from one in whose opinion I might have been justified for acquiescing, and under the authority of which I might have sheltered an opposite conduct if I had been disposed to adopt it. I was urged, from an honourable opinion I am sure, and one which was sincerely entertained by the person to whom I allude, to come forward much earlier in my own person to claim the government, as falling to me of right during your Majesty's illness, and to take the lead out of the hands of your Majesty's Ministers into my own. Such was the opinion of my uncle, the Duke of Gloucester, and he pressed it on me with all the earnestness which belonged to a sincere and fixed opinion on a subject of such moment. I beg your Majesty to remark that I do not claim any extraordinary merit for rejecting this advice; but I must urge it at least as satisfactory proof that I might have held a conduct of less moderation, and more questionable in point of dutifulness and affection, without forfeiting the esteem of a person in whom your Majesty places justly an eminent degree of confidence, and distinguishes amongst all the members of your family as peculiarly and affectionately devoted to your Majesty. I trust your Majesty will therefore acquit me during this interval of that heavy charge which I am equally incapable of deserving and of supporting without pain; I mean that of unkind and unfilial conduct towards your Majesty.

When the course of events, and the express acts and declarations of your Majesty's Ministers, drew me from this state of voluntary retirement, and placed me of necessity in a situation in which inaction would have been a crime, it is with equal confidence I challenge the whole world to fix on any one of the measures which I had occasion to adopt, a well-grounded imputation, or, as I think, even a rational suspicion, of any motive either adverse or offensive to your Majesty; and I sincerely and unaffectedly profess myself at a loss to conjecture in what part of my conduct or that of my brother, it has been possible for our common enemies to find even a plausible colour for their slander. It would be in vain for me, I know, to direct my conjectures to this or that particular circumstance, because I am quite sure that all are equally free from this reproach; and in my desire to give your Majesty complete satisfaction on this interesting subject, and to stand acquitted in your Majesty's judgment on sure grounds, I seem to have no other part left than to recite to your Majesty every act, either of mine or my brother's, during this lamented period of time, and to submit, by this means, the whole of our conduct to your Majesty's scrutiny and judgment. By the blessings of Providence your Majesty's speedy and happy recovery at once afforded me the joy of seeing your Majesty restored to the vows of your family and people, and put an early period to that anxiety, solicitude, and embarrassment which had fallen on me in that calamitous season. I deem it most fortunate that I never was invested with the trust of conducting the administration of public affairs in your Majesty's name; and the acts which I had occasion to do were, therefore, very few in number, and incapable of furnishing any important consequences. Such as they were, permit me now to lay them before your Majesty; and so far from anxiety or alarm, natural perhaps on any occasion which is thus interesting, I solemnly declare that I date from this moment the first return of that composure and peace of mind of which the cares of my new and arduous situation, succeeded and aggravated by the apprehension of your Majesty's displeasure, had deprived me for many months past. In your Majesty's candid examination of my conduct I see the sure prospect of regaining the blessings of your love and approbation; and these I shall ever deem an ample compensation for all the disquietude which my enemies have hitherto succeeded in giving me.

The first public act in which I had any share was a declaration made at my request by my brother, the Duke of York, to the House of Lords, speaking in his place as a peer of Parliament on the 15th of December.

It will be necessary to state in a very few words the subject which was then under consideration. Instead of proceeding to settle the mode in which the Government was to be exercised in your Majesty's name, your Majesty's Ministers thought proper to propose that the two Houses of Parliament should first vote an abstract proposition declaratory of their rights on that occasion. This proceeding appearing to us, both unnecessary and dangerous in itself, we could not help considering it, in the intention of those by whom it was proposed, as a measure of pure hostility to me. We were sure at least that its tendency was necessarily injurious in the highest degree to my reputation in the country. I was informed that it was not usual for Parliament to come to verbal declarations of their rights previous to exercising them, and that such a measure has only been resorted to in those cases where the jealousy of Parliament has been excited by attempts from some adequate authority to dispute or to defeat the privilege which they have asserted. The declaration of the rights of Parliament on this occasion did undoubtedly convey to the world an insinuation that they had been attacked; and as there existed at the time no authority which could give weight or importance to such an attack but mine, the eyes of the world were naturally drawn towards me, and the nation was taught to believe that

I had begun the public career to which I was unfortunately called, by some attempt or some claim inimical to the constitution and liberties of the country. I have however the satisfaction to assure your Majesty that the contrary was the case, and that I had never made, either directly or indirectly, any claim whatever. I know with certainty that no claim was ever offered to either House of Parliament by my authority, and I will venture to assure your Majesty that none was ever made or hinted at in my name without my authority. Much pains indeed were taken to misinterpret some sentiments expressed in debate by persons in whom I avow that I place confidence ; and to treat them as propositions dangerous to the rights of Parliament. I cannot in general be supposed to know correctly what passes in debate in the House of Commons, but I have reasons on which I can depend, and which enable me confidently to assure your Majesty, not only that the sentiments alluded to were not such as they were, for obvious purposes, grossly misrepresented over the whole nation to be, but that they were rendered so clear and explicit by frequent ample and satisfactory explanation that it was impossible even to misapprehend them ; and that the scandalous and libellous perversion of detached words in debate, which were so diligently dispersed from one end of the kingdom to the other, could be the work only of a policy, equally indifferent to truth, and adverse to your Majesty, your family, and the welfare and tranquillity of the nation. On the other hand, it will not be denied that in pronouncing these opinions, consonant as they were alike with the interests of your Majesty's family and the privileges of Parliament, all authority from me and all communication with me on this subject was explicitly disclaimed at the very time by the person who delivered those sentiments. In these circumstances I confess I was exceedingly anxious, first to avert a measure which I thought injurious to my credit in the nation, by removing the only ground on which it seemed possible to induce Parliament to adopt it ; and next, if that could not be obtained, but the proposition should pass, my object was to obviate and counteract its ill effects by opposing a solemn and express declaration of my own to the inference which would otherwise arise to my disadvantage out of that measure.

In this view, and in this view alone, I authorised my brother, the Duke of York, to declare in my name to the House of Lords in substance that " I had never declared any opinion whatever concerning this important question, and that, so far from urging any claim on that occasion, I was too well acquainted with and revered too much those principles which had seated the House of Brunswick on the throne of these kingdoms, to form a wish for the exercise of any power which should not be sanctioned by that House, and the representatives of the people in Parliament assembled."

The Duke of York delivered these sentiments to the House of Lords in my name, and deprecated the agitation of that delicate and dangerous question, in circumstances which could furnish no ground for such a discussion, after the declaration he had just made by my authority ; and he even entreated the House not to add to the embarrassment of a family already sufficiently afflicted, by the agitation of a question which could only tend to inflame the minds of the nation by groundless alarm, at a time when temper and composure were most essential.

Having laid this account before your Majesty, I am confident that you will discover no trace, either of an unkind or undutiful disposition towards your Majesty, in the anxiety I testified to avert the unnecessary discussion of questions so full of delicacy, and perhaps peril, as those which relate to the disposal of sovereign power, nor any disregard for the constitution and privileges of Parliament in my declaring an implicit acquiescence, under their pleasure, and disclaiming every other title. With regard to the proposition itself, which, contrary to my hopes, passed the two Houses, considering it as an act of theirs, it is now entitled to my respect, and ceases to be a fit object of my observation. But I am well assured that your

Majesty would not condemn the caution which led us to deprecate the agitation of that delicate question, and would surely not charge us on that account with any disregard for your Majesty's personal interests, or those which are most nearly personal to your Majesty—those of your family, if your Majesty had had an opportunity of being acquainted with the nature and tendency of propositions entertained, and even tendered to the nation, though unsuccessfully, indeed, at that critical and speculating period, by a person who stood the highest in authority, and in your Majesty's confidence. These propositions were indeed neither adopted by the two Houses nor countenanced by the concurrence of any one opinion besides.

The sincere respect which I entertain for the acts of the two Houses of Parliament does not, therefore, preclude me from submitting to your Majesty whether some danger might not be reasonably and sincerely apprehended, both to the Monarchy and to the Constitution in all its points, from a discussion which could furnish an opportunity for promulgating from such a quarter an opinion which went to the total extinction, for the time being, of every existing principle of our Government; throwing open to arbitrary and undefined discretion every point of our Constitution, both as to persons or powers ; and well calculated, undoubtedly, to prepare—if such a project could anywhere have existed—a competition for the sovereign authority, throughout the British empire, to the exclusion of every one of your Majesty's blood.

In this light did the opinions, distinctly and repeatedly delivered by your Majesty's Minister, Mr. Pitt, on this question of right appear to me, and I am not without grounds for supposing that they must have conveyed a similar impression to most other men; since all the support which Mr. Pitt is accustomed to find, and actually obtained throughout the strongest measures which he ventured to propose in this extraordinary crisis, could not however procure for him one assenting

voice to the sentiments I have alluded to ; and your Majesty's
Attorney-General, who must no doubt be supposed in general
to act in concurrence with your Majesty's Minister, delivered,
however, on this occasion an opinion diametrically opposite to
the doctrine of Mr. Pitt.

If such then was the complexion of the opinions delivered to
the nation by a person who was to be the author and proposer
of every measure, and to whose ambition no limits had yet
been found, your Majesty, I am sure, will not condemn the
solicitude of those who are attached to the established Constitution of your kingdom and to the rights of your Majesty's
family, when they saw this question insisted upon as a preliminary; and when the person I have described professed to
wrap up in mystery, and to conceal and withhold from the
world, the nature and extent of his projects till Parliament
should entertain a question, which, while it was obviously
unnecessary for any beneficial object, or for the attainment of
any point conformable to the regular order and spirit of the Constitution, must have been naturally the first step towards accomplishing any novel and sinister purpose. It is therefore worthy of
remark, that the proposition adopted by the two Houses, but
proposed by Mr. Pitt, was accordingly conceived in terms so
equivocal, that while they might entrap the assent of moderate
and well-meaning men, they were at the same time capable
of justifying the wildest opinions, and favouring the most
extravagant and fatal designs of others.

I leave it to your Majesty to decide what good constitutional purpose could possibly be answered by a declaration
couched in language so equivocal as to be incapable of being
fixed to any precise or determinate meaning. An attack on
the privileges of Parliament could not be very formidable
which was to be defeated by a Declaration, which does not
assert those rights intelligibly, and leaves them exactly in the
same doubt and obscurity as before. If the right of the two
Houses to interpose, and to declare in the first instance the

manner in which the temporary defect in the personal exercise
of the Royal authority should be supplied, and if the duty of
the two Houses to act in this interposition according to the
best of its judgment, was all that the Declaration meant, it
could not be necessary to make it ; for that right and duty, so
far from being questioned, were explicitly maintained by every
body without exception : and the only question was, whether
the Constitution did not furnish some fixed and certain
principle, according to which it was the duty of the two
Houses, in the present circumstances, to settle the temporary
Government ; or whether they were left, without the obligation
of any rule or principle, to an absolute and unconstrained
choice, according to their pleasure, or even according to any
loose idea of present and occasional expediency.   But, if any
arbitrary right of election, and an unconstrained discretion as
to the form and powers of the temporary Government, was
the privilege meant to be asserted, the Declaration does
certainly not answer the purpose ; and by avoiding to express
that meaning in plain and positive terms, may be thought to
leave it more questionable, and to discountenance that
doctrine by something like the authority of Parliamentary
doubt and hesitation, much more than the sentiments of any
individual could possibly do.   If no real object of constitutional importance could be sincerely proposed by him who
chose ambiguous and equivocal phrases in a Declaration of
Right, (not necessary in itself, even if it had been expressed
clearly,) I have already laid before your Majesty the view
which I cannot help entertaining of another purpose, which
might be better reconciled with this measure.

I shall only add that what I did on this occasion was
entirely approved of by both my uncles, and the Duke of
Gloucester, in his place in the House of Lords, joined my
brother the Duke of York, in deprecating the agitation of this
question.

The next act of mine which can be in any sense con-

sidered as a measure was the reply which I sent on the 2nd of
January to Mr. Pitt's letter of the 30th of December. Your
Majesty is already in possession of both these papers, and if
your Majesty will condescend to peruse them once more, I am
so confident that your Majesty will not discover a word or a
sentiment of mine which is deficient in filial affection or in a
dutiful and zealous attachment to your Majesty's interest and
honour, that I shall not think it necessary to trouble your
Majesty with much comment on that paper.

My view of the situation I was about to fill was this, that
I was to be invested with a double trust, one for your
Majesty, the other for your people; that the duties, however,
of both these trusts were fortunately not opposed to each
other, but the same. I owed it to your Majesty to preserve
entire for your Majesty, when you should resume your government, the rights, powers, and dignity of your crown such as
you had before enjoyed them; and I owed it also to your
Majesty to fulfil the objects of your Royal power by protecting
your people from foreign danger and providing for its internal
tranquillity, prosperity, and happiness. On the other hand, I was
responsible in like manner to my country for all the advantages
it can derive from a vigilant and efficient Government, and as
one means of happiness for the preservation of the Constitution
in all its parts, but more particularly in that branch which was
thus committed to my care—I mean the rights of your
Majesty's Crown—I conceived that all the existing powers
entrusted to the Crown in the regular course of the Constitution are deemed necessary for the discharge of these duties,
and are thought no more than commensurate with the object
for which alone any power whatever is delegated to sovereigns.

I was sensible that the station which I was to hold, must
out of necessity be weaker, for many obvious reasons, than the
regular government of a sovereign administering permanent
power in his own name and in his own behalf. I thought
therefore that all the powers and capacities which were deemed

necessary for enabling the Crown to maintain its own right in
the Constitution, and to discharge the functions of good
government with benefit to the people, were yet more indispensable in the representative and temporary authority which
I was to possess. I am sure your Majesty will not think these
principles wholly devoid of reason, nor will you think it
inimical to your Majesty's interest and honour, in one who was
becoming responsible for both, that he should not see himself
deprived of the natural means for preserving these objects
without anxiety and remonstrance; I can only assure your
Majesty, in the most solemn and serious manner, that this, and
this only, was the principle which induced me to complain of
the mutilation proposed to be made during your Majesty's
unfortunate inability to protect them, of the accustomed and
the most efficient powers and prerogatives of your Crown.

If these reasons might justify my apprehensions at being
entrusted with the whole duties, but with only a portion
of the power belonging to Royal authority, your Majesty will
see that it follows necessarily from the same principle that my
difficulties, and therefore my uneasiness and alarm, should be
still greater when I saw not only many powers cut off from
the authority which I was to administer, but some of those
very powers of which I was deprived erected into a distinct,
separate, independent, and perhaps, therefore, adverse authority
in the state; and those very arms which are intended for the
defence of the Crown and the service of regular government,
disposed of in such a manner as to be capable of being employed
in defeating and destroying them.

I could not, at the same time, but lament one consequence
which appeared too likely to follow from the proposed arrangement, of placing a considerable department of power and
influence in the hands of the Queen.

I had been accustomed to see her Majesty engaged solely
in domestic cares and occupations, and while her Majesty's
mind had been thus employed, I had experienced at her hands

from my infancy the strongest and most invariable marks of
parental tenderness and even of personal partiality and fond-
ness.   Her affection had always been one of the first joys
and the principal pride of my life.   It was not, therefore,
without much solicitude and pain that I perceived a scheme
formed for creating between us a rival and separate interest,
and endangering domestic harmony by political competition. I
confess, Sir, it was with the most acute pain that I saw her
Majesty set up by designing men as the head of a system,
which I must frankly and without reserve say I could not
ascribe to any solicitude for your Majesty's happiness, or
connect by any rational principle with your substantial interests,
to every one of which I thought it dangerous and adverse in
the extreme ; but which I considered as a device of private
ambition, which aimed at the accomplishment of its own projects by contention with me and opposition to the very power
it was constrained to establish in one degree or other in my
hands. By your Majesty's fortunate and auspicious resumption
of your own authority, the public evils which appeared to
menace both your Majesty's authority and the interests of your
people have been avoided.   I wish the domestic affliction
which I apprehended had been as happily averted.   But this
is a theme on which I cannot turn my thoughts without the
most sincere grief, and which I should only wound your
Majesty's feelings unnecessarily by dwelling on.

I cannot, however, quit this subject without expressing to
your Majesty the resentment I felt at seeing a system, which
appeared to me destructive of every object which I know your
Majesty, as a wise and good sovereign, as well as a father and
chief of a family, must hold most dear and valuable, justified by
a reference to the meanest and most unworthy feelings which
were supposed to exist in your Majesty's mind, and which I
felt to be a cruel slander on your Majesty's character.   The
separation of the whole of your Majesty's household, to an
extent even which could not be at first avowed, but was covered

under the equivocal and undefined sense of that word, from the
dignity, the patronage, and influence of your Majesty's representative, was defended on a ground which I am sure your
Majesty will feel to be injurious to your magnanimity and
public spirit. It was contended that your Majesty's private
and personal feelings might be wounded by the arrangements
which, without a colour of authority or probability, were
assumed as a thing intended by me, if I had had the control of
that department. This indecent argument supposed that your
Majesty would be less hurt at finding the authority and dignity
of your Crown impaired, the public service obstructed, and
your son and heir (representing yourself) degraded in the eyes of
the world, than by finding some officer of your household displaced. Sir, I deemed such sentiments abominable and detestable libels on your Majesty; yet I cannot deny myself the
satisfaction of assuring your Majesty that the supposition on
which this reasoning proceeded was as false and injurious with
regard to me as to your Majesty. I assure your Majesty that
no arrangement of the offices in your Majesty's household,
which I could have thought displeasing to your Majesty, could
possibly have obtained my consent, if I had been entrusted
with that department; and that, next to the great interests of
your Crown and people, your Majesty's personal wishes and
feelings, so far as I was capable of discovering or conjecturing
them, would have been my law in the direction of that
object.

I trust your Majesty will not, therefore, consider the
objections which I thought it my duty to make to this part of
Mr. Pitt's scheme, as indications of an undutiful disposition to
your Majesty, but will rather believe that they were founded
solely on principles of regard for your Majesty's real and permanent interests, as well as for the happiness and welfare of
your subjects. I thought your Majesty's interests would be
best provided for by maintaining the union of all the powers
and capacities of your Crown; I thought the dignity of your

Majesty's representative was in fact, in those circumstances of
your Majesty's personal retirement, the dignity of your Majesty;
and I could not see how your personal splendour was to be
better secured by detaching it from your authority, and conferring its influence on a stranger to your Crown. I know that
your first feelings were for the great interests of the Constitution and the prosperity of the people, and that all other feelings
of a private and personal nature were subordinate in your
Majesty's mind to these higher considerations. I well knew
besides, that, consistently with these objects, your Majesty's
private wishes and feelings were as sacred in my mind, and as
secure from offence in my hands, as in any to which they could
be entrusted.

There remains, before I quit this subject, one consideration
on which I confess myself anxious to say a few words, I mean
the general principle which was chosen to justify the mutilation of the powers of the Crown during the temporary government; namely, that it was necessary, in order to secure the
restoration of your Majesty to the exercise of your lawful
authority, when the recovery of your Majesty's health should
induce you to resume it. On this head I have but a word
to say: I could not help being extremely wounded by the
reflection that it should be thought necessary to cripple
Government, to disjoint the Constitution, to obstruct the present
prosperity of the people, and to endanger the future and permanent interests of your Majesty and your family, in order to
secure your Majesty against a monstrous and detestable usurpation of your throne by a son who loves and reveres you.
I am conscious that your Majesty was safer with me than with
any other persons who could have been entrusted with the
temporary representation of your Majesty; I know that if I had
been capable of the diabolical depravity which this principle
supposes, the Constitution of my country is fortunately too
strong and inflexible to leave the possibility of accomplishing
such crimes; and what is the best security of all, the virtue,

loyalty, and rational attachment, and devotion of this happy people to their Sovereign and father, afforded a better protection to your Majesty than any suspension and departure from the Constitution could have done. I profess, therefore, never to have believed that this was the true object proposed by this scheme; I considered it only as the pretext which was thought most plausible and most congenial with the affection and sensibility of your Majesty's people in that moment of public solicitude and sympathy; but intended in fact to cover objects of a very different nature, which it was obviously calculated, with much more prudence and wisdom, to effectuate. Your Majesty cannot help perceiving that this scheme of a mutilated and distracted Government suited admirably the views of those whose private ambition might be thought to require that the Government which it was to combat, and which it might hope to force, should be feeble and unable to resist it. I hope therefore your Majesty will reject that grand fundamental principle which has been too successfully imposed on part of the public, and has, no doubt, been offered to your Majesty; that in the settlement of the Government during your Majesty's indisposition, my interests were adverse to those of your Majesty; and that whatever was retrenched from that authority which was to be exercised in your Majesty's name, and on your behalf, are somehow or other to be considered as so much acquired or preserved for your Majesty. The contrary is my sincere opinion. It is my firm conviction that no part or branch of your Majesty's authority could either have been more secure by being suspended and put in abeyance, or could have been lodged in hands more faithful, or disposed of in a manner more beneficial to the interests of your Majesty's Crown and people, than by following the established order of the Constitution and placing the usual powers of the Crown entire and operative to all their purposes in the representative of your Royal authority.

The next measure I was called upon to take, was to deliver

my answer to the message of the two Houses when they offered me the Regency and acquainted me with the conditions on which it was to be established.

My answer is before your Majesty, and seems to me to furnish so little matter of reproach, and so little hold to any degree of possible misconstruction, that I shall content myself with annexing it to this paper, entreating your Majesty to observe whether it contains an undutiful word to your Majesty, or a thought that is offensive to Parliament or adverse to the Constitution.

I did not feel myself called upon to take any step subsequent to this, till it was proposed to frame a Commission in your Majesty's name, but by the sole authority of the two Houses for opening the Parliament. I learnt at the same time, that it was intended to insert my name in the Commission, and thus make me a party in that proceeding.

I authorised my brother, the Duke of York, to desire in the House of Lords, in my behalf, that my name should not stand in the Commission. He did so; and both he and my uncles, the Dukes of Gloucester and Cumberland, expressed the same desire to have their names omitted, which was accordingly done. It is certainly impossible to attribute this act to any disregard in us for your Majesty's interest and dignity. We took this measure on the very contrary principle. Not to enter at length into the discussion of a point, which by much diligence was converted into one of the most abstruse questions ever debated in Constitutional controversy, I will lay before your Majesty the general and ruling principle which governed my conduct on this occasion. I knew that whatever was necessary to be done towards supplying the exercise of the Royal authority during its temporary deficiency, must be done substantially by the authority of the two remaining branches of the Legislature, and derived, in fact, none of its validity from the assent of the third, which was known to be unattainable. A necessity for a departure from the regular

Constitution arose out of the peculiar situation of things, and of this necessity I knew that every one could judge. I saw therefore no mischief to the Constitution in submitting to an obvious necessity, while the whole world had an opportunity of considering the truth and appreciating the degree of that necessity. But I thought that if this irregular act were clothed in the regular formalities of the Constitution ; and were exhibited to the people in a form which seemed in their eyes to leave no deficiency ; and if a precedent were thus formed for enabling the two Houses to exercise by their own authority the prerogatives of the Crown in such a way as that it should not appear on the very face of the proceeding to be an act of necessity, and to be judged of and acquiesced in only as such ; a great shock would be given to the most established principles of the Constitution, by teaching us to be contented with fiction instead of reality, even on points which of all others are the most essential and the least capable of being supplied by form, and a power of innovation and usurpation would be introduced, of which it would be impossible to compute the extent, or limit the progress.

Without, therefore, presuming to question now the wisdom or propriety of the resolution taken by the two Houses, I trust your Majesty will consider these reasons as a sufficient justification for my anxiety to withdraw myself from any personal participation in a proceeding of which I entertain these sentiments.

Having laid before your Majesty everything which relates to the internal affairs of Great Britain, permit me next to inform your Majesty of my conduct in relation to your Majesty's kingdom of Ireland.

The Commissioners deputed by the two Houses of Parliament in that kingdom arrived in London, and presented to me the Address, which your Majesty will find annexed, the —— day of February.

That Address which had been voted by the two Houses of Parliament in Ireland, at a time when they still laboured under the common calamity which had afflicted every part of your Majesty's dominions, arrived, however, in England at a period when a more happy prospect had opened to this country, and the joyful hope was entertained of your Majesty's speedy recovery.

In these circumstances, I delivered the answer which is also annexed.

Your Majesty will find in that paper sentiments of regard for the Parliament and people of Ireland which their known loyalty to your Majesty's Royal House on all occasions, and their expressions of personal affection and attachment for your Majesty, conveyed in this Address, were entitled to from every one of your Majesty's family.

These are sentiments, which I am well assured your Majesty entertains also for your Kingdom of Ireland, and that so far from offending against my duty to your Majesty or risking your displeasure by delivering to a solemn deputation from their Parliament the strongest assurances of respect and affection, I could not concur more entirely with your Majesty's own gracious dispositions, nor more surely entitle myself to your Majesty's approbation. I trust, at the same time, that while I conveyed my genuine feelings on this subject, your Majesty will not discover a word in my communications with the Commissioners, which is not expressive of every degree of filial duty and love which it is possible for the most affectionate son to entertain.

The daily progress made in your Majesty's happy recovery had given me hopes that I might have an opportunity of receiving your Majesty's commands on this important business. But the caution deemed necessary at this early period of convalescence deprived me of that satisfaction, and I was constrained once more to consult my own judgment in the final answer with which the Commissioners returned to Ireland.

I have also annexed that paper, and think myself secure in leaving it to your Majesty's perusal without further observation.

I should deem this address to your Majesty imperfect, if I omitted to lay before you the few steps which I found it my duty to take respecting your Majesty's Electoral dominions and some of the foreign powers of Europe. The measures which I had occasion to take on these subjects are of a nature which require so little explanation that I need hardly do more for your Majesty's satisfaction than beg your Majesty's perusal of the papers which you will find annexed.

With regard to the Electorate of Hanover, as the suspension of your Majesty's personal government in every branch had been declared to the world by the Parliament of Great Britain, your Majesty will easily conceive that a long interval in the administration of a country circumstanced as Hanover is, could not but occasion many present inconveniences, and, yet more, furnish matter for serious reflection and vigilant attention to those who felt any anxiety for the security and tranquillity of your dominions. These considerations were enhanced by the situation of foreign affairs, and the state of continental politics at the time; and they acquired additional confirmation from intelligence which I had received. I could have no doubt, therefore, that it would be highly improper and prejudicial to your Majesty's interests that your Electoral dominions should remain longer without an ostensible authority, exercised in your Majesty's name, and in your Majesty's behalf; and the length of time required by the course which Parliament had adopted for settling the Government in this country, rendered it highly unadvisable to leave your foreign dominions in a state of dereliction until the Regency should be completed in all its formalities at home. There was no question in England concerning the person who was to exercise your Majesty's authority there in your name; nor could there be any in Hanover concerning the person on whom the administration of your Majesty's Electoral dominions in your name must fall during this interval.   In this situation the considerations I have described suggested it to me, as a duty which I owed to your Majesty, as well as to your Majesty's Electoral subjects, to leave them no longer in these critical circumstances, exposed either to foreign or domestic disturbances, and I delivered to Mr. Alvensleben the significa- tion of my intentions which your Majesty will find annexed.

A necessary consequence of this measure was the commu- nication which I made of it to the King of Prussia. My letter to his Prussian Majesty is annexed, and your Majesty will see my sole aim was to express a conformity with that system which your Majesty had thought it proper to adopt in the political administration of your German dominions.

Trusting that these steps cannot be imputed to any motive but an anxious regard for your Majesty's interests, and that they must receive your Majesty's approbation, as necessary both for the security of those dominions and the tranquillity and happiness of its inhabitants, I will detain your Majesty no longer on that subject.

Similar considerations induced me to take those measures which your Majesty will find comprised in the annexed cor- respondence with some of the foreign Courts.

All public business whatever had been suspended in the foreign department of your Majesty's Government for a con- siderable period of time, and all political intercourse between your Majesty's kingdom and foreign powers was at a stand.

It cannot be imagined that a considerable interruption in the political communication between your Majesty's kingdom and the Continent could exist without inconvenience at any period of time; but the particular circumstances of Europe rendered it peculiarly essential, at that moment, that a friendly intercourse with your Majesty's allies should be renewed and kept alive.   For this reason, it appeared to me an indispensable duty to acquaint the Prussian and Dutch ministers that the treaties of alliance contracted between your Majesty and their Courts would be faithfully observed, and the same system which your Majesty had approved would be strictly adhered to in every event which could take place in the government of this country.

I have only to express my firm assurance that your Majesty will see in these transactions no other principle than that of solicitude for the essential interests of your Majesty's Government, and a dutiful spirit of acquiescence and conformity with your Majesty's pleasure and intentions whenever I could discover them.

After having been under the necessity of fatiguing your Majesty's attention with the unavoidable length of this paper, I can only recall to your Majesty's recollection, that with the most perfect consciousness of duty and affection to your Majesty, and of zeal for the happiness of my country in every act of my life, the peculiar circumstances of hardship which I have related, left to me and my brother no choice but that of either submitting to the calumny of our enemies, and thus subscribing to our own disgrace and condemnation, or redeeming your Majesty's love, which is the first and dearest blessing of our lives, by an ample account and, we trust, a satisfactory justification of all our actions.

[With this memorial was written an introductory letter for the King's perusal, complaining in bitter terms of the Queen's treatment of her sons. This was also the composition of Sir Gilbert Elliot, and deserves insertion as a picture of the hostile spirit engendered by the discussions on the Regency, but it was not transmitted to the King. Before it was delivered to him a meeting was held on the 24th of June at Carlton House, attended by the Duke of

Portland, Mr. Fox, Lord Loughborough, Mr. Burke, Sir Gilbert Elliot, the Duke of Clarence, and the Prince of Wales. At this meeting the Duke of Portland and Lord Loughborough objected to the introductory letter as imposing upon the King the necessity of judging between the Princes and the Queen, who having entire possession of his confidence would assuredly obtain a favourable decision, the consequence of which would be, that the Princes and their friends would be forbad the Court and the Queen left entire mistress of the field. It was therefore agreed that the introductory letter should be suppressed, and that a short letter, expressing in general terms the Prince's uneasiness under his father's displeasure, and stating that he had prepared a justification of his conduct to be submitted to the King, should be substituted for it.]

[No draft or copy of this short letter recommended at this meeting has been found among Mr. Fox's papers. But it seems not improbable that a letter, published by Mr. Moore in his Life of Sheridan, from a rough copy of Mr. Sheridan's, was the letter written on that occasion. It answers to the description of the letter ordered to be written ; but if so, it was not finished or transmitted to the King before the middle of August. The original letter, written by Sir Gilbert Elliot, is subjoined.]

THE PRINCE OF WALES TO THE KING.

" Sir,

" I find myself at last not only at liberty, but I think, invited by your Majesty to throw myself at your feet and implore of your justice and paternal goodness, at least an equitable, if not a partial and indulgent hearing to the most solemn and anxious address that was ever made by a son to a father.

" During the calamitous period of your Majesty's late illness, I waited with impatience for that happy time when the recovery of your health might afford me an opportunity of appealing to your justice and affection, against the misrepresentations of those whose situations might enable them to pre-occupy your Majesty's first opinions.

" I had reason to believe that attempts would be made to prejudice me in your esteem, and God knows my apprehensions have been too well justified by the event. Urgent, however, as I felt this concern to be, I was unwilling to disturb the first hours of your returning health by any matter however important to myself, which might either fatigue your attention or agitate your spirits; I refrained accordingly from pressing any application on the subject, till I was given to understand, with a joy which was shared indeed by the whole nation, but chiefly felt by me, that your health was perfectly confirmed. Since that period I have sought every opportunity of engaging your Majesty's attention to a subject which weighed so heavily on my mind. But in vain ! Your Majesty has either been surrounded by persons whose presence rendered it improper to explain myself on delicate and confidential points ; or if ever I have had the happiness to enjoy a few moments of your presence alone, I have on such occasions been expressly enjoined either by your Majesty or the Queen to abstain from all points of business whatever.

"I was not satisfied with seeking every opportunity to make a verbal explanation at your Majesty's feet; the difficulties which opposed my personal communication with your Majesty induced me, amongst other reasons, to have recourse also to my pen; and I flattered myself, that some moments of leisure, and some periods of strength would be found for perusing the justification of a son whose accusers, I too well knew, had procured, or rather constantly possessed, the means to be heard. When I considered the interesting nature of the subject, and still more the awe which I never fail to experience in your Majesty's presence, it was my wish to address your Majesty in writing, because it would both enable me to lay the matter before your Majesty in a more correct and satisfactory form, and would afford your Majesty an opportunity of bestowing on it a more deliberate consideration than any verbal conference could do alone.

"In this view I collected some papers, which I thought important towards informing your Majesty of the transactions in which the course of events had involved me, and I proposed to annex some observations explanatory of my conduct. I delivered the papers to the Queen, requesting her to communicate them to your Majesty when she should find a convenient opportunity. I was constrained to trouble her Majesty with this application, partly by the fear of intruding unseasonably on your Majesty after your long illness, and partly by the obstacles which I found perpetually in the way of a personal interview; as well indeed as the express injunctions I had received to refrain from addressing your Majesty on business.

"Having waited for some time with great anxiety the effect of this communication, and a public intimation having been given to Parliament of the joyful event of your Majesty's recovery, I addressed to the Queen the following letter :—

" ' Dear Madam,

" ' I have this moment learned that Mr. Pitt has announced to the House of Commons that a communication is to be made to Parliament from his Majesty on Tuesday next.

" ' Your Majesty will, I am sure, have observed that notwithstanding the impatience I must naturally feel to have a fit opportunity of submitting to his Majesty a faithful statement of my conduct and my sentiments on the conduct of others, I have abstained from every idea of intruding on his Majesty's attention until the opinion of those who can best judge shall point out the proper time for submitting matters of business and public importance to his consideration.

" ' The notice given to-day I conceive to ascertain this point, and as your Majesty was graciously pleased to assure me that the papers I lodged in your Majesty's hands should be communicated to his Majesty the moment it was fit for him to attend to public business, I request from your Majesty to be informed whether the present is a proper time to make that communication, and when in consequence my brother and myself may attend his Majesty upon a subject so interesting to our feelings, and the duty we owe to his Majesty and the public.'

" This letter was written on the 5th of March; and the next day I received an answer from her Majesty, acquainting me, ' that she had taken an opportunity of mentioning to your Majesty that she was in possession of those papers, and must now leave it to your Majesty's own judgment when you would think it proper to peruse them.'

" On the day following I received another letter from the Queen, enclosing one from your Majesty to her, both of which I take the liberty of copying in this place :—

THE QUEEN TO THE PRINCE OF WALES.

" 'Kew, *March 7th,* 1789.

" ' My dearest Son,

" ' I found an opportunity of communicating to the King your letter of the day before yesterday, to which he has given me the enclosed in answer; and as this paper contains his Majesty's sentiments upon the subject, I have nothing further to say, but hope that you are convinced of my having fulfilled your wishes, and that you will believe me sincerely,

" ' My dearest Son,

" ' Your very affectionate

" ' Mother and Friend,

" 'CHARLOTTE.'

" This letter enclosed the following from your Majesty to the Queen :—

THE KING TO THE QUEEN.

" ' Kew, *March 6th,* 1789.

" ' *Friday evening.*

" ' My dearest Charlotte,

" ' As I cannot but be deeply impressed by the considera-tion of how much you must have been afflicted by the long continuance of my illness, and the events that attended it, I cannot but wish to prevent your having any further trouble concerning it; and therefore desire you will acquaint both the Prince of Wales and Frederick, that, though I do not mean to decline giving that attention to public business which may be necessary, yet that I propose avoiding all discussions that may in their nature agitate me, and consequently must for the

present decline entering on any subjects that are not necessarily
before me.

> " ' I shall ever remain,
>   " ' My dearest Charlotte,
>   " ' Your most affectionate husband,
>   " ' GEORGE R.'

"I found myself unhappily constrained to submit to this
declaration of your Majesty's pleasure, and I saw with grief
every means of setting myself right in your opinion denied me.
In this situation I could only resort to one sentiment capable
of affording me either hope or consolation.   I reflected on
your Majesty's habitual love and practice of justice, and on
the tenderness and affection which I had experienced on many
occasions at the hand of an indulgent father.   I judged that
the attempts of my enemies to deprive me of your love and
good opinion must probably have been abortive; for I could
not believe that your Majesty would either reject a reply to
any accusation which you deemed worthy of attention, or
would condemn your sons unheard on any charge, whether
grave or frivolous.   I confess, however, that the implicit
confidence I should naturally have placed in this affection was
much diminished, and very painful alarms were raised in my
mind by many circumstances which I could not help observing.
These were by degrees multiplied in such a manner as to leave
me little doubt; and I now see at length my worst fears
verified, and my misfortune too fully authenticated under your
Majesty's hand, by a clear declaration of displeasure, and an
explicit condemnation of my conduct on the tenderest point,
conveyed *in writing* to one of my brothers.   Many of the
circumstances which gave me reason to apprehend some prejudice in your Majesty's mind against me, are of a nature which
it is difficult or impossible to describe in words, or to render
sensible to others by relation, although they furnish too certain

conclusions to those who witness and are the objects of them. Although such as these, however, have often given birth to many painful reflections, I rather choose to select for my present purpose one or two of the more discernible and decisive circumstances, which can neither be controverted nor misunderstood by any one. Of these, the marked exclusion of myself and my brother from every degree of cordial and confidential communication with your Majesty, has been unquestionably one of the least equivocal, and one of the most mortifying symptoms of your Majesty's alienation; yet I would rather rely on a few recent and specific facts which are fresh in your Majesty's recollection. The very extraordinary and, I believe, unparalleled event which has lately taken place between my brother, the Duke of York, and a private gentleman, an officer in his regiment, and a person nearly connected with one of your Majesty's Cabinet-ministers, furnishes me, unfortunately, with too much matter on this subject. I do not wish to trouble your Majesty with a particular examination of all the circumstances which conducted my brother into that transaction, in which, however, I am persuaded your Majesty will be happy, on consideration, to find that the Duke of York has distinguished himself as eminently for sound judgment and an honourable character, as for the spirit and personal courage which belongs to your Majesty's blood. It is not the event itself, but some collateral circumstances attending it which I would advert to.

"Whatever the nature of Mr. Lenox's complaint was, it must be allowed that a challenge from an officer to his Colonel is an unusual transaction, and one which is extremely opposite to the general notions of discipline and subordination in the army. It must be allowed that a challenge from a private man, one of your Majesty's subjects, to a Prince of the Blood, and especially to one so nearly allied to the throne, is still more unusual; and if drawn into a practice, must be deemed productive of very important consequences to the tranquillity of the nation, and the security of the succession in your Majesty's House. Notwithstanding these considerations, the circumstance to which I would draw your Majesty's attention is, that Mr. Lenox was publicly countenanced by your Majesty's Minister the very day on which the event took place; was received the next day in a very public assembly, and on many other occasions since, with every mark of graciousness and favour by the Queen; and is not yet known to have received any signification of your Majesty's displeasure. I must also entreat your Majesty's attention to another most remarkable circumstance: the challenge was delivered to your son; and his antagonist was attended to the field by a Lord of your Majesty's Bedchamber—one who is not merely a political servant, but belongs to your Majesty's family, and is immediately attending on your person. His mother is in the family of the Queen; and he and his family have dwelt almost the whole of their lives at your Court, in your Palace, and enjoying eminently your Majesty's and the Queen's constant favour and bounty.

" Thus circumstanced, Lord Winchelsea did not think it incumbent on him to resign his situation in your Majesty's family, either before or immediately after he had accompanied your son's adversary to the field, where the preparations made by himself prove that he thought the most fatal event might be the issue of the business on which he went. Lord Winchelsea has not been dismissed from your Majesty's service, nor has he received any reprimand or other expression of your Majesty's disapprobation; but still approaches your Majesty's person, and to the world must undoubtedly appear to enjoy at Court the same grace and favour as before this extraordinary transaction. I hope your Majesty will not believe me capable of insinuating that these or any other circumstances can ever convey to my mind the most remote suspicion that to attempt the life of the Duke of York, or to be voluntarily accessary in putting it in danger, or even to be forward in espousing the quarrels of his enemies, are things not displeasing to your Majesty, much less a road to favour. I do most solemnly protest that neither I nor any of my brothers have ever for a moment harboured a thought so undutiful, so monstrous, and, we know, so false and injurious to your Majesty. We are, on the contrary, firmly convinced, and it has been often our only consolation in the midst of our afflictions, of your Majesty's tender, affectionate, and indulgent love for us and all your children. We do assure your Majesty that this is our frequent theme, and that our hearts overflow with gratitude and duty whenever we reflect on your Majesty's kind and paternal disposition, which we acknowledge with joy were never manifested more signally than in the kindness with which we were happy enough to be received by your Majesty, when we were restored to your Majesty's presence on the joyful occasion of your late recovery. On the other hand, we humbly and earnestly entreat your Majesty, on our parts, not to believe those who tell you that we do not love you. Whoever they may be, they are your enemies as well as ours. But it is in proportion to our own affection for your Majesty, to our own confidence in your love, and to the value which we set upon it, that we may contemplate with pain and anxiety every circumstance which to others may seem to render those blessings questionable. Permit me, therefore, to observe to your Majesty, that the world is so framed, and judges so grossly the appearances of things, such as they strike the eye, that undoubtedly, in this late transaction, a most ungracious impression must be made on the minds of many. They will not fail to remark that Mr. Lenox could have no difficulty in finding a second against the Duke of York out of his father's family. They will consider Lord Winchelsea as a forward volunteer in such a business. He will appear to them deserving of your Majesty's displeasure, not only for his readiness to engage in such an undertaking, but for wounding your Majesty's natural feelings, by passing from your bedchamber to a field which was to be

dyed with the blood of your family; and, above all, for daring
to presume on that, which must have been his opinion, that
this step would not indispose your Majesty against him.   He
had to consider that the public could not but be open to such
impressions, and it will appear in their eye a gross violation
of duty and attachment, to have exposed, by any action of his,
your Majesty's name and conduct to the comments of the
world, on a point so delicate and sacred.   He had a character,
as your Majesty's servant, which he ought not to have
sported with, however much as an individual he may be the
master of his own actions.   It is no vindictive desire, Sir, to
draw down your Majesty's anger on Lord Winchelsea that
dictates these observations, but my object is to show that the
impunity of Lord Winchelsea, and the continuance of his
favour, is a circumstance in this event which seems to denote
to ourselves and to the world a diminution of that favour and
partiality which generally belongs to the relation of father
and sons.   But with whatever anxiety we have contemplated
these circumstances, it is with unfeigned sorrow that I must
acknowledge them to be trivial, and their impression on our
minds to be feeble indeed when compared with other considerations of a very different import, which I cannot lay before
your Majesty without pain; but which I cannot either withhold from your notice without the suppression of a truth, fatal
indeed to our repose and happiness, but forming an indispensable part of our case, if we would offer a full and faithful
view of our true situation, with all its embarrassments and
cares.

" As soon as I had learnt the happy account of my brother's
safety, and had received the particulars of the affair from himself, I flew to Kew, in order to communicate to your Majesty
the fortunate issue of a business which had well nigh
proved so fatal.   Your Majesty received the account with all
the tenderness, affection, and anxious sensibility which belong
to your paternal goodness, and which the occasion could

inspire in the breast of the kindest father. It is a matter
then of deep affliction, as well, I am sure, as a circumstance of
great and anxious alarm, that I should be compelled to contrast the deportment of the Queen on this occasion with that
of your Majesty. But was it possible, Sir, that I should not
remark a demeanour so opposite to yours, and so different from
that which the character and affections of a mother would have
surely rendered yet more natural in her even than in your
Majesty ? Your Majesty knows that I had requested a
private audience, and that my wish was to have communicated
this event to your Majesty's ear alone. I considered the
transaction as of too delicate and of much too affecting a
nature to be broken abruptly to the Queen; and it was
therefore with regret that I found myself under the necessity
of relating in her presence an affair, the very nature of
which was agitating to a mother, and in which some circumstances were sufficiently critical and alarming to shake
even the constancy of your Majesty, and to draw from you
expressions of parental solicitude and even horror, which,
while they did honour to your Majesty's feelings, were surely
to be more naturally looked for in a mother on such an
occasion. Your Majesty is my witness, that during the
whole relation the Queen did not utter a syllable either of
alarm at the imminent danger which had threatened the life
of my brother but an hour before, of joy and satisfaction
at his safety, or of general tenderness and affection towards
him, which might appear natural in moments thus afflicting.
Nor were these the only testimonies of indifference that I
was obliged to observe. For your Majesty must well remember that the first word the Queen pronounced, and the
whole tenor of the only conversation she afterwards held, was
a defence of Mr. Lenox's conduct, strongly implying a censure
on that of my brother.

" Sir, this was a critical point of my brother's life ; the
transaction was of a new and most delicate nature. Your

Majesty's opinion was peculiarly interesting, as well as important to him. Your Majesty had not yet pronounced. Neither your Majesty nor the Queen had yet heard my brother on the subject, nor any one on his behalf. He had that very morning most narrowly escaped a violent. death. The Queen is his mother, and had that instant heard his story. In these circumstances, Sir, the first and only sentiment she expressed, implied a condemnation of his conduct, and must therefore have tended to incline your Majesty's judgment also against him.

"The Duke of York had himself the happiness of seeing your Majesty the next day, and enjoyed in that interview the inexpressible satisfaction of receiving from your Majesty every token of tenderness and sensibility which his situation could draw from the best and most affectionate parent. Your Majesty's kindness has been the subject of our admiration and gratitude ever since, and the impression it has made on us can never be erased from our hearts. Your Majesty is again our witness that at this first meeting with the Duke of York, the Queen observed a total silence on the subject which had thus affected your Majesty. This recent and interesting event was not even alluded to, and on such a day her Majesty condescended only to address my brother on the most indifferent topics. Since that period it is matter of public notoriety, and has no doubt been so of public observation, that Mr. Lenox has received the most distinguishing marks of her Majesty's approbation on every occasion on which they could be bestowed, and has been permitted, if not invited, to mix even in the personal society and amusements of your Majesty's family. This conduct I am confident he would not have dared to hold if your Majesty had been present, nor can the world suppose him to have hazarded, what must have appeared even to himself, at least, so shocking an indecorum without being well assured that it would not have been disapproved of by the Queen.

" I am sure your Majesty will not think it unnatural that these circumstances should sensibly afflict and alarm your sons, and we shall not be censured for drawing a rash conclusion, if we believe, that her Majesty's behaviour could not have been such as I have described, unless there had existed in her mind some previous dissatisfaction and some general indisposition towards us, independent of this transaction, and sufficient to extinguish entirely the natural affection and tenderness of a mother. If we observe the common course of nature and consult the happy experience of all other families, we cannot help acknowledging that Providence seems to have designed it as the part of a mother to feel and to express solicitude for the safety of her children; to absorb all other considerations in those of anxiety and tenderness at critical periods of a son's life; to plead his cause, even if it be doubtful; to heal all family differences, if such exist; to soften and conciliate towards her children the mind and opinion of their father, if it is in danger of being estranged : in examining their conduct to leave to others even the impartiality of a judge, but much more, the severe scrutiny of an adverse party, and above all, to leave to their rivals and enemies the care of fomenting the anger of their father, together with that of anticipating, and by that means, perhaps, procuring the condemnation of the world—an effect of her Majesty's unfortunate displeasure, which we have had too many occasions to feel and to lament.

" It is quite impossible, Sir, that we should behold with indifference a departure in our house alone, from that first and best law of nature which protects the harmony of other families, and which, reserving at least one indissoluble relation and one bond of affection exempt from decay, seems to have appointed maternal tenderness as the stronghold and the last sanctuary for domestic happiness, against those storms of adverse interests and rival passions which drive it from every other post.

"It is not, Sir, without a severe conflict, nor without the most acute pain, that we find at length power to express these sorrows to your Majesty. We are sensible of the sacred character and the religion as it were that surrounds and covers the subject of our complaint. Since we do not, and in our hearts cannot, acknowledge that we have merited, either by any part of our conduct, or by our most secret thoughts, the loss of the Queen's love, we feel that in lamenting that dreadful calamity we appear to be her accusers, and her accusers before your Majesty. We entreat you therefore to cast your eye for a moment on the afflicting alternative which is left to us. We cannot disguise to ourselves our true situation. The Queen's affection is estranged from us. We can neither be ignorant of nor forget a misfortune which we feel every day in a thousand shapes, both wounding our feelings and working our ruin. Her Majesty is alone possessed of your ear, and from the endearing relation which she bears to your Majesty, is naturally entitled to your confidence. In the Queen's indisposition towards us we see therefore the loss also of your Majesty's opinion and regard. Our characters and reputation in the world are not less endangered. Those who are known to approach most constantly her Majesty's person, and to enjoy the greatest share of her confidence and favour, seem to have no other language in which to express their zeal and attachment for her Majesty, than the bitterest invectives against us, and no other business or occupation than to invent and circulate from one extremity of your dominions to the other, the most gross, false, and scandalous slanders on her sons. In the meanwhile we find ourselves constrained to a silence which our enemies and even the impartial part of the world may well enough attribute to a consciousness of guilt. What choice therefore is left to us, but either to forego voluntarily your Majesty's love, and the good opinion of the world, or to tell your Majesty and the world, that without blame on our parts we are unhappy enough to have been deprived of a mother's affection, and to tender to your Majesty and the world the documents which we possess of our innocence?

" Yet, Sir, we might still be silent if even these reasons, powerful as they are, were the only grounds for our alarm, and if our fears were not at length too surely verified by the event. For if the occurrences which I have alluded to could leave us without anxiety concerning the unfortunate impressions which may too probably have been made on your Majesty's mind to our disadvantage, your Majesty must appear to have deprived us of hope on that subject, by a letter which your Majesty has written to my brother the Duke of Clarence. I trust your Majesty does not yet think us capable of perusing that unequivocal and severe declaration of your displeasure, without the most poignant grief and the deepest mortification. The love which we bear to the Duke of Clarence, and the happiness which we enjoy in our mutual affection and harmony, is our sole consolation under the many humiliating and afflicting circumstances which we experience in other branches of our family. The loss of that blessing would be a heavy blow indeed; but how much would its severity be increased, by reflecting that it comes from the hand of a parent. We see therefore with anguish, and we confess, with wonder, your Majesty, under the persuasion of others, and contrary to your own nature, labouring to hurt us in the opinion of our brother, and to deprive us both of his affection and society. It is with inexpressible grief we perceive the imputation of some monstrous but undefined guilt in us made a ground for harshness and rebuke even to him. I trust your Majesty will not be offended at seeing us sensible to such afflictions, and that you will allow, at least, that we are distinctly called upon to vindicate our conduct by one passage in your Majesty's letter. You are pleased to say, ' Though I choose to cast a veil over the unkindness I met with during my illness from the ill-advised conduct of my sons, yet I cannot but feel it, as well as the Parliament, and indeed the whole nation.'

" This, Sir, is the first explicit declaration you have made of
these unfortunate and, I must presume to say on our parts,
unmerited sentiments. Till now, we might flatter ourselves
that, however prevalent in your palace such opinions might be,
they had not reached your Majesty. Indeed, Sir, we cannot
yet consent to banish entirely a hope, which is so indispensable
to our happiness, and we would yet cling to a fond conjecture
that your Majesty has rather yielded to the importunity of
others, and condescended to adopt their suggestions, than
spoken your own opinions, or consulted your own heart on
this occasion. We have ever found your Majesty personally
kind and good to us. We most solemnly and seriously call
God to witness, that we have ever felt your goodness with
gratitude, and repaid it with affection and reverence. We
cannot, therefore, easily and rashly believe that your Majesty
should become at once cruel and unjust. Yet your Majesty will
admit, that so express a declaration of your displeasure leaves
us no choice, and that if any consideration on earth should
induce us to withhold a full and circumstantial account of our
conduct in that critical and important period of our lives to
which your censure is applied, we should subscribe to our own
condemnation, and should merit indeed the pain, heavy as it is,
of your anger and reproaches. Your Majesty cannot be offended
if we do not account your present judgment final and irrevo-
cable; for your Majesty knows that we have not been heard,
and that an opportunity to defend ourselves, although it has
been often sought by us, has hitherto been denied. It would
be therefore injurious to your Majesty's character, as a just
sovereign, to believe that your mind is not still open at least to
a fair and equitable consideration of the subject. With this
view, we humbly lay the following relation at your Majesty's
feet.

" It is submitted first, as it ought, to your Majesty. But
we are taught by your Majesty's words not to neglect the
opinion of our country, and to that country which we love and

honour, and whose good opinion is essential to our comfort and happiness, we consider ourselves bound also to address ourselves.

" I will not detain your Majesty longer from the perusal of a paper which I hope will restore us to your esteem, and regain for us the blessings of your wonted affection and confidence."

[There was no reconciliation between the Queen and the Prince of Wales till March, 1791.]

[In the "Annual Register" of 1789 it is stated, that in consequence of a vote of the House of Commons blaming the conduct of Mr. Burke, "some difference of opinion was said to have arisen in the Committee of Managers, relative to their continuance in that situation. It was resolved however to proceed." Mr. Fox, who had defended Mr. Burke warmly and ably in the House of Commons, appears to have been one of those who thought the managers ought to have paused, at least before they proceeded farther; and, therefore, to have blamed the precipitancy with which, on the day of the censure, they hurried into Westminster Hall to resume their functions. The following letter from Mr. Burke seems to have been written in reply to a communication from Mr. Fox, disapproving of their conduct.]

MR. BURKE TO MR. FOX.

"*May* 11*th*, 1789.

" MY DEAR FOX,

" The only part of your letter which has given me serious concern is the word that concludes it.

The word *me*. If I had meant to act unkindly by *you*, it must be admitted that I chose my time for an unfriendly act with very little judgment. You had just at that moment behaved most nobly, not only with regard to the cause in which we are engaged in common, but with regard to myself personally. This behaviour ought to make its due impression upon my mind at the same time, and it ought not to be forgotten speedily. I think it did affect me as it ought to do, and I am mistaken if I shall not retain it in no ungrateful memory.

" You pass by, however, this fault of mine, whatever it may be. It is certainly good to be pardoned ; but to stand in need of a pardon is not so pleasant. I am persuaded that you have received some very erroneous account of the transaction, or you could not possibly have felt, much less retained, any soreness about it. It is unlucky that things are so circumstanced that we seldom can meet, and that, with us, an explanation cannot always follow on the heels of a misapprehension. It is on Monday that I am to clear up to you the steps which I found myself obliged to take in your absence on Tuesday last.

" I hope, in the first place, that you will recollect that you never communicated to me, either by note or message, the slightest signification of what you wished to be done or omitted. Before I went down to the House of Commons, I had not the least idea that you wished me to move the House for a message to the Lords to adjourn the trial. In that state of complete ignorance I continued till it grew very late.

Several of the Committee, I think much the majority,
who had come down dressed, were in the same state
of ignorance in which I stood. Two, or possibly
three, members then came in undressed ; and from
them I learned that you had settled with them (or
with their knowledge) that the business should not
proceed for a day or two. By this time the Lords
were in their House in considerable numbers, and
robed ; and Westminster Hall had been for some
hours filled. The stream of the Committee ran
strongly for our proceeding without delay. Many,
not of the Committee, but your friends, came into
our room to enforce this opinion, and to persuade me
to lose no time in going into the Hall. It is not
necessary to trouble you with the arguments they
used ; but the importunity was general and urgent.
I will not tell you who they were whose opinions
were so strong and decided, because I choose to bear
whatever blame there was in the proceeding myself.
It certainly concurred with my own sentiments, but
I was far from pressing them ; and indeed, under the
uncertainty I stood with regard to your resolutions,
I continued very doubtful, and did not give way
until some had pledged themselves that you would
not take it amiss. In that state I did not see how I
could undertake, in an exceedingly thin House, with
such a sense of our friends against it, to move for a
message to the Lords for a third adjournment. I
felt very uneasy, and dispatched two friends to let
you know the difficulties under which I was obliged
to yield. This is a plain account of the business.

Whatever my opinions might have been, my disposition was not to go on. I have not often in my life been more ill and oppressed than I was that morning. I drank a great deal of cold water, which abated the fever that was on me ; and I never did tax myself more heavily than I was then obliged to do, to enable myself to proceed at all. It was no humour in me. I think if you were there, and had the view of things that I then had, you would have proceeded as I did ; and to this hour I cannot conceive that any other ill has happened from it, except, what indeed I consider as no small ill, that it has given you uneasiness. I might have a number of compurgators among your friends, if I thought it would be right to make your feelings on this subject generally known. An ill use would be made of it by our common enemies, who would be sure to exaggerate a thing which, I hope, hardly merits (at least I hope so) the name of a difference. Surely it is a time when those who love and trust each other, as I hope is the case with us two, ought not to permit any sourness in our minds from mistakes that could not arise from any unfriendly intention. There are enough of those who have no good will to either of us, and who will not forgive us our mistakes. Adieu ; and believe me, with some uneasy sense of your letter, but always most truly and faithfully your old friend,

" EDMUND BURKE."

[Another letter from Mr. Burke to Mr. Fox may be subjoined. It is curious on account of the

anxiety it shows on the part of Mr. Burke to pro-
pitiate Dr. Priestley and other Dissenters, and of the
exhortations it addresses to Mr. Fox to " neutralise
the acid of that sharp and eager description of men."
The letter was written about two months after the
taking of the Bastille.]

SAME TO SAME.

" BECONSFIELD, *Sept. 9th*, 1789.

" MY DEAR FOX,

 " Mr. Blair lives in my neighbourhood. I have
gained an acquaintance that I like very well, and I
have narrowly missed Sir Elijah Impey, who was in
treaty for Mr. Walker's house, which Mr. Blair has
taken. I think myself very fortunate ; but I do not
write for the purpose of communicating to you this
piece of self-gratification, but to let you know that I
find my new acquaintance, as I conjecture, a little out
of humour with you. You cannot doubt of his
attachment to your cause and your person, and therefore I think this is not quite what you would wish.
Some time ago he wrote to you at Dr. Priestley's
desire, wishing you to apply to the Prince of Wales
for his leave to dedicate a great collection of his
(Priestley's) aerial disquisitions to his Royal Highness.
He has had no answer, and is a little piqued. This
I had from Courtney. He said nothing to me on the
subject himself. It would not be amiss to write to
him, let the fortune of Priestley's application be what
it will ; though I cannot conceive what objection the
Prince can have to be considered as an encourager of

science. Besides this consideration, Dr. Priestley is a very considerable leader among a set of men powerful enough in many things, but most of all in elections ; and I am quite sure that the good or ill humour of these men will be sensibly felt at the general election. It would be material to you to gain entirely some of these Dissenters, who are already, I fancy, inclined to come over to you. This offer to dedicate to the Prince is a strong overt act of that disposition. Even if they cannot be wholly reclaimed, it would be something to neutralise the acid of that sharp and eager description of men.

" Things went off well in Yorkshire. I wish the Prince had staid a few days longer, to show himself to the manufacturing towns, which are the head-quarters of the enemy. It is very probable that he might have dislodged them. However, as it was, the Northern excursion has been of use. I suppose we are not to flatter ourselves with seeing you here very speedily. When you can come you will make us very happy. My barley had made me a little melancholy, but we are now in great spirits. We are as subject to ups and downs in our carts and waggons as those that glory carries *ventoso curru.* I wish you a good journey in yours.

" Ever very faithfully and affectionately yours,

"EDMUND BURKE."

MR. FOX TO MR. FITZPATRICK.

[*July 30th,* 1789.]

" DEAR DICK,

" I was not surprised to hear you meaned to go to
Paris, but am very much so at your having put it off.
If you go you had better come this way, as I should
be glad to talk it over with you a little, and it is
not quite impossible but I may go too. How much
the greatest event it is that ever happened in the
world! and how much the best!* If you go without
my seeing you, pray say something civil for me to
the Duke of Orleans, whose conduct seems to have
been perfect : and tell him and Lauzun, that all my
prepossessions against French connections for this
country will be at an end, and indeed most part of
my European system of politics will be altered, if this
Revolution has the consequences that I expect.

" Yours ever,

"C. J. FOX."

1790.

In the spring of this year Mr. Fox brought forward
a motion for the Repeal of the Test and Corporation
Acts. In taking this step he was fully aware that he
should provoke the High Church party to be his
enemies. But when applied to by the Dissenters to
undertake their cause, the principles he had ever held
of religious liberty, in the most full and extensive
signification of that term, prevented him from
declining the task. As a party man, the Dissenters

* The taking of the Bastile, I suppose.— J. R.

had no claim upon him.   In 1784 they had acted
heartily and efficaciously in support of Mr. Pitt ; and
it was only from their confidence in the sincerity
of Mr. Fox, that in 1789, when abandoned by Mr.
Pitt, they ventured, by the persuasion of Sergeant
Heywood, hesitatingly, and with no small fears of
a repulse, to apply to Mr. Fox to become their
champion.]

1791.

[The zeal and honesty of Mr. Fox's exertions for
the Abolition of the African Slave Trade, which,
with the aid of Lord Grenville, he may be said to
have finally accomplished, are universally known.
It may not therefore be entirely devoid of interest
to read the feelings he entertained concerning that
nefarious traffic, when the question was first brought
forward. Having been urged to take an active part in
the discussion, he replies,] " I am very much inclined
to undertake the business, but I must both read and
hear more before I engage.   I should like very much
to put down so vile a thing, if it be possible." [After
the first unsuccessful division in April, 1791, he
writes again :—] " You have heard how poor a
figure we made in numbers on the Slave Trade ;
but I spoke, I believe, very well, and indeed it is the
thing that has given me most pleasure since I saw
you ; for I do think it is a cause in which one ought
to be an enthusiast, and in which one cannot help
being pleased with oneself for having done right."

   * We have now arrived at Mr. Fox's correspondence

with Lord Holland, which will in future give the chief
interest to these volumes :—*

MR. FOX TO LORD HOLLAND.

"*May 26th*, 1791.

" MY DEAR HENRY,

 "You are very much mistaken if you do
not believe that your letters give me the greatest
pleasure, both in those parts where you speak of what
you are about, and those where you give your opinion
upon general politics. As to the latter, I *rather* agree
with you that it would be better that Sheridan should
not attend the meeting of the 14th of July, if he can
be absent without any appearance of being frightened
out of the conduct which he held last year; but I am
far from thinking that it is *always* right to give way
to unfounded prejudices. You must, too, make some
allowance for the place where you are,† which I take
to be the very centre and capital of Toryism, and
where of course, the prejudices and alarms you allude
to are more general and stronger than elsewhere. I
have not read Burke's new pamphlet, but hear a
very different account of it from yours. It is in
general thought to be mere madness, and especially
in those parts where he is for a general war, for the
purpose of destroying the present government of
France. There is a pamphlet by one Mackintosh,
which I hear a great character of, though it is
said to go too far in some respects, but I have not
yet had time to read it. I really told you what I

† Oxford.

thought, when I told you I did not think it worth your while to come up for the Libel Business ; and, in fact, there was no debate, only two speeches from Erskine and me. I am very happy to have succeeded in it, because I think the thing essentially right, and because I have reason to think that it will do me a good deal of credit, which I am sure will give you as much pleasure as myself.

" As to your studies, I am sorry they are not more intense, but not much surprised—(the Fitzpatrick indolence will come out). However, I am glad you have begun Herodotus, whom I was quite sure you would like. There is a flow, and ease, and pleasantness in him that I know in no other prose writer. I used to think the second book, about Egypt, one of the most entertaining; though perhaps the account of Xerxes' expedition and the affairs of Greece is more interesting. If you do not like algebra, I cannot help it ; the liking of such studies or not is mere matter of taste ; and if one does not feel them pleasant, I know no way of being persuaded that they are so. But with respect to Demosthenes, if you go on, and are shown the good parts of him, I think you cannot but see in him a superior force of understanding and expression to all other writers. I am so convinced of this, that if you do not feel it at first, I would advise you to read him over again, and desire some of those who admire him to point out to you the passages most to be admired, and the beauties of them ; and to make yourself quite sure that it is not owing to inattention if you

think less of him than I do. I never read anything
of his in the original, except the first Philippic, the
three Olynthiacs, and the Περι Στεφανου; but I not only
admire them very much, but the passages which I
read, ill-translated from him as I guess, in Gillies'
History this year, have greatly confirmed the opinion
I had of him. There is a force and pointedness in
him arising naturally out of the *business*, and not
produced by any far-fetched or affected antithesis,
to which all we orators are forced to have recourse,
to avoid flatness and dullness, that is, in my judgment, peculiar to him."

SAME TO SAME.

"*June 2nd*, 1791.

"DEAR HENRY,

"Mrs. Armitstead and I, and perhaps one or two
more, mean to dine at Maidenhead Bridge on Saturday, and to go after dinner on the water to see the
boys row up to Surly Hall, and I wish very much you
would come and meet us. I know you would like to
see whether things go on as well as in your time.
Pray come, and bring Canning with you, if he likes
it. The next day we go to Benson, in order to see
Nuneham, which Mrs. A. wants me to see, and there
(I mean at Benson) I depend upon meeting you, if
you do not come to Maidenhead, which I very much
wish you to do.

"We shall dine rather before four; if you do not
come, write a line by the return of the post, which I
shall get before I set out, and take care, whether you

come to Maidenhead or not, to order dinner for us at Benson, Sunday at three.

"Yours ever,

"C. J. F.

"Hastings has just finished a nonsensical and rhodomontade speech, and the trial is put off till next year. Some of it was taken from *Pierre's* speech to the Senate in 'Venice Preserved.'"

1792.

SAME TO SAME.

"ST. ANN'S HILL, *August 20th*, 1792.

"I WAS very much obliged to you, my dear Henry, for your note from Gravesend. I hope by this time you are safely landed, and have recovered your sickness, which I suppose you had plenty of during the calms which prevailed till within these few days. I do assure you we have missed you very much, but I hope you will not be long away, and that you will adhere to your first intention of coming straight home from Petersburgh, and seeing the south of Europe afterwards. Pray do not omit to write me a *true* account of Stockholm, and of such parts of Sweden as you see. I feel myself quite sure you will be disappointed, but my only doubt is whether you will own it.

"None of your three wishes are, I fear, likely to be accomplished. It is over, as you have already heard, with poor Poland, and what has happened at Paris seems to make the chance of the poor French being settled worse than ever. It seems as if the Jacobins

had determined to do something as revolting to the
feelings of mankind as the Duke of Brunswick's proclamation ; but, though it must be owned that they
have done their utmost for this purpose, yet, with
respect to mine, they have not succeeded, for the
proclamation, in my judgment, still remains unri-
valled. As to your third wish, I believe it is out of the
question, nor do I much regret it. It would be too late
to do any great and real good in regard to foreign
affairs ; and, for my own sake, when I consider the
many disagreeable circumstances that always attend
new connections, and what is much worse, the possible
discontent that might arise among the old, I do not
know whether I am not better as I am. However, if
I know myself, I never allow any considerations
respecting my own comfort or advantage to weigh with
me so as to influence my *conduct* on these occasions,
however my *wishes* may be affected by them. I have
played at tennis several times since I saw you, and
last week, two days following, single matches which
rather over-fatigued me, but I shall nevertheless be at
it again Wednesday, not to-morrow, because if it is
fine we go to the boat-race at Richmond. Adieu.
Mrs. A. desires me to give her love to you, and,
indeed, she never speaks or thinks of you without
pleasure, so properly did the Oxford man praise your
jucunditas. The Dukes of Beaufort and Portland
stand for the Chancellorship. I hope and believe the
latter is pretty sure of success, and what is very
extraordinary, Pitt and Grenville have both written
in his favour. Pray write often and long ; I will

never fail every fortnight at least, and oftener, *if need be,* as is the phrase of the friends to short Parliaments.

"Yours most affectionately,

"My dear Nephew."

SAME TO SAME.

"St. Ann's Hill, *September 3rd,* 1792.

"My dear Henry,

"Although I now expect a letter from you in a very few days, yet I am resolved to keep my promise of not letting a fortnight pass without writing. There is nothing new here, and indeed if there were I am not in the way of hearing it ; but I believe French news now is what all the world is principally interested about. I do not think near so ill of the business of the 10th of August as I did upon first hearing it. If the King and his Ministers were really determined not to act in concert with the Assembly ; and still more if they secretly favoured the Invasion of the Barbarians ; it was necessary, at any rate, to begin by getting rid of him and them. Indeed you know that from the moment of the dismission of the Jacobin Ministry, I have thought that it was absolutely necessary either that the Assembly should come round to the Feuillans, or (which seemed most according to our Whig ideas) that the King should be forced to have Ministers of the same complexion with the Assembly. However it is impossible not to look with disgust at the bloody means which have been taken, even supposing the

end to be good, and I cannot help fearing that we
are not yet near the end of these trials and exe-
cutions.   Many accounts give me great uneasiness
for the Queen, and I am more and more sorry every
day that they did not (as I think they ought to have
done) either shut her up or send her away (the last
best) after the King's escape last year.   The capture
of Longwy, especially if it is true that the Muni-
cipality forced the garrison to surrender, is a very
bad beginning of the war ; and, indeed, the way in
which the news of it was received in the National
Assembly does not appear very magnanimous.
There is a want of dignity and propriety in everything they do.   When the enemy is in a manner
at their doors, to be amusing themselves with funerals
and inscriptions, and demolitions of statues, and
creations of honorary citizens, is quite intolerable ;
and to talk so pompously of dying for liberty and
their country, before one single gallant action has
been performed by any part of their army against
the enemy, is worse than ridiculous.   And yet, with
all their faults and all their nonsense, I do interest
myself for their success to the greatest degree.   It is
a great crisis for the real cause of liberty, whatever
we may think of the particular people who are to
fight the present battle.   I wish they were like our
old friends the Americans, and I should scarcely be
afraid for them.   I hear from good authority that the
Duke of Brunswick means to quit the command as
soon as he has taken Paris, which I think very
prudent, as certainly the most difficult part of

the business will be to come afterwards. I am
heartily glad La Fayette has escaped ; for, though I
very much disapprove his conduct, I believe him to
be an honest man ; but escaped though he be, his
situation is very unpleasant, and I sincerely pity him.
I have played a good deal at tennis since I wrote,
and have quite got up my old play.

" Yours most affectionately,

"C. J. F."

SAME TO SAME.

" September, 1792.

" MY DEAR HENRY,

" Though my fortnight is not near out, Mrs. A.
says I must write to you once more before I leave
this place.   So, first of all, let me thank you for your
letter from off Elsineur, dated, as I make out by
calculation, the 24th of August, and which I received
the 5th of this month ; but the usual mode is to date
letters (from abroad especially) by the day of the
month, and not that of the week, as you do, which
cannot be made out but by such great calculators as
myself.   You talk very foolishly in making excuses
for egotism, for in letters from you it is precisely
what I want ; I wish to know everything about you.

" I should not be afraid of being an egotist if I had
anything to tell you of myself, but I have nothing.
I have shot only twice, had very bad sport, played
often at tennis, and on other days have led the life
here which you have seen, and which, though very
improperly called idle, does not furnish many events
to write to distant countries.   I had just made up my

mind to the events of the 10th of August, when the
horrid accounts of the 2nd of this month arrived,
and I really consider the horrors of that day and
night as the most heart-breaking event that ever
happened to those who, like me, are fundamentally
and unalterably attached to the true cause. There
is not, in my opinion, a shadow of excuse for this
horrid massacre, not even the possibility of extenu-
ating it in the smallest degree ; and if one were to
consider only the people of Paris, one should almost
doubt to whom one should——" [The rest torn.]

SAME TO SAME.

"South Street, *October 12th*, 1792.

"I RETURN you ten thousand thanks, my dear
Henry, for your kind letters, and I own I cannot
help feeling ashamed at your praises of my punctu-
ality, when near a month has passed since I wrote
last. I put off writing for some time, in expectation of hearing something decisive from France,
and last week I was at Newmarket, where one
has seldom time to write at all ; however, I will
now return to the exactness with which I set out,
and write regularly, however little I may have to
say. First of all, I am very glad you are quite well
again, and it was very wise to avoid the cold
climates and sleeping on the ice. Your tour,
however, will, I fear, be much less amusing than
Beauclerk's. I am sure if things had turned out
otherwise, you would have disliked to the greatest

degree the triumphant faces you would have seen
at Brunswick and at Berlin; but I do not think it
is in your nature to enjoy with a proportionable
pleasure the humbled and downcast looks which you
will now meet there. But as you wished, as you
say, ardently against the invaders, you must be
almost as much (for *quite* is impossible) rejoiced at
their flight as I am. No! no public event, not
excepting Saratoga and York Town, ever happened
that gave me so much delight. I would not allow
myself to believe it for some days for fear of disappointment; but it is now, I think, confirmed beyond
a doubt, and the whole of the negotiation, together
with the conclusion of it, by the Duke of B.'s last
manifesto, and Manstein's entreaty for an explanation, make it the most complete business in its way
that ever happened. The defeats of great armies
of invaders always gave me the greatest satisfaction
in reading history, from Xerxes' time downwards;
and what has happened in America and in France
will, I hope, make what Cicero says of *armed force*,
be the opinion of all mankind, *Invidiosum, detestabile,
imbecillum, caducum.*

"It sounds ill-natured to say so, but I own
my pleasure is heightened by all the nonsense
that was talked about the Duke of B.'s great military reputation, which, I suppose, will now be as
unjustly cried down, as it was absurdly, and without
any ground of experience, cried up. The expedition
to Spires, the behaviour of the troops on the 20th
of September (which I suppose you allude to), and

above all, the defences of Thionville and of Lisle now
give the French some right to vapour, which right,
I fear, they will greatly abuse. I do not mention
the conquest of Savoy, because, though a most
important event, it was not effected by arms, but
by the inclination of the Savoyards. Now as to
your reasoning about the Jacobins, Feuillans, &c.
I do not think it quite solid. If you admit that
the Jacobins, having the confidence of the Assembly
and country, ought to be Ministers, what can be
said for the Feuillans, who encouraged and supported
the King, in maintaining an Administration of an
adverse faction, and in using his veto and other
prerogatives in opposition to the will of the Assembly
and the nation ? He who defends even this, cannot
be a Whig. But further, I think there is not *now*
a shadow of doubt but the Ministers who preceded
and succeeded the Jacobins, not only did this, but
intentionally weakened the defence of the kingdom,
for the purpose of maintaining the King and themselves against the Jacobins by the Austrian arms.
That La Fayette and La Rochefoucauld were in this
part of the guilt I cannot bring myself to believe, but
well-meaning men may be deceived, and when so are
to be pitied ; but, that they gave into the idea of
availing themselves of the letter of the Constitution,
and of the King's using his prerogatives, indepen-
dently of, and hostilely to the Assembly, is what they
themselves would not deny, and what I must disapprove, unless I abandon every political principle of
my life. You say, you may still like the Feuillans

and hate the Jacobins, and wish the former had been
the prevalent party. Now I say, that for the reasons
I have given (partiality to persons out of the question), an English Whig must disapprove of the
Feuillant party, or quit his English principles. But
it may be said there is something in the argument
against the Feuillans, but not *for* the Jacobins. I
own I think that it goes a great way to justify the
greater part of their conduct, and to palliate even
the worst. For what people would not be driven
to madness at seeing a Ministry acting notoriously
against the nation that employed them, abusing the
royal prerogatives for the purpose of preventing the
country from defending itself by the means and by
the persons which the Assembly and the country
thought most able to defend it ; giving a veto to
the raising of an army voted by the Assembly, and
dismissing the only Ministers who were not suspected
of wishing success to the invading armies ? You will
understand that I only mean to defend the Jacobins
as far as the 10th of August inclusively ; for if they
have had any hand in the massacre of the 2nd of
September, and the killing of the prisoners at Versailles, there is no excuse, no palliation for such
cruelty and extreme baseness. There are hopes,
however, that the monsters who caused these horrors
will at last be punished. Till they are, I own that
their impunity (notwithstanding the noble speeches
of Roland, Vergniaux, &c.) throws a slur upon the
present brilliant Administration of France, which
gives pain to all true friends to liberty. It is not

enough to express horror at such execrable scenes, but no man of proper feelings could bear to be a member of a Government unable to punish the actors of them. Well, enough of French politics ; all friends to the good cause, whatever they think of Jacobins, &c., must rejoice at the defeat of the Germans, and there, I am sure, we shall agree. I have had very good sport shooting, but bad luck at Newmarket. I am here only for a few days, having come up on account of my anniversary. I saw your Uncle Dick, who is delighted, as you may suppose, at these events. He is gone to Petworth. I was glad to find that the Duke of Bedford, aristocrat as he is, wished against the invaders. It is time to finish this long lecture. So, good-bye.

"Yours affectionately.

"I am very glad to hear the Duke of Sudermania's ambition is like to do so much good. If it does, the King of Sweden's death must be allowed to have been good for Sweden as well as for France. Indeed, to the last, I do not think it would have signified. I think our Minister's declaration to the Imperial and Neapolitan Ambassadors very absurd, though I dare say it will be approved."

SAME TO SAME.

"My dear Henry,　　　　　　"November, 1792.

"I have been unpunctual again ; but the truth is, that when I am at Newmarket I have little time,

and when I am shooting, none. When I get up I
am in a hurry to get out, and when I come home, I
am in a hurry to dress for dinner ; and when I am
going to bed, I am tired and sleepy. Now here
(though I never will allow my life to be an idle one)
I can now and then find a vacant half hour, and I
will be more regular. I have three letters from you
since I wrote ; one from Hanover, and two from
Berlin. I am very much obliged to you for writing
so often, and the intelligence contained in your last
is very material. It is a difficult business to make
out ; at first I thought there was some secret agreement : but, upon reflection, I think it impossible,
though your news seems to strengthen that notion.
I think it impossible, because Dumouriez must have
been mad to have risked it. In regard to the
future, opinions are divided ; the most probable is,
that the King of Prussia will abandon the whole
thing ; but my intelligence is, that he and the
Emperor are actually concerting a renewal of their
crusade for the next spring, and as in these times,
le probable n'arrive jamais, I am inclined to believe
it. If they do, I think they risk the existence of
their monarchies, and so much the better. Some
say Custine is in a scrape, by having advanced so
far ; but before you receive this, that point will have
been determined, and you will have heard the issue.
I agree with you in disliking Dumouriez's vapouring,
but a Frenchman must be a Frenchman. I doubt
his success in Brabant on account of the influence of
the priests ; but, on the other hand, I have a great

1792.]   CHARLES JAMES FOX.

idea of the power of a French army in these moments
of enthusiasm and victory. You are come so nearly
to my opinion in our old dispute about the Feuillans
and Jacobins, that I shall say no more about it : the
latter were certainly wrong in the business of the
Regiment de Chateauvieux, and in many other
instances ; but their general policy was certainly more
solid and manly, and better adapted to the situation
of France. As to Condorcet, you seem to know some
particular ill of him which I do not ; but I cannot
help thinking the present ruling party seems to show
more sense and principle than any other has yet
shown in France. They are acting in earnest against
Robespierre and Marat, and will, I hope, convict
them. I have more fears of their acting contrary to
our wishes about the royal family, though Lord
Lauderdale and others, who are at Paris, say they
will be safe. The Committee of Insurrection, which
you mention, was *not* voted, only proposed ; but
I think they seem to act too much as if they had
voted it. However, they have got out of the Geneva
business pretty well, in which they certainly were in
the wrong. I believe the report of their going to
Italy is true, and that their first attack there will be
upon Rome, and their next on Naples. The other
report of their intending to attack Hanover I think
less likely ; but what they will do in their present
state of exultation no man can conjecture ; nothing
will surprise me. Here their success has given great
joy to us, who wish well to the good cause in general,
but I doubt whether it may not give too great spirits

to some extravagant projectors ; and I am sure, on
the other hand, that it has inspired a fear which
may be very mischievous in some very excellent
men, whom you will easily guess without my naming
them."

SAME TO SAME.

"November 23*rd,* 1792.

" I RETURN you ten thousand thanks, my dear
Henry, for your letters. I conclude as you do, that
what Prince Ferdinand says is the language of Prince
Henry, and am not at all surprised that he whom I
take to be a man of sense, should have thought
Ewart's plans as absurd for Prussia as I thought
them for England. The truth is, that the war would
have been as useless to her as to us, and in the event
of failure much more dangerous. Alliance with Russia
was always the first object with the late King of
Prussia ; and when by intrigues he had lost the friendship of the Empress, his most earnest desire was to
regain it ; and a hope of compassing that, through the
medium of Great Britain, was the true cause of the
court which he paid to the King here, during the last
years of his reign. As to poor Ewart, you know he
died raving mad, and I dare say the fact is that his
head was affected long before his death. Pitt was
not deceived by him, but by his own vanity and
presumption, and on the other hand, Ewart was most
certainly deceived by Pitt. I do not quite understand
from your last letter whether the King of Prussia
is returned to Berlin. I conclude your curiosity will
make you stay there till he does return. I do *not*

believe there is any agreement of any kind between him and the French, but there are circumstances that look like it. You say he will meet with distrust and contempt if he has not deserted the Austrians, but surely if he has in the manner which is supposed, it is an instance of perfidy, I cannot say unexampled in the history of kings (for no such instance can happen) but equal at least to any we ever read of. You have heard by this time of the complete conquest of the Netherlands by Dumouriez, so that all his vapouring promises are fulfilled. I cannot reconcile my mind (with all my partiality) to these boasting manners ; but success I suppose will put them quite in fashion. I think the mode of the Austrian Government's leaving Brussels is the most contemptible I ever heard of. The Princess, after having grossly deceived them about the action of Jemappe, and the capture of Mons, runs away and leaves behind her a declaration annulling her former acts of which the Brabanters had complained, and promising them in the Emperor's name an acquiescence in all their wishes. What a dignified moment for concession ! The French disclaim any intention of interference in Dutch affairs, but whether their disclaimer, even if sincere, is much to be relied upon, I doubt. Our Ministry are much alarmed, and have, it is said, sent Lindsay to Paris. I shall think them as mad as Ewart, if they suffer anything to draw them into a war with France, and yet it is as impossible for a nation as for an individual to say that at all events she will not fight. In this case, I think myself sure

that it can be avoided with honour, and therefore I
suppose it will be, though I do really think that Pitt
in these businesses is a great bungler.   I disapprove
the law respecting emigrants more than you do.
It is abominable ; but I do not think your other
accusations against the French well founded. Though
they are conquering, it is chiefly upon the territories
of their declared enemies, or those whom they know
to be in substance and effect so, such as the King of
Sardinia, &c.   Though the Empire has not declared
war, all the world knows it was on the point of doing
so.   It was I believe impossible to attack Hesse
Cassel without going to Frankfort, and if they remit
(which I think not improbable) the contribution
Custine has directed, I think they will be quite clear
in that quarter.   The open avowal of inhuman and
absurd doctrines by individuals ought, in my opinion,
to be *permitted* in every country ; but I really believe
they are as much detested by the generality of the
French, as by you and me.—Adieu.

" Yours most affectionately."

* On the 1st of December an order in Council was
passed, calling out part of the militia, and on the 5th
a second order called out another portion on the
southern and western coast.   This measure fore-
shadowed war, and is probably the measure alluded
to in the following letter of Mr. Fox.*

MR. FOX TO COL. FITZPATRICK.

"DEAR DICK,   " *Wednesday, December 5th*, 1792.

"I have only time to write two words. None of our friends have sanctioned this most detestable measure, and I hope none will. In the midst of a thousand unpleasant things, it gives me great satisfaction to see that your ideas of this measure and its consequences are precisely the same as mine were upon the first news of it. I believe there will not be war; if there is, I see dangers innumerable, and no chance of good. Adieu. I go to-morrow to St. Anne's, and return on Sunday to stay. I very much hope you will come sooner than you speak of; indeed you ought, for this is a moment when every right-headed man is worth his weight in gold.

"Yours affectionately."

APPENDIX.

—•—

" CHESTERFIELD STREET, *February 2nd,* 1842.

"MY DEAR ALLEN,

"I have searched in vain among my papers for a copy of the letter, supposed to have been intercepted, which I wrote to Mr. Fox from Petersburg in 1791. I can find nothing on the subject except Mr. Lindsay's note to me, in which he offered to be the bearer of it; and the fragment of a paper which I drew up with the intention of addressing it to the Duke of Portland, after Mr. Burke's article of impeachment against Mr. Fox and myself had appeared in the newspapers.

" With regard to the history of my journey to Petersburg, I must refer you to my two printed letters to the Bishop of Winchester, who, in his 'Life of Mr. Pitt,' had adopted the hearsay charge of Mr. Burke; and stated that he could prove it from documents which he had found among Mr. Pitt's papers. The Bishop's work was published in 1821, and was the first opportunity which had been given me of publicly and distinctly denying a charge which, until then, had never been publicly and distinctly made. Mr. Burke's authority for his vehement accusation, as he himself acknowledged to the editors of his works, was a story which had been told him by a friend of his connected 'with the Ministry;' but the Bishop having affirmed that he could prove the truth of it from authentic documents, I felt that it was no longer fit for me to be silent. I called upon him, therefore, in language as strong as it was proper to address to his lordship, to produce his documents. That he never did; although he was then actually preparing a second edition of his book.

" If, however, there be still lurking in the minds of any

description of persons whose opinions are worth attending to, and who—knowing nothing of me or of my letters—may think, from an indistinct general impression which they have retained of the transaction, that blame still rests upon Mr. Fox for his part in it; and who in true sincerity of heart may wish for some further explanation to satisfy them that no cause for such blame exists; all that I can say is, that there are no questions which can be put to me on the subject which I will not most willingly answer: but I must add, at the same time, that, after my reply to the Bishop, it is their business to put those questions to me, and not mine to find out, or to guess at, what they may want to know. On one point of fact, and that the only material one in this case which concerns Mr. Fox, I renew my most solemn declaration that I, and I alone, was the author, contriver—plotter—call it what you will, of that journey, and that beyond the procuring for me some letters of introduction, Mr. Fox had nothing to do with it whatsoever.

"In corroboration of this fact, I will state to you—for I remember it as if it were but yesterday—our conversation on my taking leave of him. ' Well, if you are determined to go,' said Mr. Fox, ' send us all the news : ' and on my observing to him that my letters would assuredly be opened and read, he told me that ' I might use Burgoyne's cypher ; ' and ' to puzzle them the more,' he added, ' you may put some of your figures in red ink.' This cypher was what is called a ' book-cypher,' and was used by General Burgoyne when on service in America.

" With respect to my own part in this business, I can but recapitulate my former account of it. The main points are as follow :—

" Mr. Burke had affirmed ' that I was sent by Mr. Fox to Petersburg, to frustrate the objects for which the Minister (Mr. Fawkener) was sent to treat ; and that I did frustrate some of them.'

" Now, what were those objects ? A difference, tending to hostile discussions, with Russia, had arisen in the spring of 1791, respecting the restitution of Oczakoff to the Turks ;

but the sense of the House of Commons, expressed by a very strong division against enforcing its restitution by war, induced Mr. Pitt to abandon the attempt. This division took place on the 29th of March, and somewhere between that and the 12th of April, Mr. Pitt sent off a despatch to our Minister, Sir Charles Whitworth, directing him to withhold the menacing note which he had been ordered to present on that subject. Now as I did not leave England until May, to frustrate any demand for the restitution of Oczakoff could by no possibility have been the purpose of my journey. As to the other objects of Mr. Fawkener's mission, I am in utter ignorance of them to this hour. They may have been to ascertain what part the Empress meant to take in the new state of European affairs caused by the French revolution. It is certain that he attended the conferences at Pilnitz.

" The above was the substance and the sum of Mr. Burke's charge ; and in his belief of its truth, although grounded on nothing better than what had been told him by a friend of his connected with the Ministry, he drew up a regular and elaborate article of impeachment which he addressed to the Duke of Portland and Lord Fitzwilliam, setting forth two offences committed in this instance by Mr. Fox. The one was an offence against his party in sending me as his representative without consulting with them on a matter of so much delicacy, and the other was against the State, in setting on foot communications with foreign powers, leading to concert and co-operation with them in measures hostile to the King's Government.

" My answer to both these alleged offences was simple and plain. Mr. Fox did not consult his party, because there was nothing to consult them upon. He did not send me to Petersburg as his representative, or as anything, because I undertook the journey without consulting him upon it ; and I did not ' thwart ' Mr. Fawkener, because in his mission there was nothing to be thwarted that I knew of. The Bishop said that he could prove Mr. Burke's charge. I invited him so to do by producing his proofs. He never did : and here one would think the case was at an end.

" But let it not be supposed that I mean to deny the impropriety of setting up a correspondence and concert such as Mr. Burke condemns. I subscribe, on the contrary, to everything he says of its indecorum, of its criminality, and of its danger. Such a concert would be faction in its very essence, which *party*, in the true Whig sense of that word, holds in utter abhorrence. But far different, whether tried by the common rights of social intercourse, or by the rules of a well-considered discretion, is the conduct of him who, taking a warm and open part in public affairs, and anxious for the preservation of our establishments at home and of our relations abroad, seeks to impress his hearers not only with a sense of their value, but of the value in which they are held by the leading statesmen of his country. I hold it in particular to be most important for the interests of peace, that foreigners should know what is national in our party disputes, so as to distinguish it from what is merely factious or adventitious. It was mainly owing to his ignorance of this, and of Mr. Fox's true English heart, that Napoleon threw away the opportunity of making peace with us in 1806.

" With regard to the accusation before us, resting absolutely on my supposed conversations with persons whom I met with in society, I have not the least hesitation to avow the nature of them : but I must first state what they were not. Anything in opposition to the Minister's demand for the restitution of Oczakoff, we have seen that they could not be, for he had already renounced it. Anything condemnatory of the policy which suggested the demand could have had no object, since the Commons of England had declared that policy to be erroneous, and hurtful to the best interests of our country, nor could any language that I might hold in reprobation of it exceed that of our Parliamentary leaders, Mr. Grey, Mr. Windham, Mr. Grenville ; and, if I mistake not, of Mr. Burke himself. Here, therefore, the charge falls at once to the ground ; for to suppose that Mr. Fox sent me as his representative to run about Europe, expressly to abuse Mr. Pitt, would be still more absurd than any of the idle chatter I have as yet been condemned to listen to. It is better always to search for what is true in what is probable.

" I acknowledge, therefore, without shame or regret, that,

during my residence at Petersburg, and at Vienna also, which city I visited in my way thither, I had many conversations with distinguished persons whom I met with. They are referred to in my letters to the Bishop of Winchester. The character of them all was prospective. Their tenour was to uphold, and, when the Oczakoff dispute should be over, to revert to the ancient and wise alliances of my country. Holland, as our first and best; the Netherlands, as the barrier for Holland; Austria, to maintain that barrier and continue holding it as part of her own dominions; and Russia, as a rising naval power called into our system to counterbalance the increased naval power which France had obtained by the family compact— these, in 1791, were the main pillars of the foreign policy of England, such as we had received it from King William and Queen Anne, and such as the Whig party, more especially, had incorporated into their system for the conduct of foreign affairs. All these interests were then in jeopardy; especially in the Low Countries, where the seeds of revolution had been most imprudently fostered by the enemies of the house of Austria, and where it is to be feared that our Ministers had their share in producing that state of discontent which, a year afterwards, threw those provinces into the arms of France. People forget these things. They will be reminded of them when real history begins to be written.

" Of these conversations, it is needless to say, that Mr. Fox was entirely ignorant. I never even gave him an account of them on my return. Of all blame, therefore, whether as to contrivance, or purpose, or consequences, if any blame should still attach to this journey, he must stand thoroughly exempt. What can I say more? ' *Adsum qui feci!*' I will not add, ' *mea fraus,*' but think that I might say, had any result attended my suggestions—' *mea laus omnis.*' This is high ground, but I take my stand upon it.

" Ever yours truly,

" ROBERT ADAIR."

END OF VOL. II.